SOCIAL MOBILITY
IN INDUSTRIAL SOCIETY

SOCIAL MOBILITY
IN INDUSTRIAL SOCIETY

Seymour Martin Lipset
Reinhard Bendix

With a New Introduction by the Authors

Transaction Publishers
New Brunswick (U.S.A.) and London (U.K.)

New material this edition copyright © 1992 by Transaction Publishers, New Brunswick, New Jersey 08903.
Originally published in 1959 by University of California Press.

Library of Congress Catalog Number: 91-12490
ISBN: 1-56000-606-4
Printed in the United States of America

Library of Congress Cataloging-in-Publication Data

Lipset, Seymour Martin.
  Social mobility in industrial society/Seymour Martin Lipset, Reinhard Bendix.
    p.   cm.
  Reprint, with a new introd. by the authors. Originally published: Berkeley: University of California Press, 1959.
  Includes bibliographical references and index.
  ISBN 1-56000-606-4
  1. Social mobility. I. Bendix, Reinhard. II. Title.
HT609.L52   1991
305.5'13–dc20
                                                91–12490
                                                       CIP

To the memory of
LLOYD H. FISHER
Friend, Colleague, and Counselor

Contents

vii

Part Two
Social Mobility in a Metropolitan Community

Part Three
Causes, Consequences, and Dimensions of Social Mobility

TABLES

FIGURES

Introduction to the
Transaction Edition

Political Implications of Social Mobility

Political and social stability go together, regardless whether prosperity *or* poverty prevails. More dramatic changes occur where upward *or* downward social mobility increases. This principle of "cumulative causation" has been described by a number of social theorists.

In analyzing the causes of the French Revolution, Alexis de Tocqueville noted that the potential for political upheaval increases with social improvements. He entitled chapter 4, part 3 of his The Old Regime and the Revolution: "How, though the reign of Louis XVI was the most prosperous period of the monarchy, this very prosperity hastened the outbreak of the Revolution." He called attention to a "spectacular increase in the wealth of individuals," noting that the pattern of "upward movement" continued through the American war as "private persons went on making fortunes." Seemingly, "this steadily increasing prosperity . . . everywhere promoted a spirit of unrest," a conclusion borne out by the fact that "those parts of France in which the improvement in the standard of living was most pronounced were the chief centers of the revolutionary movements."[1]

At the end of the nineteenth century, Emile Durkheim extended Tocqueville's logic in his classic work, *Suicide*, in which he emphasized that mobility, upward or downward, produces more malaise than stability. He contended that maladjustments result from "every disturbance of equilibrium, even though it achieves greater comfort and a heightening of general vitality."[2] A modern writer like James Davies has amplified these ideas in another way. He has suggested that "revolutions are most likely to occur when a prolonged period of objective economic and social development is followed by a short period of sharp reversal." The two, improvement in circumstances and then reversal, are needed to produce severe discontent, which may lead to revolution or rebellion.[3]

But stability is as self-reinforcing as change. A relatively stable growth rate in the economy, or enduring poverty, or a more or less high level of social mobility do not lead to break down. In describing the "social conditions of the Anglo-Americans," Tocqueville concluded that the widespread individual social mobility, whether upward or downward, has "political consequences." He did not know of any other country besides America, "where the love of money has taken stronger hold on the affections of men and where a profounder contempt is expressed for the theory of the permanent equality of property."[4]

More than two generations after Tocqueville, Vilfredo Pareto came to similar conclusions in his four-volume study *Mind and Society* (1917). He analyzed the consequences of divergent rates of mobility into, or out of, the dominant strata of society. Pareto concluded that the viability of a political system depends upon the openness of its elites. "The governing class is renovated by recruiting to it families from the lower classes," while it loses its less competent, "more degenerate elements." Conversely, breakdowns or revolutions occur when there is a "slowing down in the circulation of the elites . . . while among the lower strata, elements of superior quality are increasing," which in frustration support the overthrow of the established strata.[5]

These theoretical arguments about the political implications of social mobility have had special relevance for an understanding of American society, as Tocqueville anticipated. In particular, what are the reasons for the political stability of the country and the absence of proletarian class-consciousness and socialist movements? Karl Marx, Friedrich Engels, and many subsequent writers stressed that supposedly unusually high rates of social mobility apparently had the effect of reducing social tensions. During the nineteenth century these high rates seemed to result from open land frontiers as well as rapid economic and demographic growth. In the early 1850s, Marx noted that working-class consciousness was low in the United States because, "though classes, indeed, already exist, they have not yet become fixed, but continually change and interchange their elements in a constant state of flux."[6] Similarly, Engels reported that the ideal of America is a nation "without a permanent and hereditary proletariat. Here everyone could become if not a capitalist, at all events an independent man, producing or trading with his own means, for his own accounts."[7]

In their search for independence, the ambitious could go to the frontier, which had to vanish before class politics could emerge. Engels presented this "safety valve" theory in a letter to Sorge in 1892:

> Only when the land–the public lands–is completely in the hands of speculators, and settlement on the land thus becomes more and more difficult or falls prey to gouging–only then, I think, will the time come, with peaceful development, for a third party.[8]

In trying to answer the question why there is no socialism in the United States, the German economic historian Werner Sombart also emphasized social mobility. He believed that a major part of the answer was that the American worker had high "chances of rising out of his class."[9] Some seventy years after Sombart's book, Stephen Thernstrom, the doyen of historical research on social mobility in the United States, wrote that the limited

> knowledge about working-class social mobility in industrial America . . . does seem to square with the age-old belief that social classes in the United States "continually change and interchange their elements in a constant state of flux." High rates of occupational and property mobility, and selected patterns of urban migration which weeded out the unsuccessful and constantly reshuffled them together, produced a social context in which a unified "isolated mass" of dispossessed workers could not develop.[10]

Our interest in mobility, which resulted in *Social Mobility in Industrial Society*, was prompted by the question whether variations in rates of social mobility among industrialized democracies have an effect on the political radicalism or the moderation of class-conscious labor movements. We were interested in the consequences of social mobility, not simply its measurement. Lipset's first article on the subject was written in reaction to an analysis by William Petersen, agreeing with Marx and Engels that uniquely high rates of social mobility in America, which seemed to have continued till the mid-twentieth century, helped to explain the absence of viable socialist movements.[11]

This conclusion had been challenged in the 1920s by the counterthesis that widespread social mobility is inherent in all class systems so that no society is either uniquely open or closed. In support of this view, Pitirim Sorokin reported on hundreds of local studies in the late nineteenth and early twentieth centuries.[12] The thesis was also advanced on theoretical grounds by Joseph Schumpeter.[13] From these studies and subsequent national surveys it seemed evident that rates of social mobility, considered cross-nationally, had been more similar than different. Schumpeter's picturesque analogy still holds that "each class resembles a hotel or omnibus, always full, but always of different people." As he emphasized, the "persistence of class position is an illusion. . . . Class barriers *must* be surmountable, at the bottom as well as at the top."[14]

We documented this generalization in 1959, based on the results of surveys in six industrial countries, concluding that they "are comparable in their high amounts of vertical mobility."[15] This finding has been reiterated by subsequent researchers using much more sophisticated statistical methods, but its validity is confined to rates of mass mobility, that is, shifts across the divide between workers and people in the middle class. As Peter Blau and Otis Dudley Duncan have stated, there is "little difference among various industrialized nations in rates of occupational mobility between the blue-collar and white-collar classes."[16] In a more complex analysis of mobility rates in sixteen countries, including some that are less developed, David Grusky and Robert Hauser emphasize "the fundamental similarity of mobility patterns," noting that "uniformity in mobility rates is not limited to highly industrialized countries."[17] Robert Erikson and John Goldthorpe have also addressed the "Marx to Petersen" thesis that high rates of social mobility explain the relative absence of working-class radicalism in the United States. Their findings "clearly indicate that in twentieth-century America the chance of escape from the working class via worklife mobility should be *not* be thought of as exceptional."[18]

But this conclusion does not apply to patterns of movement into elite groups. On the average, American elites have been more open, and come from lower social origins, than comparable Canadian and European strata. As Blau and Duncan state, "upward mobility from the working class into the top occupational stratum of society is higher in the United States than in other countries."[19] This outcome is not surprising if we consider that university education, a prerequisite for most elite positions, has been more available in the United States than elsewhere. In any case, different rates of movement into the elites should have less effect, if any, on mass attitudes than movements into, or out of, the much more numerous middle class. As we noted, "Regardless of how open the top elite is in any country, the number of persons who can achieve positions in it is not large enough to make it a goal towards which men may realistically work."[20]

The puzzling question remains why rates of mass mobility are similar under sharply different structural conditions in industrialized as well as less developed countries. In his *The Theory of the Leisure Class* (1898), Thorstein Veblen had dealt with this question at the motivational level. He argued that there is an inherent logic of social stratification. In any hierarchical ranking of positions, the desire to maintain a high status, or to improve a lower one, is insatiable. We rephrased Veblen's insight when we wrote that people are motivated "to protect their class position in order to protect their egos, and to improve their class positions in order to enhance their egos."[21] At the same time we noted that the desire for social mobility even appears where the norms against it are as strong as they are in the rigidly stratified society of India.[22] More recently, Grusky and Hauser have used a logic similar to Veblen's in their review of data from sixteen countries. They observe that the "uniformity in mobility patterns may be the analogue to invariance in prestige hierarchies, in the sense that both may result from cross-national regularities in the resources and desirability accorded occupations."[23]

Accordingly, the puzzle with which we started remains. Given the similarity in social mobility between workers and the middle class in all the industrialized countries, American workers have had the same reasons for feeling alienated from their society as their fellow workers elsewhere as well as the same reasons for pursuing their goals collectively.[24] What, then, explains the contrast between American workers and their fellows in other industrialized countries? Why are people at the lower rungs of the social ladder in the United States less disposed than those in other Western countries to support socialist movements and join trade unions? An answer may be found in beliefs concerning class rigidities and egalitarian ideas, arising from divergent historical experience which seem more important than slight variations in rates of mobility.

In the United States, the perception of a high degree of social mobility has gone hand in hand with a strong commitment to the ideal of equality. These two propensities have helped to perpetuate the belief that even the most lowly can rise, that hard work, ambition, and intelligence pay off. Survey data collected throughout the eighties indicate that these beliefs are still held by the overwhelming majority of Americans. Contrast this with formerly aristocratic societies before World War II, in which class hierarchy and family inheritance were still emphasized. In such countries even high rates of social mobility did not mitigate the belief of those in low-status groups that their situation resulted from a rigid, "post-feudal" class structure and deprived them of opportunities to improve their condition. This social and cultural context of mobility, rather than the measurement of its rate, determine people's beliefs concerning the opportunities open to them.

> It is the American emphasis on equality as part of the democratic credo which differentiates American society from the more status-oriented culture of Europe. Data on social mobility—the bare facts and figures—cannot speak for themselves. Although continued social mobility in American society helps to sustain the belief in the "open" class system, it does not follow that in another society a similar rate of social mobility would give rise to such a belief, or encourage it. The point is that in a society in which prevailing views emphasize class differences, even a high degree of social mobility may not suffice to undermine these views.[25]

The European pattern has changed in recent decades. Britain apart, the post-feudal emphasis on status has declined in response to social changes affected by World War II, the postwar Social Democratic era, extensive economic growth, and the expansion of higher education.[26] These have moderated the effects of class consciousness on politics and have given rise to a growing belief in the existence of an open meritocratic society. It is quite another question, of course, whether in the coming decades that belief will turn into a lower- and middle-class defense of privilege against foreign workers, for whom even lower-class positions in industrial society are a step up from their previous deprivations.

Analogous questions arose in the communist world. There also, ideological egalitarianism existed alongside great inequalities in income and achievement. As Stanislaw Ossowski pointed out a generation ago, the combination between classlessness and great differences in income, which are part of the American creed, was also found in the Soviet Union. He noted that

> The Socialist principle "to each according to his merits" is in harmony with the tenets of the American creed, which holds that each man is the master of his fate, and that a man's status is fixed by an order of merit. The Socialist principle allows of the conclusion that there are unlimited opportunities for social advancement and social demotion; this is similar to the American concept of "vertical social mobility." The arguments directed against *uravnilovka* [equalization or leveling of wages] coincide with the arguments put forward on the other side of the Atlantic by those who justify the necessity of economic inequalities in a democratic society. "The maximization of effort in an achievement-oriented society calls for considerable inequality" wrote [the American sociologist J.J.] Spenger in 1953. This sentence could equally well have been uttered by a statesman in the Soviet Union or the People's Democracies.[27]

Given the recent developments in the Soviet Union, we have the advantage of hindsight in assessing Ossowski's statement. It appears that the same words have had a different meaning in the Soviet context. Classlessness, the mastery of man's fate, the belief in unlimited opportunities, opposition to an equalization of wages, and the maximization of effort: all these are part and parcel of communist ideology. On the other hand, great economic inequalities by virtue of privileged access to consumer goods plus wage differentials as an incentive, and the principle that the merit, which is rewarded, is defined by combining performance with party loyalty and by substituting, when expedient, manifest loyalty for performance: these are the attributes of the *nomen-*

klatura and of workers in the favored enterprises of the military-industrial complex.[28]

The key issue, which treated more thoroughly than even in a recent collection, is the effect of experiencing social mobility, both upward and downward, on the politics of individuals.[29] Though the findings reported from different countries vary in detail, they reiterate the conclusion of previous surveys that mobility per se is much less important in determining political attitudes and party choice than actual class position. Subjective feelings about mobility have a greater impact than objective, actual movements, a finding also reported in the literature on status congruence. But like all social science research, this new work, like our three decade old one, points up the need for further research.

Seymour Martin Lipset
Reinhard Bendix

Notes

[1]Alexis de Tocqueville, *The Old Regime and the Revolution* (Anchor Books; New York: Doubleday, 1955), 169, 175.

[2]Emile Durkheim, *Suicide* (Glencoe: The Free Press, 1951), 250. After World War II, Adlai Stevenson extended this approach to the politics of the Third World when he referred to "the revolution of rising expectations."

[3]James Davies, "Toward a Theory of Revolution," *American Sociological Review*, 27 (1962), 5.

[4]Alexis de Tocqueville, *Democracy in America*, vol. 1 (New York: Vintage Books, 1954), 53, 55.

[5]Vilfredo Pareto, *Mind and Society*, vol. 3 (New York: Dover, 1963), 1430-31.

[6]Karl Marx, "The Eighteenth Brumaire of Louis Bonaparte," (1852) *Selected Works*, vol. 2 (Moscow: Cooperative Publishing House of Foreign Workers in the USSR, 1936), 324.

[7]Engels to Florence Kelley Wischnawetsky (6/3/1886), in Karl Marx and Friedrich Engels, *Selected Correspondence, 1846-1895* (New York: International Publishers, 1942), 449.

[8]Engels to Sorge (1/6/1892), "Unpublished Letters of Karl Marx and Friedrich Engels to Americans," *Science and Society*, 2 (1938) 361.

[9]Werner Sombart, *Why is There No Socialism in the United States?* (White Plains, N.Y.: International Arts and Sciences Press, 1976), originally published in 1906.

[10]Stephen Thernstrom, "Society and Social Mobility," in S.M. Lipset and John Laslett, eds., *Failure of a Dream, Essays on the History of American Socialism* (Garden City: Doubleday Anchor, 1974), 524.

[11]William Petersen, "Is America still the Land of Opportunity?" *Commentary,* 17 (November 1953), 477-486; S.M. Lipset and Natalie Rogoff, "Class and Opportunity in Europe and the U.S.," *Commentary,* 18 (December 1954), 562-568.

[12]Pitirim Sorokin, *Social and Cultural Mobility* (New York: The Free Press, 1959), originally published in 1927.

[13]Joseph Schumpeter, *Imperialism and Social Classes* (New York: Meridian Books, 1964), originally published in 1928.

[14]Ibid., 126, 130.

[15]This book, originally published in 1959, 27.

[16]Peter Blau and Otis Dudley Duncan, *The American Occupational Structure* (New York: John Wiley, 1967), 433.

[17]David B. Grusky and Robert M. Hauser, "Comparative Social Mobility Revisited," *American Sociological Review,* 49 (February 1984), 19-38.

[18]Robert Erikson and John Goldthorpe, "Are American Rates of Mobility Exceptionally High?" *European Sociological Review,* 1 (May 1985), 13.

[19]Blau and Duncan, *The American Occupational Structure,* 434.

[20]This book, 278.

[21]This book, 61.

[22]M.N. Srinivas, *Religion and Society among the Coorgs of South India* (Oxford: Oxford University Press, 1952), 30.

[23]Grusky and Hauser, "Comparative Social Mobility Revisited", 37.

[24]Erikson and Goldthorpe, "Are American Rates . . .", 20.

[25]This book, 81.

[26]Ralf Dahrendorf has argued that the declining appeal of the Social Democratic parties is in part due to the success of their programs in the modern welfare state. See his *The Modern Social Conflict* (London: Weidenfeld & Nicolson, 1988), 116-17.

[27]Stanislaw Ossowski, *Class Structure in the Social Consciousness* (Glencoe: The Free Press, 1963), 110, 114.

[28]We are indebted to the unpublished paper by Victor Zaslavsky (Department of Sociology, Memorial University of Newfoundland), "Soviet Transition to a Market Economy: State-Dependent Workers, Populism, and Nationalism."

[29]Frederick C. Turner, ed., *Social Mobility and Political Attitudes: Comparative Perspectives* (New Brunswick, Transaction Books, 1991). This Introduction has been revised from one written for the Turner volume by Lipset.

Foreword

The study of social mobility is basic to an understanding of the functioning of modern industrial societies. The quality of a nation's leadership, its prevailing political and social philosophies, and its rate of economic development are all profoundly influenced by the relative rigidity or fluidity of its class structure.

In the present study, Professors Lipset and Bendix cast doubt on the validity of a number of widely accepted generalizations relating to social mobility: particularly (1) that there has been substantially less mobility in Europe than in the United States, (2) that social mobility tends to decline as industrial societies mature, and (3) that opportunities for entrance into the business elite become more restricted with mature industrialization. In a careful analysis of the existing literature, the authors marshal an imposing array of evidence in support of their major thesis that social mobility is an integral and continuing aspect of the process of industrialization.

This volume represents the fruits of a collaborative effort that has extended over a long period. In part the authors utilize the results of the Oakland Labor Mobility Survey which was conducted by the Institute of Industrial Relations in 1949, but they also draw on a large number of other American and foreign studies. Although many of the chapters have previously been published as articles in scholarly journals, they have been extensively rewritten, and much new material has been added. The result is an integrated treatise on social mobility rather than a collection of papers.

Both of the authors are professors of sociology on the Berkeley campus of the University of California as well as members of the staff of the Institute of Industrial Relations.

ARTHUR M. ROSS, *Director*

Preface

Research in sociology has been criticized for its lack of continuity: the problems and areas selected for investigation by scholars fail to build upon the work of the past, and attempts to form a unified, cumulative body of empirical evidence do not, as a rule, succeed. The study of social stratification and especially the recent interest in social mobility is perhaps an exception: a growing number of social scientists in many countries have conducted empirical studies in this area in the postwar decade, many of which seek to replicate previous research in their own or other countries. The great international interest in mobility research reflects not only its theoretical significance, but also its saliency as a practical political question. The International Sociological Association has played a major role in stimulating and coördinating such research.

The present volume has two distinct though, it is hoped, related purposes. The first is to bring together and analyze comparative international research on social mobility, and thus help to work toward continuity and cumulation in this area of theoretical and practical interest. The second is to present and analyze data from an empirical study of mobility in Oakland, California.

This book also represents a growing tendency in contemporary social science research: the study of specific problems through analysis of existing data which were originally collected for other purposes. Currently, academic scholars, government agencies, and commercial research organizations, through sample surveys, gather myriads of data which are only partly analyzed. A study whose primary focus was election analysis may also include material on size of family, social mobility, education, organizational memberships, newspaper reading habits, and so forth. The student of elections is only interested in that material which bears on the vote. He is not concerned with interrelations among these factors themselves, although such analysis may interest students of population, of class structure, of popular culture, or of education. It is possible, therefore, to subject data from the same survey to a variety of separate analyses all addressed to sharply different theoretical and substantive concerns. Such separate analyses, which follow up the primary analysis for which the data were originally gathered, have come to be called *secondary* analyses. This study is one such secondary analysis.

One of the great advantages of secondary analysis is that it gives scholars with limited research funds access to great amounts of data which would be very expensive to collect as part of primary analysis; among its liabilities is the fact that the secondary analyst has no control over the questions which were asked or not asked, and must sometimes be frustrated by the absence of a question, or the classification of data in ways which inhibit their usefulness to him. We believe, however, that the virtues of secondary analysis far outweigh its limitations, and that scholars should be encouraged to engage in such research.

The history of the present research is worth elaborating since it may cast some light on the reasons for its major concerns. In 1948–1949, the Institute of Industrial Relations of the University of California undertook a study of factors related to labor mobility in a sample of a large part of the population of the city of Oakland. This research was never analyzed for its primary purpose, largely because within a year of the collection of the data, the Institute joined with five other similar institutes in different parts of the country and the Bureau of the Census to do a larger study of labor mobility in six cities.[1] The principal authors of this book, then as now Research Associates of the Institute, became interested in using some of the data collected in the unanalyzed Institute study

[1] See Gladys Palmer, *Labor Mobility in Six Cities* (New York: Social Science Research Council, 1954) for the outcome of that research.

(particularly, its detailed histories dealing with every job shift made by the respondents), for elaborating knowledge concerning social mobility. Given the geographically mobile character of the California population, we felt that the type of detailed specification of social mobility patterns which these data made possible would be worthwhile. These analyses have appeared in a number of papers:

1. S. M. Lipset and Reinhard Bendix, "Social Mobility and Occupational Career Patterns," *American Journal of Sociology*, 57 (1952):366–374, 494–504.

2. S. M. Lipset and Joan Gordon, "Mobility and Trade Union Membership," in Reinhard Bendix and S. M. Lipset, eds., *Class, Status and Power* (Glencoe: The Free Press, 1953), pp. 491–500.

3. Reinhard Bendix, S. M. Lipset, and F. Theodore Malm, "Social Origins and Occupational Career Patterns," *Industrial and Labor Relations Review*, 7 (1954): 246–261.

4. S. M. Lipset and F. Theodore Malm, "First Jobs and Career Patterns," *American Journal of Economics and Sociology*, 14 (1955):247–261.

5. S. M. Lipset, Reinhard Bendix, and F. Theodore Malm, "Job Plans and Entry into the Labor Market," *Social Forces*, 33 (1955): 224–232.

6. S. M. Lipset, "Social Mobility and Urbanization," *Rural Sociology*, 20 (1955): 220–228.

7. William Goldner, *The Methodology of the Oakland Labor Mobility Study*, Berkeley: Institute of Industrial Relations, University of California; mimeographed.[2]

Concern with the study of social mobility developed through this secondary analysis led us to deal with problems that were outside the scope of the Oakland data and to seek out other material, both in published studies and on the still unanalyzed IBM cards of studies done by various agencies. These problems involved analysis of national and international patterns of social mobility. The analyses were made possible by data supplied by Angus Campbell, Jr., and the Survey Research Center of the University of Michigan from their 1952 national election study; the National Opinion Research Center and Professor Albert Reiss, Jr.,

[2] Available on request from the Institute of Industrial Relations, Berkeley, California.

from the 1947 study of occupational prestige; the Institut für Demoskopie of Allensbach, Germany, from one of their surveys of German public opinion; the UNESCO Institute for Social Research in Cologne, Germany, from their study of the 1953 election in Germany; the DIVO Institute in Bad Godesberg, Germany, from one of their 1957 public opinion surveys; and the Finnish Gallup Poll from a comparable earlier Finnish survey. Some early results of these investigations were published in the following articles:

1. S. M. Lipset and Natalie Rogoff, "Class Opportunity in Europe and the U. S.: Some Myths and What the Statistics Show," *Commentary*, 18 (1954): 562–568.

2. S. M. Lipset and Reinhard Bendix, "Ideological Equalitarianism and Social Mobility in the United States," in *Transactions of the Second World Congress of Sociology*, Vol. 2 (London: International Sociological Association, 1954), pp. 34–54.

3. S. M. Lipset and Hans L. Zetterberg, "A Theory of Social Mobility," in *Transactions of the Third World Congress of Sociology*, Vol. 3 (London: International Sociological Association, 1956), pp. 155–177.

4. Reinhard Bendix and Frank Howton, "Social Mobility and the American Business Elite," *British Journal of Sociology*, 8 (1957): 357–369 and 9 (1958): 1–14.

In 1956, Arthur M. Ross, the Director of the Institute of Industrial Relations, suggested that we collect these various articles in a volume that would bring together in one place the findings of the various investigations of social mobility that had emerged out of the early efforts to elaborate the implications of the Oakland data. In attempting to fulfill this request, it soon became evident that a simple reprinting of the original articles would not be feasible. Many important areas in the study of social mobility would not be dealt with because the study of labor mobility in Oakland had not asked questions related to them. Consequently, we decided to enlarge the scope of the original essays by including the results of various other investigations made by scholars in different parts of the world bearing on the problems dealt with in these articles: this part of the task was especially important since the literature in this field has grown enormously in the past decade.

The final product is, therefore, only in part a report on the social mobility aspects of the Oakland study. The first part of the book, chapters i–iv, does not deal with any Oakland material; the middle section, chapters v–vii, reports the Oakland findings in some detail; and the last part of the book, chapters viii–x, like the first section, integrates the findings of a variety of studies, and concludes with a statement of theoretical and practical implications of the concern with social mobility.

This book should be read, then, as an example of the growth of an intellectual concern by two sociologists. It is our hope that it will help others who plan new primary research on the causes and consequences of social mobility.

There have been many individuals involved in the various phases of this work whose contributions should be acknowledged. These include F. Theodore Malm, Assistant Professor of Business Administration in Berkeley, who helped analyze the Oakland data reported in chapter vii (Professor Malm did not participate in the reworking of the paper of which he was co-author that went into this chapter, and consequently is not responsible for materials beyond the scope of the original paper); Natalie Rogoff, of the Bureau of Applied Social Research of Columbia University, who collaborated with Lipset in some early work on comparative rates of mobility, cited above; Hans Zetterberg, Associate Professor of Sociology at Columbia University, who helped develop this work further in a paper with Lipset, and who continued his collaboration through the work on this volume, being the co-author of chapter ii; Frank Howton, now of the RAND Corporation, collaborated with Bendix in the research on which chapter iv is based; and Joan Gordon, of the Sociology Department of Vassar College, who worked with Lipset on an analysis of the consequences of social mobility for trade-union participation, which was published in an article that is not included in this book. William Goldner, Acting Assistant Professor of Business Administration at the University of California, served as the statistician of the original Oakland study, wrote the methodological report, and has given freely of his time to advise on many problems of data analysis.

Among the staff of the Institute of Industrial Relations who have contributed in important ways to different stages of this work have been Robert Blauner, Amitai Etzioni, Donald Irwin, Robert

Raschen, and Arthur Stinchcombe. Jascha Kessler of Hamilton College and John Gildersleeve of the University of California Press did much to improve the phrasing of our ideas. We are especially indebted to Jeanette Podvin of the Institute office staff who has worked tirelessly to coördinate the numerous revisions which the manuscript has undergone.

The opportunity which Lipset had to spend a year free from university obligations as a Fellow of the Center for Advanced Study in the Behavioral Sciences during 1955–1956 contributed much to advance the study to its present form. Among other experiences which the year at the Center made possible was a workshop on social mobility in which he could exchange ideas with and benefit from the experience of Alex Inkeles of Harvard University, Herbert Goldhamer of the RAND Corporation, John Atkinson and Daniel Miller of the University of Michigan.

The administrative personnel of the Institute of Industrial Relations have also contributed considerably, both through intellectual advice and through making the research facilities of the Institute available. During the initial Oakland mobility stage of the project, they were Clark Kerr, then Director of the Institute and now President of the University of California, and the late Lloyd Fisher, then Associate Director. In the past two years, Arthur Ross, Director, and Margaret Gordon, Associate Director, have encouraged our efforts in working the material into book form.

SEYMOUR MARTIN LIPSET
REINHARD BENDIX

July 3, 1958

Chapter I | Introduction to the Original Edition

In every complex society there is a division of labor and a hierarchy of prestige. Positions of leadership and social responsibility are usually ranked at the top, and positions requiring long training and superior intelligence are ranked just below. The number of leaders and highly educated individuals constitutes everywhere a small minority. On the other hand, the great majority is made up of persons in the lower strata who perform manual and routine work of every sort and who command scant rewards and little prestige. In keeping with this division between "the few" and "the many" the stratification of society has often been pictured as a pyramid or a diamond; in the first analogy, society consists of a series of strata that become larger and more populous as we move down the hierarchy of reward and prestige, and in the second, it has small numbers at the top and bottom, with the mass of the population concentrated between. However it may be depicted, the point is that men grapple with the problems of determining the number of people at each rank in their society, and that through history various methods for doing this have been devised.[1]

The term "social mobility" refers to the process by which individuals move from one position to another in society—positions

---

[1] Kingsley Davis and W. E. Moore, "Some Principles of Stratification," *American Sociological Review*, 10 (1945): 242–249. Talcott Parsons, "A Revised Analytical Approach to the Theory of Social Stratification," *in* Reinhard Bendix and S. M. Lipset, eds., *Class, Status and Power: A Reader in Social Stratification* (Glencoe: The Free Press, 1953), pp. 92–128. Both contain general discussions of the subject.

1

which by general consent have been given specific hierarchical values. When we study social mobility we analyze the movement of individuals from positions possessing a certain rank to positions either higher or lower in the social system. It is possible to conceive of the result of this process as a distribution of talent and training such that privileges and perquisites accrue to each position in proportion to its difficulty and responsibility. An ideal ratio between the distribution of talents and the distribution of rewards can obviously never occur in society, but the approximation to this ideal, or the failure to approximate it, lends fascination to the study of social mobility.

Men and women occupying positions of high status generally endeavor to preserve their privileges for their kin and heirs; indeed, a "good" father is one who tries to pass the status he enjoys on to his children, and in many societies he will try to extend it to near and distant relatives as well. Hence, in every stratified, complex society there is, as Plato suggested, a straining towards aristocracy and a limitation of mobility. This tendency never runs its full course. To see why, it is sufficient to think of the kinds of society in which there would be no mobility: either a completely closed caste system in which each variation of rank was entirely determined by the status of the family into which one was born; or a society wherein each individual would be assigned a position commensurate with his genetically determined talents, and moreover, one in which this scheme of distribution would be adequate for all social needs—such a society as Aldous Huxley depicted in his *Brave New World,* where manufactured fetuses were so treated as to produce laborers, technicians, slaves, or intellectuals. Neither of these extreme conditions is plausible.

There are two basic reasons why social mobility exists in every society:

1. *Changes in demands for performance.* Complex societies change, and whether social change is slow or rapid it leads sooner or later to a change in the demands which different positions make on those who occupy them. The few who have inherited their high positions may not have the competence to meet the responsibilities which these positions entail. Yet in a society dominated by a hereditary ruling class these few exclude able indi-

viduals from lower ranks from positions of leadership. And their failure to lead, together with their exclusion of those capable of doing so, may cause tensions which will eventuate in the rise of a new social group and a subsequent attack upon the traditional prestige of the hierarchy.

2. *Changes in supplies of talent.* Just as there are changes in the demand for various kinds of talent, there are constant shifts in the supply. No elite or ruling class controls the natural distribution of talent, intelligence, or other abilities, though it may monopolize the opportunities for education and training. As long as many of those with high abilities belong to the lower strata (and many contemporary studies suggest that this is so), there will be leaders who come from those strata. The chance for potential leaders to develop the skills which will take them up from the ranks may be small, but sooner or later some will break through. Since those who do are usually people who can adapt themselves to new ways easily, they often become the core of a new group which challenges the dominant older one.

As Karl Mannheim pointed out, every ruling class faces certain dilemmas. In what ways and to what extent will it admit to leadership those lacking the proper social background? How many qualified newcomers (who may be dangerous if they are not absorbed) will, or rather, can, the elite accept without undermining its legitimate prestige? Under what conditions can an old elite refuse to learn new roles, and yet retain its monopoly on high status? These questions indicate the important relationship between a society's internal mobility and the stability of its political regime. Alexis de Tocqueville attributed the French Revolution to the attempt of a hereditary aristocracy to maintain its privilege after its responsibilities had been assumed by other groups. On the other hand, a ruling class may admit into its ranks those from lower strata who perform key functions. The English aristocracy thus remained at the top despite a transformation of society because, though it continued its emphasis on inheritance of social status, it not only met new responsibilities but also shared its privileges with those who threatened its position. The United States supplies another good example of an open, flexible upper class. Though it never had a "blooded" aristocracy, America's old business families provided the basis for an elite group—but a group that was never strong enough to exclude the new class of financial magnates and large corporation managers. (Of course, lack of traditional caste symbols made possible easy acceptance of newcomers into the elite.) In an expanding, dynamic society, such barriers to mobility as inherited rank can be a fundamental cause of instability, since expansion calls for an increase in the number of qualified leaders. As long as the ruling group is flexible it will allow ambitious and talented individuals to rise from the lower strata; yet an ever-present tendency toward the formation of an aristocracy tends to restrict such individual mobility in any society. If the restriction is sufficiently tight, it can provoke discontent, which may result in efforts by members of deprived groups to achieve *collective or group mobility*, sometimes through a struggle to supplant the dominant group.

This perennial dilemma of every ruling class reveals but one aspect of the relationship between mobility and social stability. Another is disclosed if we consider, in terms of the lower levels of society, the shifts in society's demands for different types of skills and the imbalance between the supply of talent and the social demand for talent. Modern industrial society is different from all earlier complex structures because in it, for the first time, the populace participates in politics. For the first time, the elite has been forced to help the masses toward literacy, which has in turn widened their horizons and increased their aspirations. A mere division of the spoils of status—power and economic rewards—between the old and emergent elites may not guarantee a new political equilibrium. The lower strata must also be satisfied in order to insure the structure against revolution. There are many mechanisms by which such satisfaction can be achieved; the change in the distribution of rewards is only one of them, and a discussion of such a consequence of mobility is but a partial analysis of the problem. The same shifts in status that take place in the higher strata take place in the lower, and the results are similar; the masses may be satisfied by the presence, or frustrated by the absence, of a high rate of individual mobility from low to higher status, or satisfaction may come through group mobility such as that which results from the rise in income and job-status of certain groups of manual laborers in comparison with white-collar workers. In recent decades group mobility has been particularly noticeable: the proportion of the national income received by the lower strata has increased, the relative income of various occupations has changed, and the power of different strata to affect political decisions has been affected by the rise of trade unions and labor parties.

We should guard these generalizations against one misinterpretation in particular. The analysis of the relationship between mobility and the stability of society involves vastly more than just a study of rates of mobility. It cannot be assumed that a high rate of mobility leads to satisfaction, or that a low rate results in discontent. Emile Durkheim has suggested that stable poverty—lack of change in the situation of the lower groups—is the best soil for moderation and conservatism.[2] Nor does "success" through high mobility necessarily result in satisfaction; often it creates yet higher aspirations and a formulated hatred for one's social position. It has been pointed out that the French Revolution occurred at a time in which people on most levels of society were greatly improving their position: this very improvement seems to have led the peasants to demand further economic rights, and the rising business classes to seek social status and political power commensurate with their wealth.

THE ANALYSIS OF MOBILITY

The study of social mobility involves several analytic steps:

1. Study of the relationship between *the starting* point of a person's career and the point the person has reached at the time of the analysis. Essentially, this is a comparison of the position which an individual inherited (or his status on entering the labor market) with his current position. Such data, however, have little analytic value unless presented on a comparative basis, or in relation to an ideal-typical society, i.e., one involving equal opportunity.

2. A second major question involves the relationships between social inheritance (or starting position) and the *means of mobility*. Here we may be concerned with the degree to which given back-

---

[2] E. Durkheim, *Suicide* (Glencoe: The Free Press, 1951), 250 ff.

grounds determine the level of education, the acquisition of skills, access to people at different levels in the social structure, intelligence, and motivation to seek higher positions. The factors associated with the possession of the *means of mobility* are analyzed through much of this book.

3. As yet we have little knowledge concerning the *process of mobility*. That is, most studies have dealt with the present and initial position of individuals, ignoring the degree to which there are patterned variations in careers. Therefore, in the second part of this book we shall report data from a study which examined the *complete* job history of respondents, data which let us generalize about the amount of variation in occupational and social-status positions which occurs during given careers.

4. The ultimate reason for our interest in this subject is the study of the *consequences of social mobility*. Unless variations in mobility rates and in the subjective experience of mobility make a difference for society or for the behavior pattern of an individual, knowledge concerning rates of mobility will be of purely academic interest. Most studies of social mobility have almost completely ignored the question of social consequences. In the following chapters, we shall discuss some hypotheses on the effect of varying rates of vertical occupational mobility on status lines, beliefs about mobility, and the social stability of different countries. We shall also present some quantitative data on the political attitudes (party support) of mobile as compared with stationary individuals.

We defined social mobility as the process by which individuals move from one stratum of society to another. It should be noted that most cases of mobility—though by no means all—involve concurrent changes in more than one kind of position. A person who moves up in the social hierarchy will tend to change his friends, join new organizations, move to a new neighborhood; perhaps he will even change his religious affiliation; in some cases he will change his name; often he will alter his political attitudes. In more general terms, a person who raises his occupational status will normally seek also to raise his social status: the man who moves downward occupationally will try to retain his social position. The dynamic relationship between these different positions can be cumulative and reciprocal; that is, social status may have positive influence on one's chances for occupational advancement, and occupational status may in turn help to modify one's social status. But such relationships can also be disjunctive in the sense that the same individual may simultaneously occupy several positions which are not "in accord" with one another. For example, an individual may acquire a high occupational position, yet find himself socially ostracized because of his family background. Conversely, an upper-class family may become impoverished, but retain, at least temporarily, its high social position. It is clear that the discrepancies of status resulting from the process of social mobility have special relevance for the stability or instability of society. Much of our discussion will analyze these relationships.

This book, as was explained in the preface, is an outgrowth of a series of studies undertaken for the Institute of Industrial Relations of the University of California, Berkeley, studies which began as a secondary analysis of data collected for a labor-market survey of Oakland, California. In analyzing these data we found it necessary at many points to relate the local particulars to the larger questions of social mobility in American society. As our interest developed we attempted to examine the national aspects of social mobility more directly by relating the ideology of equalitarianism to various indexes of social mobility in the United States, and also by using several studies of the American business elite to obtain some historical perspective. This broadened inquiry suggested in turn that a proper assessment of the evidence from American society could be made only on the basis of comparative materials; accordingly we undertook a survey of the literature dealing with rates and patterns of social mobility in different countries.

In presenting these studies in one volume, we have divided them into three groups, each designed to deal with different problems. Part one, "Social Mobility as a Characteristic of Societies," (chapters ii–iv), reports in detail findings on the rates of social mobility and beliefs about mobility in various societies, and suggests reasons for the patterns revealed by the data. Part two, "Social Mobility in a Metropolitan Community," (chapters v–vii), summarizes those findings from the Oakland study that are particularly relevant to an understanding of American patterns of mobility. In part three, "Causes, Consequences, and Dimensions of Social Mobility," (chapters viii–x), we deal first with the sociological and, second, with the social-psychological approach to the study of the causes of individual mobility. This discussion of theory and of empirical findings is followed, in the final chapter, by a general theoretical discussion of the consequences of varying rates and patterns of social mobility for the integration of total societies. Although these studies of social mobility in industrial society are somewhat fragmentary, we have attempted to integrate much of the literature on America, Europe, and to some extent Asia, that seeks to relate the general analysis of total rates of mass mobility (as distinct from concern with the backgrounds of the elite) to the broader problems of social stratification in modern society.

Part One | *Social Mobility as a Characteristic of Societies*

Chapter II | Social Mobility
in Industrial
Societies

Widespread social mobility has been a concomitant of industrialization and a basic characteristic of modern industrial society. In every industrial country, a large proportion of the population have had to find occupations considerably different from those of their parents. During the nineteenth century, the proportion of the labor force in urban occupations increased rapidly, while the proportion in agriculture decreased.

In the twentieth century the West has been characterized by a rapid growth of trade and of service industries, as well as of bureaucracy in industry and government; more people have become employed in white-collar work, and the comparative size of the rural population has declined even more rapidly than before.[1] These changes in the distribution of occupations from generation to generation mean that no industrial society can be viewed as closed or static.

This apparently simple statement runs counter to widely held impressions concerning the different social structures of American and Western European societies. According to these impressions, America has an "open society" with considerable social mobility, but the countries of Western Europe (specifically England, France, Italy, Germany, the Low Countries, and the Scandinavian

This chapter was written by Seymour Martin Lipset and Hans L. Zetterberg.
[1] See Colin Clark, *The Conditions of Economic Progress,* 3d ed. (London: Macmillan, 1957), pp. 490–520.

nations) have societies that are "closed," in the sense that the children of workers are forced to remain in the social position of their parents. This judgment reflects earlier European beliefs. In the age of the French Revolution, America appeared to be a land free from traditional institutions and historical legacies: the country of the future, Hegel called it, where each man was master of his fate just as American democracy itself was the product of human reason. This notion has been reiterated in many analyses, all contrasting American and European societies.

For the most part these discussions deal with the differences between democratic and autocratic institutions; but they also express assumptions about contrasting patterns of social mobility. Sometimes the political and social aspects of the contrast between America and Europe have been linked as cause and effect: differences in political institutions and values have been cited as evidence for the assertion that the society of America is "open," those of Europe "closed"; and the supposedly greater rate of social mobility in American society has been viewed as a major reason for the success of American democracy. For example, some fifty years ago Werner Sombart referred to the opportunities abundant in America as the major reason why American workers rejected the Marxist view that there is little opportunity under capitalism, while European workers accepted it because their opportunities were more restricted.[2] Such judgments as Sombart's were, however, no more than inferences based on the general contrast between the American tradition which proclaimed the goal of opportunity for all and the European emphasis upon social stability and class differences.[3] For as a matter of fact, it is not really clear whether the different political orientation of the American and European worker reflects different opportunities for social mobility or only a difference in their ethos!

---

[2] Werner Sombart, *Warum gibt es in den Vereinigten Staaten keinen Sozialismus?* (Tuebingen: J. C. B. Mohr, 1906), p. 135.
[3] It may be noted, however, that Sombart also emphasized the subjective factor: "Consideration should also be given to the mere awareness of the worker that he could become an independent farmer at any time. This consciousness was bound to give the American worker a feeling of security and peace of mind which the European worker did not know. One can tolerate any coercive situation much more easily if one has at least the illusion that one could escape that situation if worse came to worst." *Ibid.*, p. 140. Such an awareness was, in Sombart's opinion, relatively independent of the actual number of workers who availed themselves of opportunities for upward mobility, though he did not develop this point further.

The questions implicit in these alternative interpretations can be answered today with somewhat more assurance than was possible even two decades ago because of recent research in social mobility. In this chapter we attempt to summarize the findings available for a number of countries. Since our object is to assemble a large amount of empirical evidence, it will be useful to state at the outset that *the overall pattern of social mobility appears to be much the same in the industrial societies of various Western countries.*[1] This is startling—even if we discount the mistaken efforts to explain differences in political institutions by reference to different degrees of social mobility in the United States and in Western Europe. Further, although it is clear that social mobility is related in many ways to the economic expansion of industrial societies, it is at least doubtful that the rates of mobility and of expansion are correlated. Since a number of the countries for which we have data have had different rates of economic expansion but show comparable rates of social mobility, our tentative interpretation is that the social mobility of societies becomes relatively high once their industrialization, and hence their economic expansion, reaches a certain level.

OCCUPATIONAL MOBILITY

Before World War II, studies of social mobility were usually limited to investigations of the social origins of different occupational groups, employees of single factories, or inhabitants of single communities. Since World War II there have been at least fifteen different national surveys in eleven countries which have secured from representative samples of the population information

---

[1] See S. M. Lipset and Natalie Rogoff, "Class and Opportunity in Europe and America," *Commentary*, 18(1954):562–568, and David V. Glass, ed., *Social Mobility in Britain* (London: Routledge and Kegan Paul, 1954), pp. 321–338, 344–349; P. Sorokin, *Social Mobility* (New York: Harper, 1927), pp. 414–480; S. M. Lipset and Hans L. Zetterberg, "A Theory of Social Mobility," in *Transactions of the Third World Congress of Sociology*, Vol. III (London: International Sociological Association, 1956), pp. 155–177; Sigeki Nishira, "Cross-National Comparative Study on Social Stratification and Social Mobility," *Annals of the Institute of Statistical Mathematics*, 3(1957): 181–191; Colin Clark, *The Conditions of Economic Progress*, pp. 545–564; and Robert J. Havighurst, "Educação, Mobilidade Social e Mudança Social em Quatro Sociedades—Estudo Comparativo," *Educação e Ciências Sociais*, 2 (1957): 103–131. For an annotated bibliography of articles on social mobility which appeared in the major American sociological journals between 1924 and 1953, see Raymond W. Mack, Linton Freeman, and Seymour Yellin, *Social Mobility: Thirty Years of Research and Theory* (Syracuse: Syracuse University Press, 1957).

that relates the occupations of the respondents to the occupations of their fathers. In addition, there have been a number of studies conducted in different cities of various countries. Taken together, these investigations permit the comparison of current variations in occupational mobility, as well as some estimate of differences during the past half century.

To make such comparisons and estimates is difficult. Few of the studies were made with the intention of facilitating the comparison of findings in different countries. Many of them employ systems of classifying occupations which cannot be compared with each other and the questions concerning the occupations of respondents and fathers are seldom similar. In order to use the results for a comparative analysis, we have reduced the occupational categories for most countries to the closest approximation of manual, nonmanual, and farm occupations. In presenting these materials, we make the assumption that a move from manual to nonmanual employment constitutes upward mobility among *males*. This assumption may be defended on the following grounds:

1. Most male nonmanual occupations have more prestige than most manual occupations, even skilled ones.[5]

---

[5] See National Opinion Research Center, "Jobs and Occupations: A Popular Evaluation," *Opinion News*, 9 (1947): 3–13. A comparison of occupational-prestige studies in six countries has shown a high level of agreement among these studies in the rankings of occupations. See Alex Inkeles and Peter Rossi, "National Comparisons of Occupational Prestige," *American Journal of Sociology*, 61(1956):329–339. Surveys in two additional industrial countries reveal the same prestige pattern. See Ronald Taft, "The Social Grading of Occupations in Australia," *British Journal of Sociology*, 4(1953): 181–188, and F. van Heek, *et al.*, *Sociale stijging en daling in Nederland*, Vol. I (Leyden: H. E. Stenfert Kroese N.V., 1958), pp. 25–26. Two studies in relatively underdeveloped countries, Brazil and the Philippines, show that in both, occupational evaluations agree closely with those of industrial nations. See Bertram Hutchinson, "The Social Grading of Occupations in Brazil," *British Journal of Sociology*, 8(1957): 176–189; and Edward A. Tiryakian, "The Prestige Evaluation of Occupations in an Underdeveloped Country: The Philippines," *American Journal of Sociology*, 63(1958): 390–399.

A recent report on a study of occupational prestige in Poland reports that even under Communism, "passage of the better paid skilled manual worker to the position of the slightly lower paid white collar workers ... in the majority of cases is looked on as a promotion ... [although] from the point of view of the new criteria of prestige, this should not be considered a promotion." S. Ossowski, "Social Mobility Brought About by Social Revolutions," (Working Paper Eleven submitted to the Fourth Working Conference on Social Stratification and Social Mobility, International Sociological Association, December, 1957), p. 3.

Similar findings are reported in a 1952 German study which attempted to find out whether a high-income manual job had more prestige than a low-income non-

2. Among males, white-collar positions generally lead to higher incomes than manual employment.[6]

3. Nonmanual positions, in general, require more education than manual positions.[7]

4. Holders of nonmanual positions, even low-paid white-collar jobs, are more likely than manual workers to think of themselves as members of the middle class and to act out middle-class roles in their consumption patterns.[8]

---

manual position, by asking the following question: "Who do you think receives more prestige from the population in general: A bookkeeper, who earns 300 marks a month, or a foundry worker, who brings home 450 marks a month?" The results (in percentages) were as follows:

Answer	Total sample	Manual worker respondents only
The bookkeeper............	58	56
The foundry-worker........	24	28
Don't know...............	18	16

From Erich Peter Neumann and Elizabeth Noelle, *Antworten, Politik im Kraftfeld der öffentlichen Meinung* (Allensbach am Bodensee: Verlag für Demoskopie, 1954), p. 107.

[6] The evidence on the relationship between income and occupation in a number of countries shows that the income of white-collar workers has traditionally been higher than that of skilled workers. In periods of prolonged prosperity and inflation, the gap tends to narrow considerably. However, in the United States in 1951, "in each age group beyond 35, nonfarm occupational groups could be ranked by average income in the following order: professional workers; managerial workers; clerical and sale workers; craftsmen; operatives; service workers; and laborers." Herman P. Miller, *Income of the American People* (New York: Wiley, 1955), p. 54. Similar results are reported for Germany in the data gathered in a sample survey study of the German population by the UNESCO Institute in Cologne in 1953.

[7] The median schooling reported for American males in the 1950 census for clerical and sales workers was slightly over 12 years; that of craftsmen and foremen was 9.3 years. See Lawrence Thomas, *The Occupational Structure and Education* (New York: Prentice-Hall, 1956), p. 39. The German study cited above indicates that in Germany, about 30 per cent of lower white-collar workers have more than an elementary education, compared to only 2 per cent of the skilled workers.

[8] See Richard Centers, *The Psychology of Social Classes* (Princeton University Press, 1949), p. 86; Natalie Rogoff, "Social Stratification in France and in the United States," *in* R. Bendix and S. M. Lipset, eds., *Class, Status and Power* (Glencoe: The Free Press, 1953), p. 585; Marcel Bresard, "La mobilité sociale: Le choix d'une échelle sociologique," in *Transactions of the Second World Congress of Sociology*, Vol. II, p. 399. Bresard indicates that white-collar workers and lower civil servants in France were much more likely to own property than manual workers, and that a somewhat higher proportion had automobiles and telephones. The tendency for white-collar workers to consume more like the middle class than the working class may be inferred from data on the employment of wives in Sweden. C. Arnold Anderson reports that white-collar workers are about twice as likely to have working wives as are manual workers, and that the majority of the working wives are con-

5. Low-level nonmanual workers are more likely to have political attitudes which resemble those of the upper middle class than those of the manual working class.[9]

It is true, of course, that many white-collar positions are lower in income and prestige than the higher levels of skilled manual work; however, most of these poorly paid white-collar positions are held by women, and male white-collar workers are often able to secure higher-level supervisory posts.[10] Consequently, we believe

centrated in the lower-income groups of white-collar workers. The employment of wives of manual workers is more evenly distributed among income groups. It seems that when the income of a white-collar worker goes below that required to maintain a middle-class consumption style, his wife goes to work to regain it. See "Employment, Occupation, and Socio-Economic Status of Swedish Wives in Relation to Occupation and Status of Husbands," *Statistisk Tidskrift,* 6 (1957): 3–15. See also W. H. Form and Gregory P. Stone, *The Social Significance of Clothing in Occupational Life,* Technical Bulletin 247 (East Lansing: Michigan State University, 1955). There is evidence from a number of countries which demonstrates that white-collar and manual workers have different styles of life, as indicated by divergent consumption patterns. "Comparable data for these occupational classes are available for Belgium, Czechoslovakia, Finland, Bulgaria, Norway, Germany, Sweden, the Netherlands, Japan, Denmark and Switzerland ... *Within the same income group,* manual workers spend more of their income for food than white-collar employees and officials [civil servants]." W. S. Woytinsky and E. S. Woytinsky, *World Population and Production Trends and Outlook* (New York: The Twentieth Century Fund, 1953), p. 276.

[9] Findings bearing out this statement have been reported for Great Britain, the United States, Germany, Norway, Canada, and Australia. For a summary of data on voting behavior and occupation, see S. M. Lipset, *et al.,* "The Psychology of Voting: An Analysis of Political Behavior," *in* Gardner Lindzey, ed., *Handbook of Social Psychology,* Vol. II (Cambridge: Addison Wesley, 1954), pp. 1124–1175.

[10] Gallup Poll data analyzed and kindly supplied by Dr. John Bonham show that over one-third of the British male white-collar workers held upper-level white-collar jobs in 1950–1951, as contrasted with 12 per cent of the female white-collar workers. In the U.S., 56 per cent of the male white-collar workers earned more than $3,000 per year in 1949, as contrasted with 15 per cent of women employees. See L. Thomas, *The Occupational Structure . . . ,* p. 137. In countries for which we have data, low-level male white-collar workers are considerably younger on the average than male manual workers. Thomas suggests that one explanation of this fact is that, "the clerical and sales occupations may be stepping stones for considerable numbers of young men seeking eventual positions as proprietors or managers." *Ibid.,* p. 40.

In Germany in the mid-twenties, a study of white-collar workers revealed that 20 per cent of the males and only 2.5 per cent of the females held upper-level white-collar jobs (responsible work), while 71 per cent of the females and 32 per cent of the males held lower-stratum white-collar positions. See Hans Speier, *The Salaried Employees in German Society* (New York: Works Progress Administration and Department of Social Science, Columbia University, 1939), p. 120. Speier suggested in this study that with the growth in magnitude of white-collar positions, "the chances of the male employees to exercise some authority in virtue of his position and sex becomes more intense [greater] ... the ratio between male and female employees has shifted quantitatively in favor of women and qualitatively

that using the break between manual and nonmanual occupations as an indicator of low and high occupational status is justified whenever a dichotomous division of males in urban occupations is used. It is important to remember, however, that like all single-item indicators of complex phenomena this one will necessarily result in some errors; that is, some nonmanual positions which have lower status than some manual occupations will be classified in the high group though they should be in the low."

POSTWAR NATIONAL SAMPLES

Figure 2.1 presents the inter-generational shifts between manual and nonmanual occupations for adult males in six countries. The data indicate that a large minority of the sons of the industrial labor force achieve nonmanual positions. In France this group comprises 35 per cent of the sons, in Germany 26 to 30 per cent, in Switzerland 44 per cent, in Sweden 29 per cent, in Japan 33 per cent, and in the United States 31 to 35 per cent. A smaller minority in each country declines from nonmanual to manual positions, the percentages ranging from a low of 13 per cent to a high of 38 per cent.[12]

in favor of men. The difference in stratification between both sexes has been widened. Subordinate positions are being filled still more with young and cheap female forces." *Ibid.*, pp. 121–123.

[11] See Peter M. Blau, "Occupational Bias and Mobility," *American Sociological Review*, 22 (1957): 392–399. In a secondary analysis of the NORC data on occupational prestige, Blau found that the break between manual and nonmanual occupations was the most relevant in explaining varying amounts of bias in occupational prestige ratings. His analysis is congruent with the assumption that the boundary between manual and nonmanual work is the most significant point in dichotomizing the stratification hierarchy if one is concerned with accounting for differential behavior.

[12] An analysis of mobility patterns among a sample of Russian émigrés after World War II shows a pattern similar to that reported for Western Europe and America, as the following table shows.

SOCIAL MOBILITY AMONG RUSSIAN ÉMIGRÉS
(Percentages)

Son's occupation	Father's occupation		
	Nonmanual	Manual	Farm
Nonmanual.....................	90	28	20
Manual........................	10	69	36
Farm..........................	..	3	44
Number in sample...............	265	376	541

An obvious drawback of the studies from which these data are derived is that they depend upon a "common-sense" evaluation of occupational prestige: we have sought to correct for this deficiency by elaborating in detail the distinction between manual and nonmanual occupations. However, several recent studies have attempted to give a firmer empirical foundation to the status of occupations by ascertaining first the esteem in which various occupations are held by a cross-section of the public; then, rates of social mobility were established with reference to these *known* prestige rankings, in which, for example, routine clerical jobs, are categorized as "low" even though they are nonmanual positions. The first such study was made by Professor David Glass of the London School of Economics.[13] Its sophisticated methodology has inspired researchers in Denmark,[14] Japan,[15] and Sweden[16] to proceed along similar lines. When completed, this series of studies will yield much detailed information about mobility rates. At present we can show two comparable summaries from Denmark

From R. A. Feldmesser, "Observations on Trends in Social Mobility in the Soviet Union and Their Implications," in A. Kassof, et al., *Stratification and Mobility in The Soviet Union: A Study of Social Class Cleavages in the U.S.S.R.* (Cambridge: Harvard Russian Research Center, n.d.; mimeographed).

Substantiating evidence for the high rate of social mobility in the U.S.S.R. found by Feldmesser is given in Alex Inkeles, "Social Stratification and Social Mobility in the Soviet Union: 1940–1950," *American Sociological Review*, 15(1950): 465–479.

A study of the 1957 Norwegian elections received from the Oslo Institute for Social Research after this book had gone to the publisher indicates that 22 per cent of the sons of Norwegian manual and farm workers moved up into nonmanual occupations, and that 31 per cent moved down from nonmanual to manual and farm-labor jobs. These figures are not precisely comparable with the others since the Norway survey listed farm owners separately and combined farm and manual workers.

SOCIAL MOBILITY IN NORWAY, 1957
(Percentages)

Son's occupation	Father's occupation		
	Nonmanual	Manual*	Farm owner**
Nonmanual	63	22	26
Manual*	31	70	44
Farm Owner**	5	8	30
Number in sample	153	369	253

* Includes farm workers.
** Includes self-employed in fish and lumber industries.

[13] David Glass, ed., *Social Mobility in Britain.*
[14] Studies in progress by Professor Kaare Svalastoga, University of Copenhagen.
[15] Research Committee, Japanese Sociological Society, *Social Mobility in Japan: An Interim Report on the 1955 Survey of Social Stratification and Social Mobility in Japan,* (1957; mimeographed). Two additional sources of data on Japanese

(*Footnote 15 continued on p. 23.*)

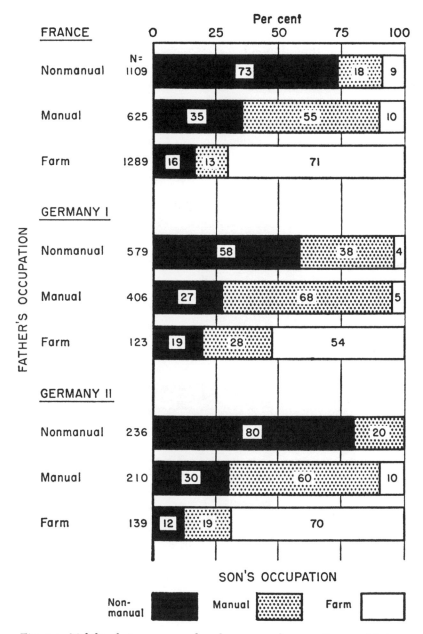

Fig. 2.1. Mobility between manual and nonmanual occupations and between
agriculture and nonagriculture. Details do not always add to 100 per cent because
of rounding. *Source.*—France: M. Bresard, "Mobilité sociale et dimension de la
famille," *Population,* 5 (1950): 553–566. Germany: (I) From data supplied by Dr.
Erich Reigratski, Cologne, Germany, from his study *Soziale Verflechtungen in der
Bundesrepublik* (Tubingen: Mohr-Siebeck, 1956); (II) From data supplied by Institut für Demoskopie, Allensbach, Germany. (*Figure continued on next page.*)

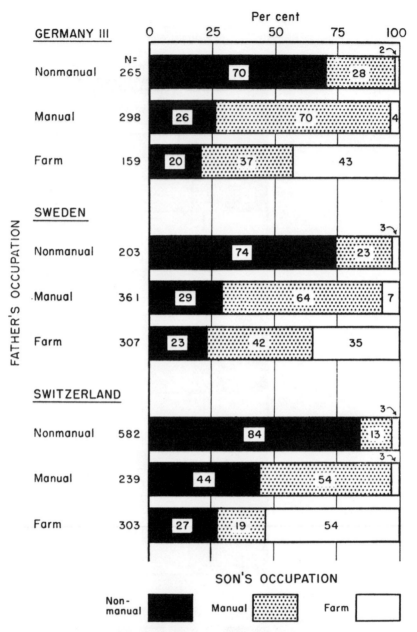

Fig. 2.1 (continued). *Source.*—Germany (III): From data supplied by DIVO, Frankfurt A.M. Sweden: From data collected by H. L. Zetterberg, partly reported in "Sveriges fem rangrullor," *Vecko-Journalen*, 48 (1957): 40. Switzerland: Recalculated from information supplied by Professor Roger Girod.

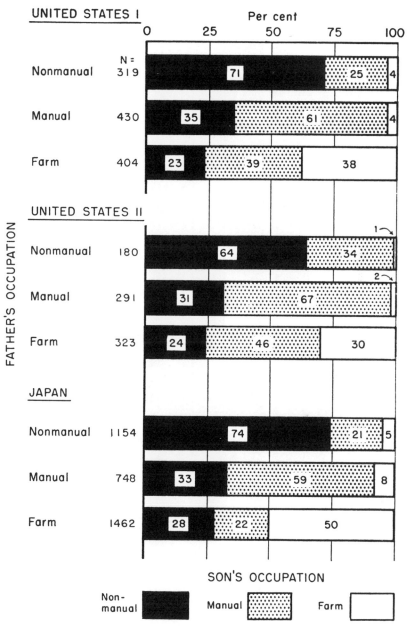

Fig. 2.1 (continued). *Source.*—United States: (I) Derived by Dr. Natalie Rogoff from data published by the National Opinion Research Center in "Jobs and Occupations," *Opinion News,* September 1, 1947, pp. 3–33; (II) From data supplied by the Survey Research Center of the University of Michigan from their study of the 1952 presidential election. Japan: Research Committee on Stratification and Social Mobility of The Japanese Sociological Association, *Social Stratification and Mobility* (Tokyo: 1956; mimeographed), p. 13.

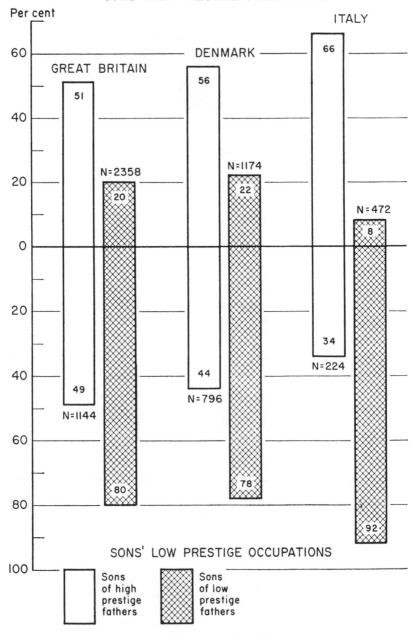

Fig. 2.2. For explanation see foot of facing page.

and Great Britain, and a reasonably comparable study from Italy (see figure 2.2). We find here evidence of considerable upward mobility from the occupational categories of manual workers, farm workers, and routine nonmanual employees into farm-ownership and high-level nonmanual positions. In Denmark 22 per cent of them rise in this way; in Great Britain, 20 per cent; and in Italy, 8 per cent. Downward mobility between these categories appears to be greater: 44 per cent in Denmark, 49 per cent in Great Britain, and 34 per cent in Italy. The actual decline is probably not as great as shown by these figures. The classification employed in these studies, which grouped together positions of comparable prestige regardless of whether these were in the farm or nonfarm sectors of the economy, is, whatever its merits on other grounds, likely to exaggerate the rate of downward mobility, since sons of farmers who come from the rural middle class and go to the city are more likely to become manual workers than young men from the urban middle class.[17] This consideration does *not* apply as much to Great Britain, which has a very small proportion of its population engaged in farming, but it does apply to agricultural countries like Denmark and Italy. A method of mobility analysis that is quite adequate for the former country might, therefore, be misleading in the latter countries.[18]

mobility, received after the present manuscript had gone to press, describe changes in occupational structure as a consequence of industrialization and the influences on mobility of education. These data appear congruent with the earlier findings above. See Kunio Odaka, ed., *Shokugyô to Kaisô* (Occupation and Stratification) (Tokyo: Mainichi Shimbunsha, 1958); Japanese Sociological Society, *Nihon Shakai no Kaisô teki Kozô* (The Stratification System in Japanese Society), (Tokyo: Yuhikaku, 1958).

[16] Studies in progress by Professor Gösta Carlson, Sociological Institute, Lund University.

[17] For documentation see chapter viii.

[18] The Japanese researchers computed so-called indices of association which measure the relationship between fathers' and sons' occupational status by calculating

Fig. 2.2. Mobility between occupations of high and low prestige. Occupations of high prestige are high levels of nonmanual occupations and farm owners, except in the high-prestige data for Italy, which include all nonmanual occupations and well-to-do peasants. Occupations of low prestige include routine nonmanual occupations, manual occupations, and farm occupations, except the low-prestige data for Italy, which include only manual occupations (including farm workers) and poor peasants. *Source.*—Great Britain: Calculated from David Glass, *Social Mobility in Britain.* Denmark: Computed from data furnished by Professor K. Svalastoga, Copenhagen, Denmark. Italy: L. Livi, "Sur la mesure de la mobilité sociale," *Population,* 5 (1950): 65–76.

A third method of determining the relationship between the occupations of fathers and sons—the method least useful for comparative purposes—has been employed in two Scandinavian studies, one in Finland, the other in Sweden. Respondents were themselves asked to identify the social class to which they and their fathers belonged. Since the meaning of class identification varies considerably from country to country, and the two studies used very different social-class categories, we will not discuss them here.[19]

The lack of comparable classifications in nationwide surveys of social mobility makes it difficult to conclude this summary with more than general impressions. Moreover, we must bear in mind that we deal here exclusively with a single index to complex and quite diverse societies, so that inferences can carry us only part of the way and should be made with caution. Yet, the value of a comparative approach to social mobility becomes apparent when we set side by side for each country the figures which are most clearly indicative of upward, downward, and total mobility across the line between the middle and the working class (table 2.1). Because of the varying systems of occupational classification the Italian figures cannot be compared with any of the others, and the British and Danish figures can be compared only with each other. The remainder, however, are reasonably comparable.

The figures in the first column give the proportion of all sons of manual workers who now occupy middle-class positions. In the second column the figures indicate the proportion of all sons of middle-class fathers who are now in manual occupations. In order to get some index of the total mobility in society, the figures in the third column were computed: out of all the sons of fathers in urban occupations who are themselves in urban occupations, those who were mobile in either direction were added together,

"the ratio of actual to the expected number of sons who, having category 1 fathers, arrive in category 1." See D. Glass, ed., *Social Mobility in Britain*, pp. 194–195. The British researchers also used this index, which is arrived at by calculating the expected number on the assumption that sons are distributed on a random basis among occupational categories. It should be noted that the Japanese indices of association show a slightly greater tendency for Japanese to remain in the father's occupational prestige class than for the British. See Research Committee, Japanese Sociological Society, *Social Mobility in Japan*, p. 10, and Glass, *Social Mobility in Britain*, p. 199. See also p. 27, n. 24.

[19] For a presentation of the results of these studies see Lipset and Zetterberg, "A Theory of Social Mobility," p. 165.

TABLE 2.1

COMPARATIVE INDICES OF UPWARD AND DOWNWARD MOBILITY
(Percentages)

NONFARM POPULATIONS

Country	Upward mobility (Nonmanual sons of manual fathers)	Downward mobility (Manual sons of nonmanual fathers)	Total vertical mobility (Nonfarm population mobile across the line between working and middle class)
United States[a]	33	26	30
Germany[b]	29	32	31
Sweden	31	24	29
Japan	36	22	27
France	39	20	27
Switzerland	45	13	23

POPULATIONS WITH RURAL AND URBAN OCCUPATIONS CLASSIFIED TOGETHER

Country	High prestige occupation sons of fathers in low prestige occupations	Low prestige occupation sons of fathers in high prestige occupations	Proportion mobile across high and low occupation prestige lines
Denmark	22	44	31
Great Britain	20	49	29
Italy	8	34	16

SOURCES: See figures 2.1 and 2.2.
[a] Average of three studies: two cited in figure 2.1, and the third computed from data in R. Centers, "Occupational Mobility of Urban Occupational Strata," *American Sociological Review*, 13 (1948):203.
[b] Average of three studies cited in figure 2.1.

and this figure was expressed as a percentage of the total. For example, of those persons in the nonfarm population of the United States who were sons of fathers in nonfarm occupations, 30 per cent had either fallen into a manual position from their fathers' nonmanual position, or had risen from their fathers' working-class occupation into a middle-class one. Though this is, to be sure, a very crude index, it should give a rough indication of the fluidity of the urban occupational structure. It expresses the proportion of the native urban population which has, in one way or another, "changed class."

The first impression one gains from table 2.1 is that all the countries studied are characterized by a high degree of mobility. From one generation to another, a quarter to a third of the non-farm population moves from working class to middle class or vice versa. Second, there is among the first six countries a high degree of similarity in this total mobility rate. The total range is between 23 and 31 per cent, and five of the six countries (United States, Germany, Sweden, Japan, France) range between 27 and 31 per cent. Such narrow differences lead quickly to one interpretation: total mobility rates in these countries are practically the same.[20]

This similarity does not hold, of course, if the relationship between parental occupations and sons' occupations are compared in terms either of upward or of downward mobility, rather than the total amount of mobility. Then it appears that there is considerable variation among countries in the degree to which a father's occupation is an asset or a handicap. Thus, we see that the sons of middle-class fathers are more likely to fall in status in the United States and Germany than they are in Japan, France, or Switzerland. There is less variation in the degree to which a working-class family background handicaps a man in securing a nonmanual position; only Switzerland stands out as permitting higher rates of upward movement than the other countries.[21] Given the variations in the methods of collecting data, it would be premature to place much reliance on these differences.

Information about career patterns might yield results different from those cited above. The length of the step up or down the ladder of occupations might well be substantially greater in one country than in another, although in each the same proportion of the population could obtain better positions than their fathers when we compare them solely in terms of movement across the

[20] Data from Morris Janowitz' study of social mobility based on a survey conducted by DIVO in 1955 in Western Germany indicate lesser opportunities for personal social mobility in Germany as compared to the United States, than are shown by the three German studies we have cited in figure 2.1. However, Janowitz included both men and women in his sample. Since quite recent data supplied by DIVO from a 1957 survey indicate that German women have a much lower rate of social mobility than men, this factor could account for these apparently contradictory findings. Morris Janowitz, "Social Stratification and Mobility in Western Germany," *American Journal of Sociology*, 64(1958): 6–24. The considerably greater upward mobility of German men as compared to women is also reflected in sharply different levels of aspiration. A study of Hesse youth aged 14 to 21 found that 64 per cent of the males were striving "for a higher social position than your father's" as compared with 34 per cent of the females. See "Intensität des Aufstiegs-strebens," *Offene Welt*, 54 (1958): 102.
[21] For a detailed discussion of the high rates of social mobility in Switzerland, see Roger Girod, "Mobilité sociale en Suisse: changements de milieu d'une génération à l'autre," *Revue de l'institut de sociologie*, 1957, No. 1, pp. 19–32.

manual-nonmanual line. Studies of intra-generational mobility have been made in the Netherlands[22] and Sweden.[23] The Dutch study shows that intra-generational mobility has increased over the past few decades; the Swedish study, that advancement from general and industrial labor was slower in the depression years 1930–1935 than in the war years 1940–1945. Both studies support the proposition that intra-generational mobility increases with industrial expansion.

Finally, it should be mentioned that the fact that one country contains a greater percentage of mobile individuals than another, does *not* mean that that country approximates a model of equal opportunity more closely. There may be *more mobility* in one country than in another, and yet *less equality* of opportunity. For example, if a country is 90 per cent peasant, even with completely equal opportunity most children of peasants must remain peasants. Even if every nonpeasant position should be filled by a peasant's son, only about 11 per cent of the sons of peasants could change occupation; an upward mobility rate of 9 per cent would indicate complete equality of opportunity. On the other hand, if a country undergoes rapid economic transformation and the proportion of nonmanual positions increases to, say, one-half of all positions, then anything less than a 50 per cent upward mobility rate would indicate inequality.[24]

Our major finding in this section is that the countries involved are comparable in their high amounts of total vertical mobility.

[22] J. J. M. van Tulder, "Occupational Mobility in the Netherlands from 1919 to 1954," in *Transactions of the Third World Congress of Sociology*, Vol. III (London: International Sociological Association, 1956), pp. 209–218. An earlier Dutch reference is F. van Heek, *Stijging en daling op de maatschappelijke ladder* (Leiden: E. J. Brill, 1945).

[23] C. Arnold Anderson, "Lifetime Inter-Occupational Mobility Patterns in Sweden," *Acta Sociologica*, 1 (1955):168–202.

[24] For statistical techniques developed to handle this problem, see Rodolfo Benini, *Principii di Demografia* (Florence: G. Babèra, 1901), pp. 129–138; Emily Perrin, "On the Contingency between Occupation in the Case of Fathers and Sons," *Biometrika*, 3 (1904): 467–469; Donald Marvin, "Occupational Propinquity as a Factor in Marriage Selection," *Publications of the American Statistical Association*, 16 (1918): 131–150; Natalie Rogoff, *Recent Trends in Occupational Mobility* (Glencoe: The Free Press, 1953), pp. 29–33; David V. Glass, ed., *Social Mobility in Britain*, pp. 218–259; see also Frederico Chessa, *La Transmissione Ereditaria delle Professioni* (Torino: Fratelli Bocca, 1921), for an early presentation of the logic of this approach. Several critical papers on this technique appear in *Population Studies*, 9 (1955). An important recent critique may be found in Edward Gross, *Work and Society* (New York: Thomas Y. Crowell, 1958), pp. 150–154.

The reservations and cautions which are in order do not invalidate this finding, which a number of other researchers in this area, such as Pitirim Sorokin, Robert Havighurst, Natalie Rogoff, David Glass, and Colin Clark, also agree is warranted by the extant statistical data. In this connection, it is worth reporting that the Australian-British economist, Colin Clark, "found [it] *rather surprising,* [that] of the sons of French urban manual and clerical workers, a higher proportion succeeded in securing 'social promotion' than in the U.S.A."[25]

URBAN MOBILITY IN DIFFERENT COUNTRIES

Studies based on recent national samples can be supplemented in a number of countries by studies of mobility in individual cities.

Recent surveys of samples of the population of two Asian cities, Tokyo, Japan, and Poona, India, show high rates of social mobility. The Japanese study indicates that about one-third of the

---

[25] Colin Clark, *The Conditions of Economic Progress,* 3d ed., p. 554. Clark also found British mobility patterns somewhat similar to those of the United States, and that "Italy is a society of much greater hereditary stratification than any of the other countries examined."

In "Class and Opportunity in Europe and America," Natalie Rogoff has pointed out that the French mobility survey that she had previously cited as suggesting higher rates of mobility in the United States than in France actually does not do so. (See "Social Stratification in France and the United States.") The French study used fewer occupational classes than the N.O.R.C. one with which it was compared—e.g., the American analysis counted movement among unskilled, semiskilled and skilled as social mobility, while the French used only one category, *ouvrier,* for all three—and since there were fewer classes in France there was less mobility. It is obvious that one can increase or decrease the proportion who are "mobile" by increasing or decreasing the number of classes among which movement may take place.

It is interesting to note, moreover, that not only can the same data yield different statistical conclusions depending on whether or not comparable classifications are used, but the same statistical results may yield widely divergent interpretations, even in the same book. Citing the first Rogoff comparison which suggested greater mobility in the United States than in France, Jessie Bernard writes: "The relative mobility which prevails in a society is, however, apparently more closely related to its technology than to its historic tradition. Thus, for example, one study which compared occupational mobility in the United States and France found that although mobility was greater in the first—67.5 per cent as compared with 48.3 per cent—both showed a great deal of mobility in spite of the feudal tradition in one and the frontier tradition in the other." Jessie Bernard, "The United States," *in* Arnold M. Rose, ed., *The Institutions of Advanced Societies,* (Minneapolis: University of Minnesota Press, 1958), p. 610. In the same book François Bourricaud, in the chapter dealing with France, cites these data from the early Rogoff study to argue that "the mobility of the French workers is absolutely and relatively low." *Ibid,* p. 487.

To this note on the varying interpretations of data one must add that the comment of Colin Clark, quoted in the text, that French workers have greater opportunities

sons of fathers employed in manual occupations were in non-manual jobs when interviewed, and that about 30 per cent of those coming from nonmanual family backgrounds had become manual workers, while the Indian survey found that 27 per cent of those of manual origin had risen into the middle classes, and that about one-quarter of those whose fathers were in nonmanual positions had become manual workers.[26]

In Helsinki, Finland, there is considerable mobility among youth of 21 to 24 years of age. Close to half (45 per cent) of the sons of manual workers either had nonmanual positions, or were attending institutions of higher learning and were, therefore, preparing for high-level occupations.[27]

A comparable high rate of mobility in another Scandinavian capital is indicated by a study of young residents of Stockholm

---

for advancement than Americans is also based on a comparison of American data with the results of the same French mobility survey cited by Rogoff, Bernard, and Bourricaud. The French data which have been the subject of so many varying interpretations are those reported in Figure 2.1 above, and also form the basis for our conclusions about the relative amount of social mobility in France.

[26] A. G. Ibi, "Occupational Stratification and Mobility in the Large Urban Community: A Report of Research on Social Stratification and Mobility in Tokyo, II," *Japanese Sociological Review*, 4(1954):135–149; N. V. Sovani and Kusum Pradhan, "Occupational Mobility in Poona City Between Three Generations," *The Indian Economic Review*, 2 (1955): 23–36. The Indian study, which uses a 10-class occupational breakdown, suggests that urban India has a very mobile society. While these Asian urban studies indicate high rates of social mobility, data from a small sample in the city of Melbourne, Australia, have led two writers to conclude that "a comparison between these Australian data and data on social mobility from the United States and certain Western European countries suggests that there is much less mobility from manual to nonmanual occupations in Australia." Ronald Taft and Kenneth F. Walker, "Australia," *in* Arnold M. Rose, ed., *The Institutions of Advanced Societies*, (Minneapolis: University of Minnesota Press, 1958), p. 143. Although Taft and Walker go on to give a psychological explanation of why there is less social mobility in Australia than in other countries, we frankly doubt their factual conclusion. The Melbourne data on which they rely—reported in O. A. Oeser and S. B. Hammond, *Social Structure and Personality in a City*, (London: Routledge and Kegan Paul, 1954), p. 239—are reports on the occupations of fathers and grandfathers of the children in *one* grade in two Melbourne elementary schools. Even if these data were representative of some larger population, meaningful comparisons could not be made since Oeser and Hammond coded rural and urban occupations in the same categories while the other studies that are cited by Taft and Walker differentiated them. Combining rural and urban occupations, as we have noted earlier, increases the amount of downward mobility and reduces the incidence of upward mobility, since the urban-dwelling sons of farm owners are much more likely to be manual workers than are the sons of urban businessmen, and the sons of farm laborers are much less likely to move up into the urban middle class than are the sons of urban manual workers.

[27] Based on data kindly supplied by Dr. Erik Allerdt of the University of Helsinki.

in 1949.[28] It reports that more than half of the sons of manual workers who grew up in the city were in nonmanual occupations at the age of 24. This report, however, exaggerates the inter-generational mobility in Stockholm because the researcher did not know the occupations of fathers of migrants to the city. Another postwar study of employees in the major industrial enter-prises in two Swedish cities reveals that 47 to 49 per cent of the male nonmanual workers came from working-class homes, and that 56 to 58 per cent of the female nonmanual workers had working-class backgrounds.[29] Supplementary evidence on the composition of the white-collar unions (TCO) in Sweden indi-cates that 31 per cent of the members have fathers in the working class.[30] All these studies support the evidence from figure 2.1. However, the Anderson data on intra-generation mobility suggest that this may be a recent phenomenon.[31] A lower rate of mobility was found in a provincial Swedish city before World War II: only 13 per cent of the white-collar workers employed in industries had fathers who were industrial workers.[32]

In a recently published article that compared the findings of two additional studies of urban mobility, Robert Havighurst has sug-gested that there is more upward and downward mobility in Sao Paulo, Brazil, than in Kansas City, Missouri. However, much of the difference reflected in the findings—40 per cent of the Sao Paulans moved up and 17 per cent moved down, as compared with only 33 per cent upward and 12 per cent downward movement in Kansas City—can be explained by differences in the number and nature of the strata used to compute mobility in the two studies. The Brazilian research employed *six* Edwards-type occupational strata, while the Kansas City investigators employed only *four* Warnerian social classes. In order to make a better comparison, one can apply a two-fold division for both samples: recomputing

[28] Gunnar Boalt, "Social Mobility in Stockholm: A Pilot Investigation," in *Trans-actions of the Second World Congress of Sociology*, Vol. II (London: International Sociological Association, 1954), pp. 67–73.
[29] T. T. Segerstedt and A. Lundquist, *Människan i Industrisamhället*, Vol. II (Stockholm: Studieförbundet Näringsliv och samhälle, 1955), p. 295.
[30] F. Croner, *Tjänstemannakaren i det moderna samhället* (Stockholm: Gebers, 1951), p. 319.
[31] C. Arnold Anderson, "Lifetime Inter-Occupational Mobility."
[32] E. Arosenius, *Yrkesväxlingen fran en generation till en annan i en medelstor svensk stad* (Gleerup: Lund, 1936), p. 25.

the Brazilian data by means of a manual-nonmanual break and dichotomizing the Kansas City data into the two higher and the two lower classes. When this is done, both cities show fairly similar degrees of mobility. In Sao Paulo 30 per cent moved up from manual social backgrounds to nonmanual occupations, and in Kansas City 29 per cent of the sons of lower-class fathers moved

TABLE 2.2

SOCIAL MOBILITY IN AARHUS AND INDIANAPOLIS

(Percentages)

Son's occupation	Father's occupation							
	Aarhus: 1949				Indianapolis: 1940			
	I	II	III	IV	I	II	III	IV
I: Professional, business executive and self-employed.	38	23	14	32	33	21	10	11
II: Clerical and sales.	20	28	12	12	29	42	17	15
III: Manual.	41	48	73	52	38	37	72	70
IV: Farm.	1	1	1	4	. .	. .	1	4
Total.	100	100	100	100	100	100	100	100
Number in sample.	8,220	1,990	12,469	3,928	1,791	1,092	5,372	1,635

SOURCES: Indianapolis data are taken from Natalie Rogoff, *Recent Trends in Occupational Mobility* (Glencoe: The Free Press, 1953), p. 45; the Aarhus materials come from Theodore Geiger, *Soziale Umschichtungen in einer Dänischen Mittelstadt* Vol. III, no. 1, Acta Jutlandica (Copenhagen: Ejnar Munskgaard, 1951), Appendix table 1.

up into the middle classes. Nineteen per cent of the Brazilians were downward mobile compared to 16 per cent of those in Kansas City.[33]

Two excellent studies of social mobility—one in a Danish and one in an American city—permit a second even more detailed comparison of mobility in two somewhat comparable provincial cities (table 2.2). It is clear that there is no substantial difference in the patterns of social mobility in Aarhus and Indianapolis.

[33] Robert J. Havighurst, "Educação, Mobilidade Social e Mundanca Social. . . ." The original Kansas City data appear in Richard P. Coleman and Warren A. Peterson, "Social Structure of the Kansas City Area," (Unpublished research memorandum, Committee on Human Development, University of Chicago, 1956), which is cited in Robert J. Havighurst and Bernice Neugarten, *Society and Education,* (Boston: Allyn and Bacon, Inc., 1957), p. 53. The Brazilian data are from Bertram Hutchinson, ed., *Trabalho, Status e Educação,* (Rio de Janeiro: Brazilian Center of Educational Research, 1958).

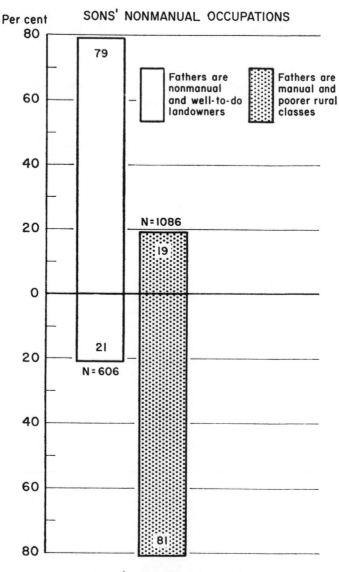

Fig. 2.3. Social mobility in Rome, 1950. *Source.*—Computed from Alessandro Lehner, "Sur la mesure de la mobilité sociale," in *Transactions of the Second World Congress of Sociology*, Vol. II, p. 123.

The Japanese, American, and Scandinavian urban studies indicate a high rate of social mobility comparable to the corresponding national data. A study completed in Rome, Italy, in 1950, on the other hand, supports the conclusion derived from the national sample data that Italy has a lower rate of mobility than the other countries (see figure 2.3).

OCCUPATIONAL MOBILITY—1900 TO 1939

Most of the data presented so far were gathered after the end of World War II, in a period of prosperity that followed on the heels of great dislocations. There is no doubt that dislocations and prosperity both tended to increase the rate of social mobility. Indeed, it has been argued that the high rates of social mobility in Europe were a product of the upheavals caused by war and political change, whereas in the United States similarly high rates were a concomitant of an expanding economy.[34] There is plausibility to this argument, but we should be wary of it since it involves a black and white contrast between the political instability and economic stagnation of Western Europe and the political stability and economic expansion of the United States. Whatever its merits in the political sphere, this explanation does not appear to fit the data on social mobility. As early as 1927 Pitirim Sorokin, after an extensive analysis of the data then available, rejected the contention that in terms of occupational mobility the United States has a more "open" society than the industrial countries of Europe.[35] And there is evidence that the entire twentieth century has been characterized by expansion of the urban and industrial structures of Western Europe as well as of the United States (except for the 1930's). We should, therefore, expect to find high rates of social mobility in Western Europe even before World War I, over

---

[34] Herbert Luethy, "Social Mobility Again—and Elites," *Commentary*, 20 (1955): 271. The effect of major social crises such as depressions, wars, and revolutions on mobility patterns is a relatively unexplored but important element. There is evidence, for example, that one of the factors related to downward mobility in Western Germany is the presence of a large refugee population from the East. A study, based on a random sample of 1,800 residents of Schleswig-Holstein reports that 15 per cent of older refugees (52–60) and 20 per cent of younger ones (32–40) held positions in 1953 which were lower in occupational status than the ones they had in 1939. The corresponding figures for permanent residents of the province are 6 per cent for both the older and younger groups. See the forthcoming book by Karl Martin Bolte, *Berufsprestige-Berufsmobilität*.

[35] Pitirim Sorokin, *Social Mobility*, pp. 414–480.

and above any mobility that may have been caused by the dislocations of war, political upheavals, or economic crises: and the
available data substantiate this expectation.

From the 1890's on, a large number of studies of social mobility
have been made in various countries of Europe, especially in
Germany. Unfortunately, none of these were made on samples
of the national population, and most deal with the social origins
of men in selected occupations or factories. Yet, with few excep-
tions, these researches indicate high rates of upward and downward mobility—rates quite comparable to those found by more
recent studies.

The largest single study was made by the German trade union
of white-collar workers in the late 1920's. Questionnaire data were
secured from over 90,000 white-collar workers. Almost a quarter
of the males in this group, 23.9 per cent, came from working-class
families.[36] Moreover, mobility was probably increasing at the time
the study was made, since the proportion of white-collar workers
of manual origin was highest among the young. Of those white-
collar workers who were less than thirty years old, 32 per cent
had manual workers as fathers, as compared with only 19 per
cent for men over thirty. Hans Speier, writing in Germany in 1929,
concluded, on the basis of his examination of a large number of
German studies, that: "At the present time the working-class is
the main recruiting stratum for white-collar workers."[37]

Several other German studies made before World War I also
indicate that the pattern of upward mobility into the middle class
was then similar to that of the present. A study of the Krupp Mills
in Essen, made in 1906, reported that about 30 per cent of the
sons of manual workers who had been employed by Krupp for

---

[36] Gewerkschaftsbund der Angestellten, *Die wirtschaftliche und soziale Lage der
Angestellten* (Berlin: 1931), p. 43; see also Speier, *The Salaried Employees in
German Society*, pp. 86–98. The data for this study are based on the membership
of the liberal white-collar union. Speier estimates that 20 per cent of the members
of the conservative union, and 50 per cent of the members of the socialist one were
the children of manual workers. The 23.9 per cent of white-collar workers who
were sons of working-class families in the 1920's compares with 31 per cent in the
nationwide sample study of 1950. However, the two samples were collected
differently and one cannot conclude on this basis that the mobility of workers into
the white-collar group has increased.

[37] Speier, *The Salaried Employees . . .* , p. 95.

more than thirty years were in nonmanual positions.[38] An 1895 study of the pattern of mobility of migrants to Karlsruhe reported that 25 per cent of the *grandsons* of migrants (almost all of whose grandfathers had been in lower-class occupations) were in professions and 15 per cent were in other nonmanual jobs.[39] An analysis of the occupations of the sons of over 4,000 members of the German printers union in 1910 revealed that a majority of them were in nonmanual occupations.[40]

In Great Britain an excellent study done in 1912 reported that over two-thirds of owners, directors, and managers in the cotton industry had begun their careers either as manual workers or in low-status clerical positions.[41] The researchers, surprised by their own findings, attempted to check them by interviewing company executives, union leaders, and economic historians of the industry. They found general agreement with their findings. Sidney Webb, the Fabian leader, commented, "In Lancashire I think that practically all mill managers are taken from the ranks of the Spinners' Union."[42] Although this study of the cotton industry is certainly not representative of British industry in general, it does cast doubt on the validity of the assumption that British society was comparatively closed. The authors, who had conducted a number of studies of social mobility in Britain before World War I, concluded by saying:

> The spread of technical education and the improvement of general education have greatly stimulated the vertical mobility of the population. As the century has advanced, the need for education, general, technical and commercial, has become more specialized and intricate. In all the principal centres of the cotton industry in Lancashire we found a vigorous interest taken in technical education. Generally speaking, the ablest of the young wage earners attend in the evening at technical classes. . . . Of the best students an appreciable number rise to positions as managers or independent employers in industry.[43]

---

[38] Ehrenberg and Racine, "Kruppsche Arbeiterfamilien," *Archiv für exakte Wirtschaftsforschung*, 6(1912):383.

[39] Otto Ammon, *Die Gesellschaftsordnung und ihre natürlichen Grundlagen* (Jena: Verlag Gustav Fischer, 1895), p. 145.

[40] Sorokin, *Social Mobility*, p. 452.

[41] S. J. Chapman and F. J. Marquis, "The Recruiting of the Employing Classes from the Ranks of the Wage Earners in the Cotton Industry," *Journal of the Royal Statistical Society*, 75 (1912): 293–306.

[42] Quoted, *ibid.*, p. 305.

[43] *Ibid.*, p. 306.

A recent study of an English steel-rolling mill (1956) indicates that there is at present a comparable pattern of social mobility in English heavy industry."[44] For most of its history, the plant had followed a policy of promotion from the ranks. Though this was being replaced to some extent by recruitment of men from college, still 65 per cent of the staff as a whole was of manual social origin, as was 36 per cent of the top management.[45] Such evidence as this does not support the conventional impression that opportunities for upward social mobility have been great in the United States, but not in Europe.

We have to note, also, substantial downward social mobility. The studies of the social origins of workers in various factories and trades made from 1890 to 1930 indicate that a large proportion of the German working class had fathers who were either self-employed or in nonmanual occupations. In some factories, this group constituted over 50 per cent of the manual work force. This downward mobility was a consequence of shifts in the German economy before World War I, as factories replaced handicraft work. Analyses of Nazism have suggested that the fear of downward mobility in the 'twenties and 'thirties played a major role in winning the German middle class to Nazism.[46] Yet the available evidence indicates that the amount of downward mobility had been great in many other countries—not only in Germany—since the beginning of the century, thus raising a question about the importance which the fear of losing occupational and social status must have had as a precipitant of Nazism.

Two other studies of social mobility before World War I should be mentioned together because, in both, information on the occupations of fathers and sons was obtained from marriage license records. The studies were made in Indianapolis in 1910, and in Rome, Italy, in 1908. Although the same methodology was em-

[44] W. H. Scott, *et al.*, *Technical Change and Industrial Relations* (Liverpool University Press, 1956).

[45] *Ibid.*, p. 202.

[46] For example, H. H. Gerth, "The Nazi Party," *American Journal of Sociology*, 45 (1940): 524–529. Of course, the fear of downward mobility here referred to involves intra-generation mobility, while our data are on mobility between generations. Further, this mobility is generally conceived to be pauperization (downward *consumption* mobility) rather than proletarianization (downward *occupational* mobility). Nevertheless, the great amount of (presumably) anxiety-producing downward mobility before the rise of Nazism cannot be dismissed as a factor, even though its importance may have been exaggerated.

ployed, the two cities differ in so many respects that it is not possible to use the results of these studies as comparable indicators of social mobility in the two countries (see table 2.3). For example, because the Italian capital had such a large proportion of white-collar workers and officials, the proportion of nonmanual sons of nonmanual fathers was significantly higher than in the more industrial community of Indianapolis. Yet, the percentages of

TABLE 2.3

Social Mobility in Rome and Indianapolis Before World War I

(Percentages)

	Father's occupation					
Son's occupation	Rome: 1908			Indianapolis: 1910		
	Nonmanual	Manual	Farm	Nonmanual	Manual	Farm
Nonmanual..........	73	22	17	59	21	25
Manual..............	27	76	74	40	78	64
Farm...............	..	2	9	1	1	11
Total..............	100	100	100	100	100	100
Number in sample.....	1,017	1,503	547	2,363	5,205	2,685

Sources: Rome: F. Chessa, *La Transmissione Ereditaria delle Professioni*, p. 28; Indianapolis: N. Rogoff, *Recent Trends in Occupational Mobility*, p. 44.

nonmanual sons of manual fathers show clearly that there was considerable upward social mobility in both cities before World War I.

The studies we have cited are certainly limited in many respects. They do not enable us to estimate the possible extent of variation in social mobility rates among different countries in the period from 1900 to 1939. However, we do not believe that social research will be advanced as rapidly as it should be if we wait with our interpretations until limited and inadequate data are replaced by ample and methodologically sound research findings. The data we have surveyed appear to indicate that mobility, as measured by movement across the manual-nonmanual dividing line, has been considerable in many countries of Western Europe as well as in the United States. Roughly comparable rates of mobility have been found under so many different social and economic conditions and in so many otherwise divergent samples that it may be more plausible to believe that the cause of mobility lies primarily in the economic expansion made possible by a given level of industrialization than to believe that it lies in the spasmodic dislocation of war and political upheaval. The overall finding certainly does not mean that there may not be important differences among countries which may be revealed once we have comparative studies of more detailed variations in occupational status, such as the effort now under way by S. M. Miller under the auspices of the International Sociological Association to compare systematically in a detailed way studies of social mobility in over twenty countries. But until such better evidence is available it does entitle us to reject the banality that the societies of Western Europe are "static" but American society is "open."[47]

ELITE MOBILITY

Comparisons of the social mobility rates of several countries can also be made tentatively on the basis of several studies dealing with the "circulation of the elites."

There is some evidence to suggest that a much larger proportion of American than of European professionals come from working-class families.[48] Since professional work everywhere requires attendance at institutions of higher learning, this finding is congruent with our knowledge that a larger percentage of workers' sons attend universities in America than in Europe.[49] But this gen-

---

[47] It is certainly not unusual for social research to discover discrepancies between scientific facts and popular images of reality. A recent example, perhaps less weighty than that of comparative social mobility, concerns a study of turnover of university faculty and administrative personnel in close to 900 colleges and universities. Less turnover was found among head football coaches than among university presidents, deans, registrars or head librarians. There can be little doubt that most people, including university faculty members, would state that there is much more turnover among head football coaches than among other administrative personnel. See National Educational Association, *Teacher Supply and Demand in Colleges and Universities* (Washington: 1957), p. 11.

[48] Some of the studies presented in figure 2.1 give data about professionals separately. A. Touraine and J. D. Reynaud of the Centre d'études sociologiques of Paris are currently writing a monograph which will report in detail the findings concerning the social origins of professionals in various countries. This monograph, together with the one mentioned earlier by S. M. Miller, will probably be published as a special number of the journal, *Current Sociology*, in 1959 or 1960.

[49] C. Arnold Anderson, "The Social Status of University Students in Relation to Type of Economy: An International Comparison," in *Transactions of the Third World Congress of Sociology*, Vol. V (London: International Sociological Association, 1956), pp. 51–63.

eralization cannot be readily corroborated by direct studies of the background of professionals, since American studies include free and salaried professionals as well as semiprofessionals under one heading, while most European research classifies only free professionals (physicians, lawyers, etc.) in this category.

A number of studies have examined the background of high-level civil servants. They indicate that French, German, Dutch, British, and Swedish civil servants come from families of higher social status than their American peers,[50] a finding that probably reflects national variation in the status of civil-service positions. In much of Europe, high civil-service positions are considered appropriate and even desirable for men coming from families with elite backgrounds, whereas in the United States this has been generally true only for the diplomatic service. Conversely, studies of members of legislatures and cabinets suggest that American politicians as a group come from families of higher status than do Europeans.[51] This difference is probably related to many factors: to the presence or absence of labor parties and of class-conscious politics, to the different structure of political parties in Europe and America, and so forth. In Europe more workers are motivated to enter politics and there is more opportunity for them to do so than in the United States.[52]

[50] See Reinhard Bendix, *Higher Civil Servants in American Society* (Boulder: University of Colorado Press, 1949), pp. 22–32, esp. p. 29 for a comparison of German and American data; Thomas Bottomore, "Higher Civil Servants in France," in *Transactions of the Second World Congress of Sociology*, Vol. II, pp. 143–152; Robert Catherine, "La fonction publique," *in* Maurice Duverger, ed., *Partis politiques et classes sociales en France* (Paris: Armand Colin, 1955), pp. 109–154; H. E. Dale, *The Higher Civil Service of Great Britain* (London: Oxford University Press, 1941), pp. 22–62; R. K. Kelsall, *Higher Civil Servants in Britain from 1870 to the Present-day* (London: Routledge and Kegan Paul, 1955); Sten-Sture Landström, *Svenska ämbetsmäns sociala ursprung* (Uppsala: Almquist och Wiksell, 1954), pp. 96–99; A. van Braam, 'Sociale herkomst en mobiliteit van ambtenaren," in F. van Heek, *et al., Sociale stijging en daling in Nederland*, I, pp. 201–211.

[51] Donald R. Matthews, *The Social Background of Political Decision Makers* (Garden City: Doubleday, 1954); M. McKinney, "The Personnel of the 77th Congress," *American Political Science Review*, 36 (1942): 67–75; Mattei Dogan "L'origine sociale du personnel parlementaire français élu en 1951," *in* Maurice Duverger, ed., *Partis politiques . . .* , pp. 291–327; J. F. S. Ross, *Parliamentary Representation* (London: Eyre and Spottiswoode, 1948), pp. 58–83, 260–274.

[52] Sweden appears to represent a mixture of these two tendencies. Since the turn of the century there has been a slow trend towards a larger percentage of civil servants with a working-class background, a trend which is somewhat at variance with the general European pattern. But although the Social Democrats have had control of the *Riksdag* and of the government for the past twenty years, the propor-

A number of studies of the social origin of the business elite in different countries have also been completed in the past few years. We know of such studies for Germany,[53] Great Britain,[54] the Netherlands,[55] Sweden,[56] Switzerland, and the United States.[57] They vary in the methods of collecting data, in the classification employed for describing the social background of the elite, and above all in the definition of the elite. But despite much methodological uncertainty some conclusions stand out. Approximately 60 per cent of the samples of business elite in Britain, the Netherlands, Sweden, and the United States have businessmen as fathers, of whom about 15 per cent are small businessmen. The Swiss data indicate that about 50 per cent had fathers in business. (The German study's system of classification makes it useless for comparative purposes.) Between 10 and 15 per cent of these groups have manual-working-class or lower-white-collar origins. There is, however, a variation among countries in the proportion of business leaders who come from rural backgrounds which corresponds to the importance of agriculture in the national economy. There are also intercountry variations in the proportion of business leaders

tion of civil servants from the working class has not increased more than could be expected from the earlier trend, when non-socialist parties were in power. See Landström, *Svenska ämbetsmäns . . .* , p. 98. W. L. Guttsman, "The Changing Social Structure of the British Political Elite, 1886–1935," *British Journal of Sociology,* 2 (1951): 122–134, reports that the entry of workers into cabinet posts is almost entirely through the Labor Party, with 20 of the 24 ministers of working-class origin being from the BLP.

[53] Heinz Sachtler, *Wandlung des Industriellen Unternehmers in Deutschland seit Beginn des 19 Jahrhunderts* (unpublished dissertation, University of Halle: 1937).

[54] G. H. Copeman, *Leaders of British Industry* (London: Gee and Company, 1955); The Acton Society Trust, *Management Succession* (London: The Acton Society Trust, 1956), p. 26; and R. V. Clements, *Managers: A Study of Their Careers in Industry* (London: Allen and Unwin, 1958).

[55] P. Vinke, "The Vertical Social Mobility of the Chief Executive Groups in the Netherlands," in *Transactions of the Third World Congress of Sociology,* Vol. III, pp. 219–229.

[56] Sten Carlsson, *Svensk Stands-Circulation, 1680–1950* (Uppsala: Lindblads, 1950), pp. 134–142; the educational background of another sample of Swedish executives is reported in Sune Carlsson, *Företagsledning och företagsledare* (Stockholm: Nordisk Rotogravyr, 1950), pp. 95–113.

[57] The Swiss data, which report on a national sample of 118 "Directeurs," are presented in Roger Girod, "Ecole, université et sélection des membres des couches dirigeantes: le cas de Genève" (Paper presented at the Fourth Working Conference on Social Stratification and Social Mobility of the International Sociological Association, Geneva, December, 1957). See chapter iv of this book, which contains a methodological discussion and summary of business-elite studies in the United States.

from professional-family and civil-service backgrounds. Sweden and Britain seem to have a larger percentage of businessmen from professional and civil-service origins than does the United States.

Today few elite positions can be achieved without higher education, and the organization of a country's higher educational system is therefore relevant to this discussion. Popular images and fictional accounts depict the American businessman as uneducated. On the basis of studies in the United States, Britain, and Sweden, this must be myth, for American businessmen have more formal education than their European counterparts. But this fact has to be seen against the organization of higher education in Europe and the United States, and the values placed on education on the two continents. Almost 20 per cent of white Americans of university age attended college in 1950, as contrasted with less than 4 per cent of West Europeans.[58] Consequently, since the percentage of high-level positions is not five times greater in America than in Europe there must be a great difference in the amount of education required for them. Americans enter college somewhat earlier than the English and two years earlier, on the average, than Europeans. The American is about eighteen when he enrolls— still a minor—and the American college keeps him for a required four years even if he can pass all his examinations after the third year, which insures that when he graduates to the job market he will be an adult ready to assume a responsible position. Thus, in America a college education becomes an almost necessary requisite for a position of responsibility, and its completion is timed to coincide with becoming an adult. In Europe, on the other hand, a university degree is considered necessary only for a professional career, fewer go to the university, and many begin their business careers without completing or even attending a university. Hence, it should not be surprising that American big businessmen have more schooling than their British colleagues and that the latter start work at a younger age than the Americans.

Another aspect of this contrast should also be pointed out. European universities have generally retained the medieval organiza-

---

[58] Includes Denmark, Sweden, Switzerland, Netherlands, Germany. C. A. Anderson, "The Social Status of University Students . . . ," p. 53. Of course such comparisons are only rough indicators, since the content of the education at preuniversity levels is very different in Europe and America, and since some professional training done by the universities in America is done by apprenticeship in Europe.

tion which required them to graduate only physicians, lawyers, civil servants, and clergymen. They have generally refused to accept new faculties such as engineering, business, education, applied arts, social work, home economics, nursing, and others commonly found in American universities. Training for these occupations and professions is not given in the universities, but in special technical schools, which tend to be rated lower than the universities. And although those who practice these applied professions must be classed as members of the occupational elite, they have less prestige than the traditional professions.

Through this mechanism of two higher educational systems which vary in status the traditional elites of a number of European countries appear to have reconciled themselves to one of the requirements of modern industrial society—large numbers of executives and professionals with lower-class backgrounds. It is noteworthy that despite these and other important differences between American and European business elites, their social backgrounds are, for the most part, quite similar. This fact reinforces the assumption that modern economic structures create vacancies at the executive and professional levels, and that the necessity of filling them creates comparable opportunities for upward mobility in different industrial societies.

STATUS MOBILITY

The previous discussion should not be interpreted to mean that occupational mobility is the sole or even the primary basis for assessing the availability of opportunities in an industrial society. An individual may rise occupationally and economically and yet find himself excluded from those social groups to which, he feels, his economic position entitles him to belong; this exclusion may have an adverse effect on his later career, though this need not be true. The degree of emphasis on "aristocratic" values and privileges, that is, on the inheritance of position, may therefore be reflected in the extent to which men claiming high status because of their family's position will accept as social equals those who have but recently climbed the economic ladder. Few studies bear directly on this problem, but the most nearly relevant data deal with intermarriage across class lines by contrasting the occupations at marriage of husbands and wives, the occupations of the fathers of the bride and groom, and the husbands' occupations with those of their fathers-in-law.

The most detailed European study comparing the class status of husbands and wives is based on all marriages in the state of Bavaria in 1927; comparable American material is from one of the earliest, but in many ways best, of American studies, based on Philadelphia marriage licenses for the years 1913 to 1916.[50] These studies (see figure 2.4) clearly suggest that barriers to marriage across the manual-nonmanual class line are equally strong (or weak, depending on one's interpretation) in Germany and America. Moreover, the more detailed analysis of the various Bavarian mobility statistics by J. Nothaas shows us the degree of openness of German society:

> The Bavarian statistics on marriage show that the women of the working class, whether gainfully employed or not, have a relatively high chance of rising socially. In some occupational groups the proportion of women rising into higher strata through marriage amounts to as much as two-fifths. Conversely, the wives of manual workers come, to a comparatively large extent, from higher social strata. The percentage varies between twenty-five and fifty per cent, according to the occupational group; the remainder is supplied by the working class itself. In fact, the proportion of the higher classes is still greater, if we are to classify the married women not according to their occupation but according to their social origins [fathers' occupations].[60]

[50] For Bavarian data see "Sozialer Auf-und Abstieg im Deutschen Volk: Statistische Methoden und Ergebnisse," Heft 117 of *Beiträge zur Statistik Bayerns* (Bayerisches Statistisches Landesamt, 1930). For Philadelphia materials see Donald Marvin, "Occupational Propinquity . . . ," pp. 131–150. After going to press we located, through the courtesy of Dr. Martin Bolte of the University of Kiel, one of the earliest but nevertheless most comprehensive statistical analyses of mobility via marriage in different countries: Rudolfo Benini, *Principii di Demografia*, pp. 126–158. In this book, which was published in 1901, Benini worked out for the first time, so far as we know, an "index of attractiveness" which relates mobility rates to differences in potential for mobility of different groups. This index was then computed for the extent of intermarriage among groups which varied in interests, age, marital status, place of birth, nationality, occupation, and religion. Benini compared the premarital occupational-status background of the husband and that of the wife or her family and concluded that it affected marital opportunities less than education, national origin, or religion. His data also indicated considerable upward social mobility via marriage in a number of European cities in the 1890's.

[60] J. Nothaas, *Social Ascent and Descent in Germany* (New York: State Department of Social Welfare and Department of Social Science, Columbia University, 1938), pp. 28–29. A recent survey of intermarriage in Schleswig-Holstein indicates that there is more class intermarriage among young people of the present genera-

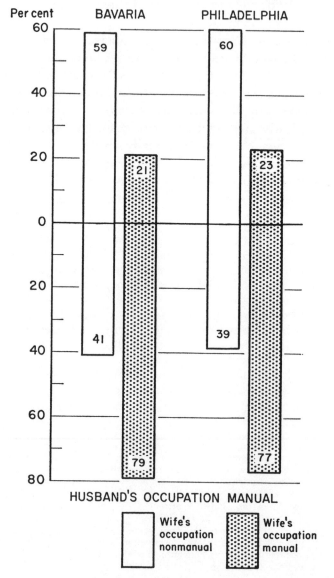

Fig. 2.4. Occupations of marriage partners, Bavaria and Philadelphia.

More recent European studies tend to confirm the belief that European society provides relatively frequent opportunities for marriage between the classes. *Social Mobility in Britain* also analyzed the rates of mobility through marriage by comparing the relationship between the occupations of fathers of husbands and wives. The author then compared his findings for England and Wales with those of an American study, and concluded that, "So far as the basic material permits comparison . . . the results of the analysis suggest that the pattern and degree of status association between brides and grooms probably is about the same in the U. S. A. as it is in England and Wales."[61] In a general way this finding is also supported by the study of the city of Aarhus, Denmark, which included data on mobility through marriage. Although the author of this study compared the occupation of the husband with that of his father-in-law, and we are therefore unable to contrast his findings with those of the British and American studies, the results nevertheless indicate a rate of social mobility through marriage which is much higher than would be expected if the notion were valid that for intimate relations European society puts extreme emphasis on status background. For example, 30 per cent of the daughters of middle-class fathers were married to manual workers, and 41 per cent of the women of working-class parentage had husbands in non-manual occupations.[62]

---

tion than of their parents' generation. Upward social movement through marriage was more common for women than it was for men. Irmela Pedell, "Die Entwicklung sozialer Heiratskreise seit dem 19. Jahrhundert," (Unpublished paper given in the Sociological Seminar, University of Kiel, under the direction of Dr. Martin Bolte, 1958).

[61] J. R. Hall, "A Comparison of the Degree of Social Endogamy in England and Wales and the U.S.A.," *in* David Glass, ed., *Social Mobility in Britain*, p. 346. This conclusion is necessarily tentative, since the American and British studies employed different occupational classifications; in addition, the American study omitted all rural residents and children of farmers, and the British analysis was based on a total population sample. The English material has also been compared with data on intermarriage in Kiel, Germany, that was reported in I. Langner, "Soziale Heiratskreise in Geschichte und Gegenwart," (University of Kiel dissertation, 1949). Dr. Pedell concludes that the degree and patterns of class intermarriage in the German city are quite similar to those in England. Irmela Pedell, "Die Entwicklung sozialer Heiratskreise . . . ."

[62] Theodore Geiger, *Soziale Umschichtungen in einer Dänischen Mittelstadt,* Vol. XXIII, no. 1, Acta Jutlandica (Copenhagen: Ejnar Munskgaard, 1951), appendix table 18.

High rates of interclass mobility through marriage were also found in large-scale research in Aberdeen, Scotland. Almost half (46 per cent) of Aberdeen women with professional and managerial class origins married skilled-worker husbands, and 40 per cent of the wives of professionals and managers had fathers who were skilled workers. The interchange between the skilled workers and the lower working-class strata was even more marked. It should be noted, however, that intermarriage between the extremes—between the two upper strata and the two lower strata—accounted for less than 2 per cent of all marriages. The Scottish study also indicates that mobility through marriage is only the final stage of a process of upward occupational mobility: the daughters of lower-strata fathers who married upward had already gained entrance into white-collar occupations through superior intelligence and education.[63]

High rates of interclass marriages are also reported in France by Marcel Bresard. For example, 32 per cent of male manual workers married daughters from nonmanual strata, and 16 per cent married daughters of farmers. Similarly, 31 per cent of the men in lower-white-collar occupations married daughters of workers, and 14 per cent married daughters of farmers. As in the Scottish study, intermarriage between the extremes of the status hierarchy was quite infrequent.[64]

Though less valuable in assessing the part played by marriage in social mobility, data on the relationship between the occupations of Swedish wives and those of their husbands throw some light on intimate cross-class associations. C. Arnold Anderson found in 1945 that in Sweden, 17 per cent of the urban-middle-class husbands had wives working in manual occupations, and in 38 per cent of working-class families with both husband and wife working, the wife worked in a nonmanual occupation.[65]

Marriage is, of course, not only a vehicle of social mobility for women: a recent Danish study gives statistical weight to the

[63] R. Illsley, "Social Class Selection and Class Differences in Relation to Stillbirths and Infant Deaths," British Medical Journal, Dec. 24, 1955, pp. 1520–1524.

[64] Marcel Bresard, "Mobilité sociale et dimension de la famille," Population, 5 (1950): 533–566; figures computed from table, p. 541.

[65] C. Arnold Anderson, "Employment, Occupation, and Socio-economic Status of Swedish Wives," pp. 8–9.

popular notion that the marriage a man contracts is an important factor in *his* subsequent mobility. Kaare Svalastoga found that one of the most significant indicators of the social mobility of a married male was his wife's social origin. Although more than half (53 per cent) of those males from manual worker origins who "married up" were upwardly mobile occupationally, only 37 per cent of those who married on the same level were upwardly mobile. Conversely, only 38 per cent of the men stemming from nonmanual origins whose fathers-in-law were also nonmanual workers descended in occupational status, as compared to 58 per cent of nonmanuals whose fathers-in-law were manual workers.[66]

The similarity between those mobility patterns of Europe and America that are created by interclass marriages is in some ways even more interesting than the similarity between the patterns of occupational mobility. Before locating these data, we had guessed that comparative materials on interclass marriage patterns would reveal that in Europe there are fewer marriages across class lines than in America, on the assumption that there is more emphasis on family background in most European countries than in the United States. These studies, however, suggest that there may be something wrong with our image of status structures; or rather, with our assumptions concerning the action these structures make imperative. Apparently, Europeans maintain patterns of behavior which emphasize gradations of status much more visibly and rigidly than American patterns, yet at the same time find differences in status no greater barrier to marriage. Perhaps the better defined the *status* of individuals in a society, the less *conscious* emphasis there need be to maintain status barriers. This may explain why in England there are no restrictions to the admission of Jews to the leading social clubs, or schools such as Eton and Harrow, although barriers or quotas exist in comparable American clubs and schools.[67]

The great concern with background which W. Lloyd Warner

---

[66] Kaare Svalastoga, "An Empirical Analysis of Intrasocietary Mobility Determinants," (Working Paper Nine submitted to the Fourth Working Conference on Social Stratification and Social Mobility, International Sociological Association, December, 1957). The percentages given here were computed from data presented by Svalastoga.

[67] Howard Brotz, *A Survey of the Position of the Jews in England* (New York: American Jewish Committee, 1957; mimeographed), p. 5.

has shown to be characteristic of parts of American society may be a reaction to the feeling of uncertainty about social position in a society whose manifest values deny anyone the right to claim higher status than his neighbor.[68] As Brotz has remarked,

> In a democracy snobbishness can be far more vicious than in an aristocracy. Lacking that natural confirmation of superiority which political authority alone can give, the rich and particularly the new rich, feel threatened by mere contact with their inferiors. This tendency perhaps reached its apogee in the late nineteenth century in Tuxedo Park, a select residential community composed of wealthy New York businessmen, which, not content merely to surround itself with a wire fence, posted a sentry at the gate to keep nonmembers out. Nothing could be more fantastic than this to an English lord living in the country in the midst, not of other peers, but of his tenants. His position is such that he is at ease in the presence of members of lower classes and associating with them in recreation. (For example, farmers ride to hounds in the hunts.) It is this "democratic" attitude which, in the first instance, makes for an openness to social relations with Jews. One cannot be declassed, so to speak, by play activities.[69]

In cultures which accept the idea of aristocracy, and which explicitly recognize the existence of classes, it may be possible for an individual to ignore distinctions of status in a number of social contexts without feeling that he has thereby jeopardized his social or economic position. But much more information than we now have is needed to test this hypothesis—and even then other hypotheses would be required to explain the similarity of mobility rates we have reported.

RELIGIOUS VALUES AND MOBILITY

The evidence we have surveyed so far tends to refute the hypothesis that social mobility is relatively low where status stability and class differences are emphasized and relatively high where equal opportunity for all is highly valued. Instead, we find that rates of social mobility are markedly similar in the several countries of Western Europe and the United States, at any rate as far as our crude measures permit this judgment. In all probability, present differences in social mobility are related to the rates at

---

[68] W. Lloyd Warner and Paul S. Lunt, *The Social Life of a Modern Community* (New Haven: Yale University Press, 1941), pp. 92–104.

[69] H. Brotz, *A Survey of the Position of the Jews in England*, pp. 8 f.

which different countries are urbanizing and industrializing, though the differences in these rates must be large before they are reflected in the measures of mobility which we have employed.

So far, we have examined the gap between prevailing opinion and social fact by considering the available data on social mobility. This procedure is at fault in that we took account of opinions only in terms of certain stereotypes. There is one area, however, in which the relationship between opinions and the facts of social mobility can be examined with more exactitude. We refer to the hypothesis that Protestantism, especially Calvinism, encourages occupational achievement, and hence social mobility. Before Max Weber initiated his studies of the Protestant Ethic in the early stages of capitalism he suggested to one of his students an investigation of the contemporary relevance of religious belief to economic achievement.[70] Since it was well known that industrial development had been greater in Protestant than in Catholic countries, it was worth while to inquire whether or not the different work ethics of contemporary Protestants and Catholics were still reflected in the economic arena. Data available for the United States, Germany, England, and the Netherlands permit some test of the hypothesis that religious values still affect social mobility and economic achievement.

In America the study of the relationship of social mobility to religious affiliation is complicated by the ethnic differences between Catholics and Protestants. Catholics comprise a much larger proportion of recent immigrants than do Protestants. Melville Dalton has suggested that foreign-born workers are less oriented toward occupational achievement than their native-born colleagues.[71] Hence any examination of the differences in occupational achievement between American Catholics and Protestants should distinguish the effects of recent immigration from the impact of religious differences.

Data collected by Samuel Stouffer indicate that the occupa-

[70] Max Weber, *The Protestant Ethic and the Spirit of Capitalism* (London: George Allen & Unwin, 1930), chap. i, where the author discusses the results of an investigation by Martin Offenbacher, *Konfession und soziale Schichtung*, Volkswirtschaftliche Abhandlungen der Badischen Hochschulen, Vol. IV, No. 5 (Tuebingen: J. C. B. Mohr, 1900).

[71] Melville Dalton, "Worker Response and Social Background," *The Journal of Political Economy*, 55 (1947): 323–332.

tional distribution of third-generation Catholics and Protestants differs from that of immigrants and the sons of immigrants, but that there is little or no difference between the occupational status achieved by third-generation Catholics and Protestants, except that more Protestants than Catholics are farmers. (See table 2.4.) On the other hand, among those with a recent-immigrant back-

TABLE 2.4

OCCUPATIONAL DISTRIBUTION OF WHITE MALES: 1955
(Percentages)

Occupational group	Father or respondent foreign born		Native-born sons of native-born fathers	
	Protestant	Catholic	Protestant	Catholic
Professional and semi-professional......	10	5	8	9
Proprietors, managers and officials......	17	17	12	14
Clerical and sales.....................	10	8	12	15
Craftsmen and foremen...............	20	23	20	23
Operators...........................	16	23	17	18
Unskilled...........................	4	8	9	8
Service.............................	6	10	5	5
Farmers............................	17	6	16	9
Farm labor.........................	..	..	2	..
Nonmanual.........................	37	30	32	38
Manual and service..................	46	64	51	54
All occupations[a]	100	100	100	100
Number in sample....................	230	278	1,343	212

SOURCE: Calculated from data collected by Professor Samuel Stouffer for his study of civil liberties.
[a] Details do not always add to totals because of rounding.

ground Protestants are in higher positions than Catholics. Thus the occupational difference between the two religious communities disappears once the ethnic factor declines. It is difficult to estimate the extent to which the variations among those of recent-immigrant background derive from religious differences. Among first- or second-generation immigrants almost all Protestants are from English-speaking parts of the British Commonwealth, from Scandinavia, or from Germany; the bulk of the Catholics are from Italy, Slavic countries, and Ireland. Or to put it another way, the Protestant immigrants come from ethnic groups with high status, while the Catholics are members of ethnic groups with low status.

The Protestants come from countries where educational attainment is high, the Catholics from poor countries in which the lower classes receive little education. Hence even the difference between Catholic and Protestant immigrants may be related to ethnic rather than to religious factors, an interpretation that is given

TABLE 2.5

MOBILITY PATTERNS OF WHITE AMERICAN CATHOLICS AND PROTESTANTS
RELATED TO IMMIGRATION BACKGROUNDS: 1952
(Percentages)

Immigration background and respondent's occupation	Father's occupation					
	Protestants			Catholics		
	Non-manual	Manual	Farm	Non-manual	Manual	Farm
One or both parents foreign born						
Nonmanual..............	68	38	29	70	39	.. [a]
Manual.................	28	62	16	30	61	.. [a]
Farm...................	4	..	55	..	..	.. [a]
Number in sample........	(25)	(29)	(38)	(20)	(83)	.. [a]
Both parents native born						
Nonmanual..............	74	43	38	77	34	38
Manual.................	25	52	42	23	66	44
Farm...................	1	4	20	..	..	19
Number in sample........	(95)	(139)	(113)	(26)	(32)	(16)

SOURCE: Calculated from data collected by Survey Research Center, University of Michigan.
[a] Too few cases.

support by the fact that there is relatively little difference in the occupations of first- and second-generation German-American Catholics and Protestants.

To state that ethnic derivation rather than religion is the main reason for the difference between the occupations of American Catholics and Protestants does not rule out the influence of religion on rates of social mobility, although it strongly suggests that it should be ruled out. Other studies, however, permit an explicit test of the mobility relationship. The data collected in the Michigan Survey Research Center study of the 1952 Presidential election indicate that Protestants as a group showed somewhat more upward mobility than Catholics. However, four-fifths of the

Protestants, but only two-fifths of the Catholics, had native-born parents. When we again differentiate between Catholics and Protestants in terms of how long their families have been in this country, we find no significant difference between the two groups. (See table 2.5).

The conclusion that religion does not affect rates of mobility in the United States, derived from the two national samples examined, is reinforced by a third study based on a sample of 2,205 men employed in three white-collar occupations—salesmen, engineers, and bankers. The authors of this study conclude that, "Among the men in these three white-collar occupations, there is apparently no relationship between being Catholic or Protestant and being upward or downwardly mobile either from the occupational status or stratum of one's father or from one's previous status or stratum in the labor force."[72] Information on the aspirations of the men interviewed also indicated no relationship "between religious affiliation and either income goal or work oriented plans for the future."[73]

---

[72] Raymond W. Mack, *et al.*, "The Protestant Ethic, Level of Aspiration and Social Mobility: An Empirical Test," *American Sociological Review*, 21 (1956): 299. It is possible that American Catholics are even more mobile than American Protestants. A recent study in New Haven indicates that Catholics who are successfully mobile in the economic structure convert to Protestantism in order to facilitate their movement in the status system. This fact means that any survey which compares Catholics and Protestants at a given moment lists a number of the successful as Protestants even though they were reared in Catholic households. "As individuals moved toward middle class status, they have become either leaders in the Roman Catholic Church or members of Protestant denominations, principally Congregational or Episcopal. . . . upward mobility has led to greater defections from the Roman Catholic Church than is true of either Protestants or Jews." A. B. Hollingshead and F. Redlich, *Social Class and Mental Illness*, (New York: John Wiley, 1958), p. 101. A thorough analysis of the phenomenon of the successful in America converting to high-status churches may be found in E. Digby Baltzell, *Philadelphia Gentlemen: The Making of a National Upper Class*, (Glencoe: The Free Press, 1958), pp. 223–246.

[73] Mack, *et al.*, "The Protestant Ethic . . . ," p. 300. These findings call for a comment on the relationship demonstrated in McClelland, *et al.*, "Religious and Other Sources of Parental Attitudes toward Independence Training," *in* D. C. McClelland, ed., *Studies in Motivation* (New York: Appleton-Century-Crofts, 1955), pp. 389–397. They found that their sample of Catholics had less training for independence, which is closely related to motivation for achievement (see the summary of this material in chapter ix), than had their sample of Protestants. This may seem inconsistent with the observations on the lack of relationship between religious values and mobility. But the authors picked that part of the Catholic population which is most affected by ethnic variables, which we have found to explain most of the variation in rates of social mobility. "We selected our [Catholic] informants from those parents whose children had at least one grandparent born in the 'Old Country.' " *Ibid.*, p. 396 n.

Data bearing on the same problem have been collected in three European countries which have Catholic minorities: Germany, England, and the Netherlands. The German materials, gathered by the UNESCO Institute in Cologne and based on a national sample of the population, show identical rates of mobility for Catholics and Protestants (see table 2.6).[74] The British study is more limited in scope since it is concerned only with educational achievements of school children in Middlesbrough, England, a community containing a Roman Catholic minority of 20 per cent,

TABLE 2.6

SOCIAL MOBILITY AND RELIGIOUS AFFILIATION IN GERMANY: 1953
(Percentages)

Religious affiliation and father's occupational group	Son's occupation			Number in sample
	Nonmanual	Manual	Farm	
Protestants				
Nonmanual	65	33	2	123
Manual	35	60	4	351
Farm	19	30	52	161
Catholics				
Nonmanual	70	27	3	124
Manual	33	63	4	317
Farm	21	27	52	164

SOURCE: UNESCO Institute at Cologne.

largely immigrants from Ireland. The researchers, studying the factors that determine admission to Grammar School (the university-oriented high school), found that a larger proportion of Catholics of working-class origin (16.8 per cent) than Protestants with the same background (10.5 per cent) were admitted to Grammar School. The authors attribute this in part to the interesting fact that "the children of unskilled workers form a very large group amongst the Catholics, and their relatively superior average intelligence [as compared with the children of unskilled Protestants] must account to a great degree for the proportionately larger yield of Catholic pupils." These data suggest that in Britain

[74] This finding for Western Germany is confirmed by a more recent study by Morris Janowitz, who also found virtually no differences between Catholics and Protestants, both with respect to inter-generational and intra-generational mobility. Morris Janowitz, "Social Stratification and Mobility in Western Germany."

as in America, the children of low-status Catholic immigrants tend to move up disproportionately, and to obtain positions in the total occupational structure roughly similar to those of the largely native-born Protestant population. Whether this assumption is valid or not, the fact remains that the British data do not show a positive link between Protestantism and social mobility, and (if anything) suggest the reverse pattern. The Dutch study is limited to an examination of the background of employees in the Philips works, and reports that religious affiliation is among the factors which seem to have little bearing on the success of individuals.[75]

These recent investigations in four countries indicating no significant differences between the mobility rates of Catholics and Protestants obviously raise questions about the validity of generalizations based on data from before World War I that purport to show greater achievement by Protestants. It is significant that when Kurt Samuelsson, a Swedish scholar, recently replicated the most frequently cited study of the influence of religion on achievement (made at the end of the nineteenth century by Martin Offenbacher), he found that it contains serious methodological errors.[76] These errors invalidate its conclusion that German Protestants show higher rates of educational and economic achievement than Catholics. For example, Offenbacher had reported that 59 per cent of the graduates of *gymnasien* (university-oriented high schools) were Protestant in 1895–1896. Samuelsson points out, however, that if the proportion of Catholics and Protestants in *gymnasien* is compared holding the ratio of the two religious groups in the population sampled constant, then the difference almost completely disappears. Similarly, when the enrollment of members of the two denominations in higher *Bürger* schools is compared, Catholics attend them in ratios identical with their proportion in the population in the cities examined by Offenbacher. Samuelsson concludes his reëxamination of the relationship between religious affiliation and high school enrollment in Germany in the 1890's

---

[75] See Jean E. Floud, *et al.*, *Social Class and Educational Opportunity* (London: Heinemann, 1956), pp. 134–138. I. E. van Hulten, *Stijging en daling een modern grootbedrijf* (Leiden: Stenfert Kroese, 1954), p. 116.

[76] Kurt Samuelsson, *Ekonomi och religion*, (Stockholm: Kooperativa forfundets, 1957), pp. 150–153. Max Weber leaned heavily on Offenbacher's work. See the notes on pages 188 and 189 of *The Protestant Ethic*.

by saying that in communities with such schools, the proportions of Catholics and Protestants in attendance faithfully reflected their proportions in the population as a whole.

Similar errors were made by Offenbacher in reporting and interpreting data dealing with the economic wealth of Catholics and Protestants. He reported that the taxable property of German Protestants was much higher than that of Catholics. According to Samuelsson, however, this is only true on an absolute basis. If the two are compared percentagewise, it turns out that the Protestants owned 60 per cent of the book value of all taxable property, but that they also constituted 60 per cent of the German population at the time.

These findings, which reverse the conclusions of a major empirical investigation of the relationship between religion and achievement at the turn of the century, added to the materials reported here dealing with postwar studies in a number of countries, give further weight to the conclusion, derived from the cross-national researches presented earlier, that differences in national value systems are not related to variations in social mobility. We do not desire at this point to enter into the controversy among economic historians as to whether the thesis that the Protestant ethic had causal significance in promoting economic achievement in the early period of capitalism was valid for that time or not. It is worth noting, however, that these findings about the absence of a more recent relationship are congruent with Max Weber's belief that variations in the religious-economic ethos had lost whatever effect they had had during its early stages.

Since asceticism undertook to remodel the world and to work out its ideals in the world, material goods have gained an increasing and finally an inexorable power over the lives of men as at no previous period in history. . . . But victorious capitalism, since it rests on mechanical foundations, needs its support no longer. . . . Where the fulfillment of the calling cannot directly be related to the highest spiritual and cultural values, or when, on the other hand, it need not be felt simply as economic compulsion, the individual generally abandons the attempt to justify it at all.[77]

---

[77] Weber, *The Protestant Ethic*, pp. 181–182. See also R. K. Merton, *Social Theory and Social Structure* (Glencoe: The Free Press, 1949), pp. 123–133. Perhaps only the degree of religious interest, as opposed to secular orientation to economic advancement, now plays a role. Gerhard E. Lenski, "Social Correlates of Religious

We have seen that broad national differences in value orientation toward social mobility seem to have little effect on the actual
amount of mobility within industrial societies, and that Catholics
and Protestants do not show any appreciable differences in upward
movement. But this is not to assert that, for individuals and subgroups, values have no role in the mobility process. Just as differences in lower-class and middle-class values result in differential
momentum toward upward movement, so, especially, those values
of ethnic and religious groups within a society which affect child
rearing and motivation greatly influence mobility patterns. One
of the best examples is the Jews, who at least in the United States,
have markedly higher rates of upward mobility than non-Jews,
according to a number of studies. The higher mobility of Jews is
of course related to the traditional Jewish respect for learning
and education. But education alone cannot account for the phenomenon: when this factor is held constant Jews still consistently
outdistance non-Jews in occupational achievement. Nathan Glazer
has suggested that the historical experience of Jews in Europe
has imbued them, far more than other American ethnic groups,
with the "middle-class" values—the Protestant ethic—so valuable
in achieving success in business and intellectual pursuits. In
America, "the Jewish workers violated most of the patterns of
lower-class behavior," and with respect to organizational memberships, leisure time activity, and patterns of education and delin-
quency, they were hardly distinguishable from "the non-Jewish
as well as the Jewish middle class."[78]

Interest," *American Sociological Review*, 18 (1953): 533–544, found that those who
were upward mobile were much more likely to report little interest in religion than
were the stable or downward mobile. This relationship seems to exist strongly
among American Jews, who, according to a number of studies, are both more upwardly mobile and less religiously observant than other major ethnic and religious
groups in the United States.

[78] S. Joseph Fauman, "Occupational Selection Among Detroit Jews," in Marshall
Sklare, ed., *The Jews, Social Patterns of an American Group*, (Glencoe: The Free
Press, 1958), p. 124. Nathan Glazer, "The American Jew and the Attainment of
Middle-Class Rank: Some Trends and Explanations," *ibid.*, pp. 138–146. For an
insightful comparison of the achievement values of American Jews and Italians, see
Fred L. Strodtbeck, "Family Interaction, Values, and Achievement," *ibid.*, pp.
147–165.
A recent study of mobility among evangelical Christians in Sweden suggests
that among them also, group norms facilitate mobility. The "nonconformists" were
originally recruited primarily among workers and small-scale farmers. They
adopted strict norms. Liquor, commercial entertainment, ostentation, novels, and

MOBILITY TRENDS AND SOCIAL STRUCTURE

Several different processes inherent in all modern social structures have a direct effect on the rate of social mobility, and help account for the similarities in rates in different countries: (1) changes in the number of available vacancies; (2) different rates of fertility; (3) changes in the rank accorded to occupations; (4) changes in the number of inheritable status-positions; and (5) changes in the legal restrictions pertaining to potential opportunities.

By examining the relationship between these features of the social structure and the trends of mobility in different countries, we may be able to account for the similarities and differences among these trends.

1. The number of vacancies in a given stratum is not always, or even usually, constant.[78] For example, in every industrialized or industrializing country, the increase in the proportion of professional, official, managerial, and white-collar positions and the decline in the proportion of unskilled-labor jobs creates a surge of mobility, which is upward—provided these positions retain their relative standing and income. More and more people are needed to manage industry, to distribute goods, to provide per-

---

colored weeklies were prohibited. Thus the nonconformists could save the money their friends spent on such items. This has had certain interesting consequences for their position in society.

In non-churchgoing working class homes, 9 per cent of the youth 12 to 27 years old have savings of more than 1,000 crowns. The corresponding figure is twice as high (19 per cent) for working-class nonconformist youths. Evidently capital accumulates quicker among those who, because of their religious conception, are prohibited from wasting it on "the vanity of this world." Of the adult nonconformists from working-class homes, 36 per cent have more or less realized their plans to start an enterprise of their own; this compares with 28 per cent of those who grew up in working-class homes in which the parents did not go to any church. Twenty-four per cent of those with nonconformist parents have more than 12,000 crowns in annual income; only 16 per cent of the others. Persons growing up in working-class homes in which one parent goes to the Lutheran state church tended, on both points, to be in between those from areligious and nonconformist homes. See Hans Zetterberg, "Tror Ni på Gud?" *Vecko-Journalen*, 48 (1957): 31.

[79] In commenting on an earlier published version of the views presented here, Stanislaw Ossowski, of the University of Warsaw, reminded us that we had ignored a major factor creating opportunities for mobility, "Mass death, due e.g., to war especially to civil war, or to mass emigration of certain sectors of the population." See S. Ossowski, "Social Mobility Brought About by Social Revolutions." There can be no doubt that Professor Ossowski is correct in suggesting that such events must be considered as one of the major causes of contemporary social mobility, even though we may hope that "mass death" is not endemic to the nature of modern industrial society.

sonal services, and to run the ever-growing state bureaucracy. A comparison of the ratio of administrative (white-collar) to production (manual) workers in manufacturing industries over the last half-century in the United States, the United Kingdom, and Sweden shows that the correspondence in trends is very great. Thus, in the United States in 1899 there were 8 administrative employees per 100 production workers, in 1947 there were 22 administrative employees per 100 production workers, and in 1957 there were 30 administrative employees per 100 production workers.[80] The corresponding rise in Britain between 1907 and 1948 is from 9 to 20 administrative employees per 100 production workers, and in Sweden the number rose from 7 to 21 between 1915 and 1950. In none of these countries did the proportion of those self-employed in urban occupations decline.

2. An important determinant of upward mobility is the difference in rates of fertility. In all industrialized countries for which we have data, fertility tends to vary inversely with income.[81] Although changes in the economic structure are increasing the proportion of persons engaged in high-level occupations, the families of men who are now in such occupations are not contributing their proportionate share of the population. Consequently, even if every son of a high-status father were to retain that status, there would still be room for others to rise.

A similar consideration also applies to the process of urbanization. In all industrialized countries the urban centers continue to grow, requiring migrants to fill new positions or to replace urbanites, who characteristically fail to reproduce themselves. Although the urban birth rate is below reproduction level, the proportion of the population living in large cities (100,000 and over) grew in England from 26 per cent in 1871 to 38 per cent in 1951; in Germany from 5 per cent in 1870 to 27 per cent in 1950; in France, from 9 per cent in 1870 to 17 per cent in 1946; and in the United States from 11 per cent in 1870 to 30 per cent in 1950. And, as we shall show in chapter viii, the process of migration into urban

---

[80] Reinhard Bendix, *Work and Authority in Industry* (New York: Wiley, 1956), pp. 211–226.

[81] An exception is the big cities of Sweden in the earlier part of this century. However, data in the 1935 census indicate that differential fertility was at that time a characteristic of the nation as a whole.

areas permits a large proportion of the sons of workers who grow up in metropolitan centers to fill the newly created or demographically vacated middle-class positions, while the manual jobs left open are filled by migrants from small towns or rural areas.

3. In our rapidly changing world some positions lose, some gain, prestige. Thus, a person can be mobile in the eyes of society without changing his job. Admittedly, most of these losses or gains are barely noticeable within one generation. For example, a rating of twenty-five occupations made in 1925 was compared with a rating made in 1947, and a correlation of .97 was obtained, indicating practically no change.[82] However, another study of the same period has indicated that government positions in the United States have enhanced their prestige since the 'twenties.[83] Moreover, the addition of new occupations may sometimes inadvertently alter the prestige of certain ranks; for example, the emergence of the occupation of airplane pilot during the last generation served to deglamorize such occupations as ship captain and locomotive engineer. And significant changes in a given profession such as were effected in those of physicist, mathematician, and others by the atomic research programs during World War II, are also likely to better—or to lower—its prestige. However, we do not have studies with which to test such guesses.

4. In modern social structures there is a relative decline in the number of inheritable positions.[84] Many middle-class fathers in salaried positions have little to give their children except a good education and motivation to obtain a high-status position. If for any reason, such as the early death of the father or family instability, a middle-class child does not complete his higher education, he is obviously in a poorer position, in terms of prospective employment, than the son of a manual worker who completes college. Clearly, some of the children of the middle class are so handicapped, others simply do not have the ability to complete college or to get along in a bureaucratic hierarchy, and many of these fall into a status below that of their fathers. Whatever the

---

[82] Martha E. Deeg and Donald G. Paterson, "Changes in the Social Status of Occupations," *Occupations*, 25 (1947): 205–208.

[83] M. Janowitz and Deil Wright, "The Prestige of Public Employment: 1929 and 1954," *Public Administration Review*, 16 (1956): 15–21.

[84] See chapters iii and iv.

reason, persons of middle-class origin who fall in status leave room for others of lower-class background to rise.

The importance of this factor is emphasized by the sharp increase in the educational level among the working classes. No nation approaches the United States in terms of the number of university students who come from the working class. Even sons of working-class Negroes in the United States are more likely to go to college than sons of European workers.[85] The effect of the difference in university attendance among workers on the two continents, of course, is reduced by the fact that higher education is a more certain way of achieving a privileged position in Europe than in the United States.

5. Many earlier legal restrictions upon the right of a person to create a new and higher occupational status for himself have been removed. The abolition of the guild system is the classic example of this. All the countries we have discussed in this chapter have legal guarantees of the freedom of occupational choice. A peculiar consequence of such guarantees is the phenomenon of "increased upward mobility" during depressions. In these periods many manual workers are fired and cannot find jobs in their normal occupations. To survive, many of them become small entrepreneurs and, thus, according to the conventional classification, move upward on the social ladder.

These five explanations do not, of course, account for *motivation*. If mobility is to occur, individuals must aspire to higher positions. It is common sense to assume that people do not like to move downward, preferring to keep their rank or to improve it; but a theory of motivation must seek to explain the emotional rationale behind men's desire to improve themselves. Such an explanation is contained in Veblen's analysis of factors in patterns of consumption which reflect social mobility.

Those members of the community who fall short of [a] somewhat indefinite normal degree of prowess or of property suffer in the esteem of their fellowmen; and consequently they suffer also in their own esteem since the usual basis for self-respect is the respect accorded by one's neighbors. Only individuals with an aberrant temperament can in the long run retain their self-esteem in the face of the disesteem of their fellows.

[85] Anderson, "The Social Status of University Students . . . ," p. 57.

So as soon as the possession of property becomes the basis of popular esteem therefore it becomes also a requisite to that complacency which we call self-respect. In any community where goods are held in severalty it is necessary in order to ensure his own peace of mind that an individual should possess as large a portion of goods as others with whom he is accustomed to class himself; and it is extremely gratifying to possess something more than others. But as fast as a person makes new acquisitions and becomes accustomed to the resulting new standard of wealth, the new standard forthwith ceases to afford appreciably greater satisfaction than the earlier standard did. The tendency in any case is constantly to make the present pecuniary standard the point of departure for a fresh increase of wealth; and this in turn gives rise to a new standard of sufficiency and a new pecuniary classification of one's self as compared with one's neighbors. So far as concerns the present question, the end sought by accumulation is to rank high in comparison with the rest of the community in point of pecuniary strength. So long as the comparison is distinctly unfavorable to himself, the normal average individual will live in chronic dissatisfaction with his present lot; and when he has reached what may be called the normal pecuniary standard of the community, or of his class in the community, this chronic dissatisfaction will give place to a restless straining to place a wider and ever-widening pecuniary interval between himself and this average standard. The invidious comparison can never become so favorable to the individual making it that he would not gladly rate himself still higher relatively to his competitors in the struggle for pecuniary reputability.[86]

The following hypotheses seem to be implicit in this passage:

1. The evaluation (rank, class) a person is given in his society determines in large measure his evaluations of himself.

2. A person's actions are guided, in part, by an insatiable desire to improve even a favorable self-evaluation. Hence, if a given pattern of high consumption (such as a new car every year) is esteemed by a society, the individual will try to increase his consumption, since he thereby increases his opinion of himself.

Because a person's self-evaluation reflects the ranking he receives from his fellows, he will either try continually to increase his prestige rank as an individual, or he will seek group support for his claims to prestige. In either case, it may be said that people like to protect their class positions in order to protect their egos, and improve their class positions in order to enhance their egos.

---

[86] Thorstein Veblen, *The Theory of the Leisure Class* (New York: The Modern Library, 1934), pp. 30-32

Societies with visible class distinctions, like that of Germany, are therefore likely to produce strong ego needs for invidious distinctions, because a favorable self-evaluation depends upon such distinctions. And since, as we have seen, such emphasis on class distinctions is also compatible with a good deal of mobility, the invidious distinctions are maintained most vigorously by those who have managed to rise in spite of them. It is probable that the drives favoring the acquisition of high status *and* the maintenance of the rank-order are stronger in such societies than in countries like the United States, where less emphasis is placed on class distinctions, and where, accordingly, a favorable self-evaluation requires fewer of the visible appurtenances of status. That is to say, distinctions of status are not very invidious in the United States. There are, it is true, extreme means of upward mobility: some individuals do everything possible to get ahead, as Schulberg illustrated in his novel, *What Makes Sammy Run?* The *concern* with status may likewise go to extremes: some individuals and groups try to maintain the values of family ancestry as the major buttress of their high status, as Marquand showed in another novel, *Point of No Return*. These examples certainly reflect the cultural norms which stress or seek to negate social mobility, but such extreme forms of "social climbing" or of "status monopoly" tend to be caricatures (though they certainly exist outside of novels) which deviate from the national pattern of an equalitarian ethos. This pattern stimulates mobility, of course, since existing distinctions of status and of wealth are regarded as transitory; indeed, mobility itself is highly valued as a badge of equality. On the other hand, mobility is not a cultural norm where distinctions of status are strongly emphasized, and in such societies widespread mobility may, therefore, require a great tolerance of deviance from accepted norms, or a tightly knit solidarity among groups which seek to advance collectively.

The distinguished Indian anthropologist, M. N. Srinivas, has given a striking example of the latter in an analysis of his own society. He contends that group mobility, shifts in the status of castes, has *always* been possible in the operation of the caste system. Srinivas states:

The caste system is far from a rigid system in which the position of each component caste is fixed for all time. Movement has always been possible, and especially so in the middle regions of the hierarchy. A low caste was able, in a generation or two, to rise to a higher position in the hierarchy by adopting vegetarianism and teetotalism, and by Sanskritizing its ritual and pantheon. In short, it took over, as far as possible, the customs, rites, and beliefs of the Brahmans, and the adoption of the Brahmanic way of life by a low caste seems to have been frequent, though theoretically forbidden.[87]

The fact that there is constant striving for upward mobility in the most status-ridden society in the world, adds considerable weight to the hypothesis derived from Veblen, according to which a system of stratification is a fundamental source of mobility motivation in and of itself. Apparently, there are imperatives which prompt men to resist and reject an inferior status and these imperatives persist regardless of the way in which any given society has legitimated inequality. Srinivas even suggests that the stronger the norms against social mobility, the greater the desire for it: "It is possible that the very ban on the lower castes' adoption of the Brahmanical way of life had an exactly opposite effect." The description of the spread of Brahman customs in Indian society sounds very much like Veblen's analysis of the way in which upper class consumption patterns spread in America through "emulation." "In the case of the numerous castes occupying the lowest levels, Brahmanical customs reached them in a chain reaction. That is, each group took from the one higher to it, and in turn gave to the group below."[88] The consistency of these

---

[87] M. N. Srinivas, *Religion and Society among the Coorgs of South India* (Oxford University Press, 1952), p. 30.

[88] M. N. Srinivas, "A Note on Sanskritization and Westernization," *The Far Eastern Quarterly*, 15 (1956): 483. A great deal of general evidence, as well as specific examples, of social mobility in nonindustrial societies has been summarized in Bernard Barber, *Social Stratification* (New York: Harcourt, Brace, 1957). For example, in the early feudal period, military prowess could lead to the achievement of knighthood; in the later feudal era, mobility "through service in the administrative and legal bureaucracies of the great princes and monarchs" was more common (pp. 482–483). In prerevolutionary France, families of the bourgeoisie could eventually gain entrance into the nobility by emulating the latter's style of life over a long period of time. Successful marriages were key factors in this process (pp. 346–349, 387–389). In seventeenth-century England performance of political roles as royal officials often led to elevation to the peerage (p. 409 f.). Evidently there has always been considerable turnover among the hereditary nobility: data cited by Barber indicate that of 1,547 Swedish noble families registered in 1626, "only *two* lasted for nine generations in direct male succession" (p. 425). The same seems to be true of non-Western societies: the evidence of Francis Hsu shows "at least

findings with Veblen's general theory suggests an important line of inquiry: comparative study of similarities in social structures, particularly those of their stratification systems.

THE CONSEQUENCES OF SOCIAL MOBILITY

Although it appears, then, that the *amount* of social mobility is largely determined by the more or less uniform structural changes of industrialized societies and is therefore much the same in all such societies, it should be emphasized that the *consequences* of that mobility have been most diverse. To take an extreme example: if a Negro in South Africa obtains a nonmanual position, he is a ready candidate for leadership in a movement of radical protest. But if a white American from a working-class family makes the same move, he usually becomes politically and socially conservative. Perhaps the most important key to an explanation of such varying consequences of mobility across the line between manual and nonmanual occupations, is the concept of *status discrepancies*. Every society may be thought of as comprising a number of separate hierarchies—e.g., social, economic, educational, ethnic, etc.—each of which has its own status structure, its own conditions for the attainment of a position of prestige within that structure. There are likely to be a number of discrepancies among the positions in the different hierarchies that every person occupies simultaneously, for, as Georg Simmel pointed out, every person maintains a unique pattern of group affiliations. Mobility merely adds to these discrepancies by creating or accentuating combinations of a high position in one rank and a low one in another; for example, a high position in an occupation combined with a low ethnic status, or a high position in the social-class hierarchy (based

a moderate amount of social mobility persisting over a long span of Chinese history." F. L. K. Hsu, "Social Mobility in China," *American Sociological Review,* 14 (1949): 764–771. "A good deal of social mobility" over a long span of time in Indonesia is reported by J. M. Van Der Kroef, "The Changing Class Structure of Indonesia," *American Sociological Review,* 21 (1956): 138–148. Similarly Kingsley Davis has pointed out that there has always been "a certain amount of gradual social mobility" in the Indian caste society. K. Davis, *The Population of India and Pakistan* (Princeton University Press, 1951), chapter 18. While the typical pattern has been for entire castes or subcastes to rise, westernization and the consequent weakening of the caste system is providing more opportunities for individual social mobility. The effect of these processes of industrialization and urbanization on increasing mobility in Latin America is discussed by Barber, pp. 496–498.

on the status of people with whom one associates) combined with a low income.

The few analyses of the psychological dimension of this problem that have been made indicate that status discrepancies may cause difficulties in personal adjustment because high self-evaluations in one sphere of life conflict with low ones in another. Durkheim, for example, suggested that both upward and downward mobility result in increased suicide rates by increasing the number of persons who find themselves in an *anomic* situation, one in which they do not know how to react to the norms involved.[89] Studies of mental illness have suggested that people moving up in America are more likely to have mental breakdowns than the nonmobile.[90]

Since it is primary-group relations which give individuals the psychic support which "protects" them against suicide and mental illness, the hypotheses developed by Janowitz and Curtis on the social consequences of occupational mobility may help explain the above findings. They suggest that social mobility is likely to have disruptive consequences on primary group structures, such as family, clique, and friendships, but that the integration of secondary group structures is less likely to be influenced. They further suggest that primary group strains will be greatest for extreme upward-mobile and downward-mobile families and least for stable and moderately upward-mobile families; greater for intra-generational than for inter-generational mobility.[91]

Of greater interest in the present context are studies which focus attention upon structural sources of status discrepancies, rather than upon the psychological adjustment to the experiences which typically result from these discrepancies. For example, in a society in which there is a marked difference between the con-

---

[89] E. Durkheim, *Suicide* (Glencoe: The Free Press, 1951), pp. 246–254.

[90] A. B. Hollingshead, R. Ellis, and E. Kirby, "Social Mobility and Mental Illness," *American Sociological Review*, 19 (1954): 577–584. A. B. Hollingshead and F. C. Redlich, "Schizophrenia and Social Structure," *American Journal of Psychiatry*, 110 (1954): 695–701. The possibility that the same factors cause social mobility that cause mental illness is suggested by Evelyn Ellis, "Social Psychological Correlates of Upward Social Mobility among Unmarried Career Women," *American Sociological Review*, 17 (1952): 558–563.

[91] Morris Janowitz and Richard Curtis, "Sociological Consequences of Occupational Mobility in a U. S. Metropolitan Community," (Working Paper One submitted to the Fourth Working Conference on Social Stratification and Social Mobility, International Sociological Association, December, 1957).

sumption patterns of the working class and the middle class, status discrepancies are more likely to arise from occupational mobility than in societies in which the consumption patterns of workers and middle-class persons are similar.[92] Unfortunately, only in the field of political values do we have comparative data on the differential consequences of social mobility.[93] The data derived from a number of European and American studies (table 2.7) indicate that in America the successfully mobile members of the middle class are more conservative (that is, more often Republican) than those class members who are in a social position comparable to that of their parents. In Germany, Finland, Norway, and Sweden, on the other hand, the former group is more radical (that is, more often Social Democratic or Communist).

The data from these five countries suggest that individuals moving up occupationally in Northern Europe where shifts from one class to another require major adjustments in living style are more likely than comparably successful Americans to retain links to their class of origin. In the United States there is also presumably less concern with personal background in much of the middle class, and more likelihood that the successful individual need only change his residential neighborhood to bring his economic and

---

[92] See chapter iii.

[93] Some of the various consequences of status-discrepancies which might be investigated on a comparative basis are suggested in the following works: E. V. Stonequist, *The Marginal Man* (New York: Scribners, 1937); Thorstein Veblen, "The Intellectual Pre-eminence of Jews in Modern Europe," reprinted from *Essays in Our Changing Order*, in *The Portable Veblen* (New York: The Viking Press, 1950), pp. 467–479; Georg Simmel, "The Stranger," in *The Sociology of Georg Simmel*, translated by Kurt Wolff (Glencoe: The Free Press, 1950), pp. 402–408; Joseph Greenblum and Leonard I. Pearlin, "Vertical Mobility and Prejudice: A Socio-psychological Analysis," in Bendix and Lipset, eds., *Class, Status and Power* (Glencoe: The Free Press, 1953), pp. 480–491; B. Bettelheim and M. Janowitz, *The Dynamics of Prejudice* (New York: Harpers, 1950); G. E. Lenski, "Status Crystallization: A Non-Vertical Dimension of Social Status," *American Sociological Review*, 19 (1954): 405–413; and "Social Participation and Status Crystallization," *American Sociological Review*, 21(1956):458–464; and W. F. Kenkel, "The Relationship between Status Consistency and Politico-Economic Attitudes," *American Sociological Review*, 21(1956):365–368; Peter M. Blau, "Social Mobility and Interpersonal Relations," *American Sociological Review*, 21 (1956): 290–295; E. E. Lemasters, "Social Class Mobility and Family Integration," *Marriage and Family Living*, 16(1954):226–232; Daniel Bell, ed., *The New American Right* (New York: Criterion Books, 1955), pp. 41–54, 192–195; Melvin M. Tumin, "Some Unapplauded Consequences of Social Mobility in a Mass Society," *Social Forces*, 36 (1957): 32–37.

TABLE 2.7

PARTY CHOICE OF GERMAN, FINNISH, SWEDISH, AND AMERICAN
MIDDLE-CLASS MEN RELATED TO THEIR SOCIAL ORIGIN

Country and party choice	Father's occupation					
	Manual		Nonmanual		Farm	
	Per cent	Number in sample	Per cent	Number in sample	Per cent	Number in sample
Germany: 1953						
Social Democratic.........	32	200	20	142	22	58
Finland: 1949						
Social Democratic and Communist.............	23	357	6	356	10	183
Sweden: 1950						
Social Democratic.........	47	135	20	315	..	..
Norway: 1957						
Labor and Communist.....	49	61	29	73	24	46
United States: 1952						
Democratic..............	22	67	30	79	34	59

SOURCES: The German data are from a study made by UNESCO Institute at Cologne, Germany; the Finnish data were supplied by Dr. Erik Allerdt and were collected by the Finnish Gallup Poll; the Swedish data are from H. L. Zetterberg, "Overages Erlander?" *Vecko-Journalen*, 48 (1957): 18 and 36; the Norwegian figures are recomputed from data provided by the Oslo Institute for Social Research; the American data are from material supplied by the Survey Research Center of the University of Michigan.

his social status into line.[94] These findings seem related to variations
in the working-class vote. In Germany and Sweden, the skilled
workers are more radical than the semi- and unskilled; in America,
Britain, and Australia, the skilled workers are more conservative.[95]
This leads us to the hypothesis that skilled workers experience
more status rejection in these North European countries, so

[94] The conclusion that the upward mobile in America are even more conservative
politically than those who are nonmobile in high-status positions is reinforced by
another study of the 1952 election, based on a sample of young voters 21 to 24
years of age in Cambridge, Mass. See Eleanor E. Maccoby, "Youth and Political
Change," *Public Opinion Quarterly*, 18 (1954): 35. Data secured from a sample of
American business leaders also support the conclusion that the socially mobile in
America are less likely to be Democrats than sons of upper- and middle-class
parents, though the differences are too small to be significant. These latter findings
are from a study conducted by the M.I.T. Center for International Studies.

[95] See S. M. Lipset and J. Linz, *The Social Basis of Political Diversity* (Stanford:
Center for Advanced Study in the Behavioral Sciences, 1956; mimeographed.) Data
from the Swedish Gallup Poll for different Swedish elections, and from a 1953
study of German elections conducted by the UNESCO Institute at Cologne, and
the 1957 study conducted by DIVO indicate that the better paid and higher
skilled Swedish and German workers are much more likely to vote for the left
parties than the lower paid and less skilled.

that their higher economic status results in frustrations, while the other countries mentioned may give the highly paid skilled worker more real opportunities to aspire to middle-class status. The differences between the working- and middle-class styles of life may also be an important factor, since in America it is presumably easier to take on middle-class consumption patterns. A suggestive indication that the retention of working-class political values by upward-mobile persons is related to other working-class elements in their style of life, is indicated by the following data

TABLE 2.8

RELATIONSHIP BETWEEN SOCIAL ORIGIN, CONSUMPTION PATTERNS, AND VOTING BEHAVIOR AMONG MEN IN SWEDEN
(Percentages)

Voting	Manual from manual homes		Nonmanual from manual homes		Nonmanual from nonmanual homes	
	Without car	With car	Without car	With car	Without car	With car
Non-Socialist.........	15	14	38	74	79	83
Socialist..............	85	86	63	26	21	17
Number in sample.....	221	72	78	55	170	145

SOURCE: From H. L. Zetterberg, "Overages Erlander?"

(see table 2.8) from Sweden: white-collar workers who have risen from working-class backgrounds will generally continue to vote for the working-class party unless they change their style of consumption (symbolized here by the automobile); on assuming a middle-class consumption pattern, they also adopt the voting pattern of the middle class.

This attempt to interpret what little data we have on the consequences of upward mobility in different cultures rests on the unproven assumption that in Europe men who move up in the economic hierarchy find it difficult to adjust to the life style of higher levels, while in the United States men can more easily fulfill the requirements of the social position that corresponds to their economic success.

It should be noted that most of the studies dealing with mobility and politics indicate that the upward and downward mobile are more likely to be apathetic, to abstain from voting and to show low levels of political interest, than the stationary. This finding conforms to a general pattern revealed in many voting studies: that individuals subject to cross-pressures—pulls in different political directions resulting from exposure to varying appeals— react to this conflict by withdrawal from involvement. Conversely, the more homogenous one's political environment, the more decisively one may act. The mobile individual, who is in many ways a marginal man, retaining old ties and experiences, is more likely to be subjected to cross-pressure than the nonmobile person.[96]

In cases of downward mobility we should not expect, nor do we find, variations among different countries. In all countries, manual workers coming from middle-class backgrounds should be expected to desire to return to the higher class, and hence should be likely to retain middle-class values and patterns of behavior. A number of national surveys in different countries provide evidence from the political sphere for this generalization. Two European studies, one German and the other Finnish, indicate that manual workers whose fathers and grandfathers were all manual workers are more likely to back leftist parties than are those whose families have been working-class for only two generations (father worker, but grandfather middle class or rural), and that those with two generations of working-class background are in turn more disposed to vote leftist than those whose fathers were not workers (see table 2.9).

A number of studies conducted in the United States (see table 2.10) and Norway permit a two-generation mobility analysis for these countries. The results are similar to those indicated for Germany and Finland, since American and Norwegian sons of workers tend to vote for the more liberal or radical of the available candidates.[97]

The results of voting studies in five countries provide considerable support for the hypothesis that downward mobile persons are less likely to identify with the political and economic organ-

[96] For a further elaboration and presentation of evidence regarding the cross-pressure thesis, see S. M. Lipset, *et al.*, "The Psychology of Voting."

[97] A nationwide survey of intended vote in Norway's 1957 elections found that 91 per cent of manual and farm workers whose fathers were workers were supporting left (Labor or Communist) candidates. But only 69 per cent of those workers whose fathers were in white-collar positions and only 59 per cent from farm-owning families were voting left. Data received from Oslo Institute for Social Research.

TABLE 2.9

VOTING SUPPORT OF LEFT PARTIES AMONG MANUAL WORKERS IN GERMANY AND FINLAND
RELATED TO SOCIAL ORIGINS OF FATHERS AND GRANDFATHERS

GERMANY: 1953

Social origins	Per cent voting for Socialists and Communists[a]	Number in sample
Both grandparents workers..........................	75	108
Father worker (one grandfather other)...............	61	242
Father rural......................................	38	75
Father middle class...............................	24	89

FINLAND: 1948

Social origins	Per cent Socialists	Per cent Communists	Total per cent leftist	Number in sample
Father and paternal grandfather workers..........................	51	31	82	573
Father worker (grandfather other)......	55	23	78	444
Father rural.......................	56	11	67	378
Father middle class.................	34	8	42	50

SOURCES: The German data were analyzed from the results of a study conducted by the UNESCO Institute in Cologne, Germany; the Finnish data were supplied by Dr. Erik Allerdt of the University of Helsinki and are based on two surveys conducted by the Finnish Gallup Poll. The German materials are based on reports of occupations by respondents, the Finnish study asked respondents to report social class, giving them a choice of "worker, middle-class, and agrarian class."
    [a] Communists are only 1 or 2 per cent.

izations of the working class than manual workers who inherit their class status. Thus, the process of social interchange through which some men rise in status and others fall weakens the solidarity and the political and economic strength of the working class.[98] The majority of the men who rise to middle-class status become politically conservative (more in America than in Europe but still a majority on both continents), while a large minority of those who are reduced to working-class status in the United States, and

[98] Additional supporting evidence for this point of view is found in studies of active union members and union leaders. The less social mobility a worker has experienced, either in terms of father's occupation or his own career patterns, the more likely he is to participate actively in his trade union. Arnold Tannenbaum and Robert Kahn, *Participation in Union Locals* (Evanston, Ill.: Row, Peterson, 1958), pp. 142–148, and S. M. Lipset and Joan Gordon, "Mobility and Trade Union Membership," *in* Bendix and Lipset, eds., *Class, Status and Power*, p. 493. Another survey found that 67 per cent of local union leaders in Columbus, Ohio, were sons of urban wage earners. Glenn W. Miller and Edward J. Stockton, "Local Union Officer—His Background, Activities and Attitudes," *Labor Law Journal*, 8(1957):33.

a majority of men mobile downward in Europe, remain adherents of conservative movements.

While the notion that the socially mobile are more likely to be prejudiced against ethnic groups than the stationary has become rather common, the available evidence is quite ambiguous and cautions against any simple interpretation. The study of Greenblum and Pearlin, based on data gathered in Elmira, New York, in 1948, presents the only positive evidence for this relationship: they found that both upward and downward mobility was associated with heightened ethnic prejudice. Bettelheim and Janowitz found greater prejudice among the downward mobile, and somewhat *less* among the upward mobile, than among the stationary.[99] Without presenting any data, the authors of *The Authoritarian Personality* state that upward mobility is associated with ethnocentrism and that downward mobility is associated with anti-ethnocentrism![100] It is, therefore, not surprising that one of these authors in an article discussing her more recent research, concludes that "instability of status *per se* goes almost as often with ethnic tolerance as it does with ethnocentrism."[101]

The uncertainty about a definite relationship between mobility and prejudice is further emphasized by the results of a recent study by Martin Trow, who found no association between authoritarianism and social mobility in a systematic sample of adult males in Bennington, Vermont.[102] Again, in a study in Guilford County, North Carolina, *no* relationship was found between attitudes toward desegregation and upward occupational mobility.[103]

---

[99] Greenblum and Pearlin, "Vertical Mobility and Prejudice." Bettelheim and Janowitz, *Dynamics of Prejudice*.

[100] T. W. Adorno, *et al., The Authoritarian Personality*, (New York: Harper, 1950), p. 204.

[101] Else Frenkel-Brunswik, "Further Explorations by a Contributor to 'The Authoritarian Personality,'" in Richard Christie and Marie Jahoda, eds., *Studies in the Scope and Method of "The Authoritarian Personality,"* (Glencoe: The Free Press, 1954), p. 232.

[102] Martin A. Trow, *Right-wing Radicalism and Political Intolerance*, (Unpublished Ph.D. dissertation, Columbia University, 1957), pp. 110 f. This study, which dealt with the determinants of the support of McCarthyism, found in general no relation between mobility and such support.

[103] Melvin M. Tumin, "Readiness and Resistance to Desegregation: A Social Portrait of the Hard Core," *Social Forces*, 36(1958):261. No mention was made of downward mobility in this article.

TABLE 2.10

VOTING BEHAVIOR OF AMERICAN WORKERS, BY FATHER'S OCCUPATION

Proportion supporting the Democrats among a national
sample of American male workers: 1952[a]

Father's occupation	Per cent Democratic	Number of respondents
Worker..	62	119
Middle class....................................	54	37
Rural...	58	87

Proportion supporting Democrats among a sample of Detroit members
of the United Automobile Workers: 1952[b]

Father's occupation	Per cent Democratic	Number of respondents
Semiskilled or unskilled...........................	81	125
Skilled...	74	55
White collar......................................	60	42
Farmer...	71	61

Radical or conservative attitudes of a national sample
of male American workers: 1945[c]

Father's occupation	Per cent radical or moderate	Per cent conservative	Number of respondents
Workers...........................	75	25	236
Middle class.......................	60	40	50

[a] Based on an analysis of data supplied by the Survey Research Center of the University of Michigan.
[b] From A. Kornhauser, *et al.*, *When Labor Votes* (New York: University Books, 1956), p. 43.
[c] From R. Centers, *The Psychology of Social Classes* (Princeton University Press, 1949), p. 180.

CONCLUSIONS

In this chapter we have presented evidence concerning varying amounts, causes, and consequences of social mobility in different countries. The results of this analysis may be summarized as follows:

1. There is relatively little difference in rates of social mobility, as measured by the shift across the manual-nonmanual line, in countries for which sample survey data exist.

2. There is considerable national variation in the social origins of those in professional work, a fact which is related to the dif-

ferences in available openings for university study in different countries.

3. There is national variation in the social origins of high-ranking civil servants, a fact which is related to different educational opportunities and perhaps to the status of the civil service in different countries.

4. There seems to be relatively little difference in the backgrounds of high-level business leaders in Sweden, Britain, Switzerland, the Netherlands, and the United States.

5. Opportunity to enter the political elite through the electoral path is greater in Europe than in America, a fact which stems from the difference in the political-party systems on the two continents.

6. The similarities in rates of mass mobility (manual to non-manual) among countries with such diverse social structures, suggest that propensity for mobility can not be correlated with national cultural patterns, since some cultures encourage and others discourage social mobility.

7. The religious values of Protestantism and Catholicism do not appear to be related to significant differences in mobility rates at the present time.

8. Instead of supporting the assumption that value differences cause variations in mobility rates, the data support the hypothesis that mobility patterns in Western industrialized societies are determined by the occupational structure.

9. The findings are compatible with Veblen's analysis of the ways in which consumption patterns spread down the class structure. Our hypothesis is that the desire to rise in status is intrinsic in all persons of lower status, and that individuals and groups will attempt to improve their status (and self-evaluation) whenever they have any chance to do so.

10. There is little material available concerning the consequences of social mobility, but some evidence of their nature could be secured from the realm of politics. It appears that upward movement in America has an effect on political behavior which differs from the effect of upward movement in Germany and Scandinavia. In America, persons who move up into the middle class are more conservative than those born into it, whereas in the European countries studied the latter are more conservative

than the former. The downward mobile, however, behave similarly in all countries: they vote more conservatively than the stationary members of the class into which they have fallen.

In effect, the principal impression which may be derived from the summary of mobility studies around the world is that no known complex society may be correctly described as "closed" or static. Although the paths of mobility and the extent to which the mobile may enter or leave different strata are not the same in all such societies, the number of persons in each who are able to rise above the position of their parents is large enough to refute the statement that "class barriers are insurmountable."[104] There is now more evidence to document this than has ever existed before, thanks to the researches of sociologists in many lands, but the conclusion is not so new or startling as it might seem—as witness the American saying, "Three generations from shirt-sleeves to shirt-sleeves," the German proverb which refers to "the third critical generation," the old Lancashire maxim, "Clogs to clogs in three generations," and the Chinese saying that "a family may rise from rags to riches in three generations and go back to rags in the next three."[105] Although the materials which we have

---

[104] Joseph Schumpeter, *Imperialism and Social Classes* (New York: Meridian Books, 1955), p. 124. "This is in accord with a very widespread popular notion that not only governs our evaluation of and emotional reaction to matters in the field of class, but has also gained entry into scientific circles—for the most part only as a half-conscious axiom, attaining the dimensions of an axiomatic rule only in the case of Marxist analysis. The modern radical critique of society often rests on this asserted law."

[105] *Ibid.*, p. 129; see Sir Josiah Stamp, "Communication," *The Economic Journal*, 36(1926): 687. In this letter, Stamp reports a communication from Professor Haensels of the State University of Moscow, U.S.S.R., in which Haensels indicates that "he has for some years been investigating the power of the inheritance factor in producing uneven distribution of wealth and has collected over a thousand biographies of rich men in many countries. His conclusion has been that 'inheritance has no great importance in the uneven distribution,' the greater part being made in one generation by self-made men, and 'only in a few instances of settled property is wealth kept through the successive generations.' He remarks that the German proverb, 'the third critical generation'—compare our Lancashire saying: 'from clogs to clogs in three generations'—has proved to be true after a particular study of wealthy people in Hamburg over three generations."

For the report on the Chinese maxim, see Karl Wittfogel, *Oriental Despotism*, (New Haven: Yale University Press, 1957), p. 313. For a summary of the literature bearing on social mobility in historic China, see Derk Bodde, *China's Cultural Tradition*, (New York: Rinehart and Company, 1957), pp. 68–77. There is considerable controversy among students of China concerning the rates of upward mobility through the examination system. It seems evident, however, that at all

examined here give us no good basis for generalizing about non-industrial societies, there is much evidence from historians of Western society as well as from contemporary students of basically nonindustrial societies that such societies have also been characterized by considerable mobility.[106] The difference between the pace of mobility in China and the Western world that these maxims suggest in their contrast between six and three generations as the length of the cycle may reflect the difference between nonindustrial and industrial societies. Both have considerable mobility. But industrial societies have more frequent and especially *more rapid* movement.

The conclusion that widespread social mobility is not only compatible with the existence of social classes, but even with a general emphasis on inheritance of social status, was stated forcefully by Schumpeter in 1926 in his brilliant essay on social classes:

> [The] assumption as to the insurmountability of class barriers for individual families does not accord with the facts. The persistence of class position is an illusion, created by the slowness of change and the great stability of class character as such and of its social fluid. Class barriers *must* be surmountable, at the bottom as well as at the top . . . there is constant turnover. Entries and exits occur continually—the latter directed both upward and downward. Class composition is forever changing, to the point where there may be a completely new set of families. . . . The process always goes on, though at times extremely slowly and almost imperceptibly, impeded by legal and other barriers which every class, for obvious reasons, seeks to erect. *For the duration of its collective life, or the time during which its identity may be assumed, each class resembles a hotel or an omnibus, always full, but always of different people.*[107]

times a minority, which some estimate at from 10 to 20 per cent and others considerably higher, coming from "commoner" or "new blood" background successfully embarked on the path to high status and power through the government examination system.

[106] J. Schumpeter, *Imperialism and Social Classes*, pp. 127–129; and references in footnote 88. See also Henri Pirenne, "Stages in the Social History of Capitalism," *in* R. Bendix and S. M. Lipset, eds., *Class, Status and Power*, pp. 501–517.

[107] *Ibid.*, pp. 130, 126; first emphasis is Schumpeter's; second is ours. For a recent critical discussion of some methodological difficulties faced in attempting the kind of international comparisons of mobility rates we have made in this chapter, see Karl Martin Bolte, "Vom Umfang der Mobilität in unserer Gesellschaft," *Kölner Zeitschrift für Soziologie und Sozialpsychologie*, 10(1958), esp. pp. 49–55.

Chapter III | *Ideological*
Equalitarianism
and Social Mobility
in the United States

The data presented in the preceding chapter raise questions about the validity of the widely-accepted belief that the United States is *the* land of opportunity. Yet how can we account for the persistence of the assumption that in this country the position of an individual's family is less likely to determine his social and economic destiny than in Europe? And how is this image related to patterns of social mobility?

Many political analysts have declared that the political stability or instability of an industrial society is determined by its rate of social mobility: one with a high rate is stable, one with a low rate is not. (This distinction is sometimes formulated as the difference between "open" and "closed" societies, but these terms are very misleading.) A revolutionary like Marx and a conservative like Tocqueville agreed, for example, that the American political system was sustained in part by the opportunity that farmers and workers had to attain positions of prominence and privilege; but since American and Western European societies probably have similar rates of social mobility, their reasoning is not conclusive. Differential rewards, inherited privilege, *and* social mobility exist in *every* society. And since the rate of social mobility is high in *all* industrial societies, it may be necessary to account for political stability by other factors, one of which appears to be the cultural value attributed to social mobility.

The emigration of German intellectuals after the revolution of

1848 illustrates the importance of such evaluations. This emigration meant that many of the most talented people in German society found it impossible to remain in their homeland; hence in Europe there was bitterness toward the political conditions which forced this important group of active liberals to seek their fortunes abroad. From the American point of view the same emigration testified to the freedom and opportunities which beckoned from the United States; hence the movement of political refugees across the seas contributed to a buoyant optimism. And, if we consider more recent events, it is easy enough to see that the *same* degree of social mobility will be viewed optimistically if it is thought to be a result of expanding opportunities in a politically stable society, and pessimistically if it is seen as a result of changes brought about by two world wars and the political upheavals of totalitarianism.

Cultural traditions, and especially cumulative political experience, may result, therefore, in a massive difference between the values that two different societies assign to social mobility, and the effect that such values have on the social structure, *even though the actual proportion of mobile persons is the same in both.* Thus, where, as in the United States, social mobility receives positive encouragement, the existing opportunities for upward mobility probably help to sustain the acceptance of the social and political order by the lower classes. But such opportunities probably cannot shake the distrust of the prevailing order that exists among lower-class persons in such countries as France where the dominant historical image is one of an unfair distribution of opportunities, in which little mobility occurs. The distinctively American combination of opinion and social fact in this field is, in our judgment, the product of six factors: (1) the absence of a feudal past, whose legacies could have been perpetuated under capitalism to strengthen the claim to legitimacy of the new class of capitalists;[1] (2) the continuous high rate of social mobility in American society, which has tended to support the belief in the value of an "open class" society; (3) the increase in educational opportunities, which has been especially important in sustaining

---

[1] The significance of such legacies for the stability of the social structure of capitalism has been analyzed by Joseph Schumpeter, *Capitalism, Socialism and Democracy* (New York: Harper, 1951), pp. 134–139.

the belief in a continuing expansion of opportunity; (4) the patterns of business careers at the bottom and at the top, which seem to reflect and support the same belief; (5) the presence of immigrants and racial minorities on whose shoulders the children of previous generations of immigrants or of more-or-less segregated ethnic groups could rise; and (6) the combination of relative wealth and mass production of consumer goods, which has had the effect of minimizing the differences between the standard of living of the working class and the middle class. In commenting briefly on each of these factors, we shall attempt to give a general interpretation of the role of social mobility in American society.

IDEOLOGICAL EQUALITARIANISM

We can only speculate when we attempt to assess the effects of the absence of a feudal past in America. Clearly it has not meant the absence of status distinctions—which have frequently been every bit as invidious, though more surreptitiously introduced, on this side of the Atlantic as on the other. But it has led to, among other things, an ideological equalitarianism, which is not any the less important because it has been contradicted on every side by the existence of status differences. No act is perhaps as symbolic of this ideology as Thomas Jefferson's order to have a round table replace the rectangular one at the White House because this would relieve him of the necessity of stipulating the order of precedence at official receptions. This act was not a denial of the existing differences in rank and authority; it was rather a testimony to the belief that these were the accidental, not the essential, attributes of man. Among men of equal worth it is not in good taste to insist on the accidental distinctions which divide them.

Such ideological equalitarianism has played, and continues to play, an important role in facilitating social mobility in the United States. It enables the person of humble birth to regard upward mobility as attainable for himself, or for his children. It facilitates his acceptance as a social equal if he succeeds in rising economically. It mitigates the emotional distance between persons of different social rank. And it fosters in any existing elite the persuasion (however mistaken this may be) that its eminence is the result of individual effort, and hence temporary. The point to emphasize is, not that these beliefs are often contradicted by the experience of those who hold them, but that this equalitarian ideology has persisted in the face of facts which contradict it. We would suggest that the absence of hereditary aristocracy has done much to foster this persistence. Americans have rarely been exposed to persons whose conduct displays a belief in an inherited and God-given superiority and also demands that others demonstrate (by deferential behavior) their recognition of this superiority.

The existence of ideological equalitarianism in the United States is generally acknowledged, but interpretations of its significance vary widely. One of these interpretations holds that this ideology is a delusion which must be dispelled by presenting the people with the hard facts of status differences. Accordingly, W. Lloyd Warner has called for systematic, explicit training to combat half-knowledge and confused emotions, in order that the adult student will learn "what he needs to know about our status order, how it operates, how he fits into the system, and what he should do to improve his position or make his present one more tolerable."[2] Whatever may be said of the usefulness of such studies, we find it difficult to believe that significant numbers of Americans are not aware of the existence of status differences. We doubt that instruction of the kind envisaged by Warner will have any notable effect upon the belief in equal opportunity. All the available evidence points, rather, to the fact that people continue to believe in the "equalitarianism" of American society despite their daily familiarity with economic inequality and status distinctions.

Another interpretation of ideological equalitarianism takes a much more optimistic view. In his great work on the American Negro, Gunnar Myrdal has pictured the dilemma which arises for every white American out of the profound contradiction between the theory of equal rights and the practice of racial segregation.[3] In the actions prompted by this deep moral conflict Myrdal sees the lever that can be used to bring about progressive

[2] W. Lloyd Warner, *et al.*, *Social Class in America* (Chicago: Science Research Associates, Inc., 1949), p. v. It is perhaps paradoxical that a theory of class which emphasizes reciprocal status evaluations, should, nevertheless, justify itself on these grounds. The very ambiguity of these evaluations is an important part of the evidence, and an approach that deliberately eliminates this ambiguity in the name of scientific accuracy may obscure this part of the evidence.

[3] See G. Myrdal, *The American Dilemma* (New York: Harper, 1942).

social change. This too we find difficult to accept. It is our belief that *this* approach overemphasizes the urgency of a moral conflict. We would not deny that the conflict is present and that it has often led the way from equalitarian theory to equalitarian practice. Indeed, this conflict and its resultant social agitation is a mainspring of the American liberal tradition. Yet the available evidence indicates that the development of both the theory and the practice of "equalitarianism" among the white majority has been aided by the continued presence of large, ethnically segregated castes. That is, one of the reasons why the belief in this system has been sustained is because opportunities to rise socially and economically have been available to "majority-Americans," and a disproportionate share of poverty, unemployment, sickness and all forms of deprivation have fallen to the lot of minority groups, especially fifteen million Negro Americans.

Our own interpretation of "ideological equalitarianism" differs from these overpessimistic or overoptimistic views. We think that the equalitarianism of manners is not merely a matter of belief, but a reality: differences in status and power have no great effect upon the casual social contacts which set the tone of everyday human relations. This is linked to the fact that these differences have not been elaborated ideologically as they have in Europe. Surely this has not diminished these differences of status and power, but it has helped to prevent the ideological hardening of interest- and status-groups, so that the representation of collective interests is a thing apart from the intellectual life of the country. As a result, Americans frequently think of the differences of status and power, not as being what they really are, but rather as differences in the distribution of material goods. This well-known materialism of American society can also be thought of as an ideology—an ideology which purports to measure men by the single yardstick of material success. As such it is unlike the class and status ideologies of Europe; it involves instead quite an idealistic belief in equality, for all the differences in material status which it accentuates.'

' This belief may be reflected even in the behavior of the very rich. In the late nineteenth and early twentieth century a number of American millionaires went out of their way to emphasize their wealth and superiority by a distinct style of life. Of course, those men have their imitators even today: for example, some Texas

Such ideological equalitarianism implies an ideal which is best expressed by the familiar phrase, "equality of opportunity." It is conceivable that a people might adhere to such an ideal for some time even in the face of declining opportunities for occupational advancement. Some of the evidence concerning the response to the experience of the Great Depression suggests that the traditional belief in America as the land of opportunity imparted to people a spirit of resilience which helped to sustain them through great adversity.[5] However, it is our guess that *a sharp and lasting decline* in the opportunities for occupational advancement would jeopardize these beliefs and lead to a change in the system of values.[6] Such a decline has not yet occurred.

"EQUALITY OF OPPORTUNITY" IN THE UNITED STATES

Data on social mobility—the bare facts and figures—cannot speak for themselves. Although continued social mobility in American society helps to sustain the belief in the "open" class system, it does not follow that in another society a similar rate of social mobility would give rise to such a belief, or encourage it. The point is that in a society in which prevailing views emphasize class differences, even a high degree of social mobility may not suffice to undermine these views.

But although it cannot by itself give rise to a widespread belief in the existence of opportunities, social mobility may be counted upon to sustain such a belief where it already exists. It is therefore important, in making an assessment of ideological equalitarianism in American society, to determine the extent to which its assumptions are borne out by the evidence. Of course, to speak of "equality of opportunity" is to speak vaguely. Yet the phrase

---

oil millionaires. But the generally accepted style of behavior of the upper class tends to emphasize the similarities between their way of life and that of the average man. For related comments see D. Riesman, *Thorstein Veblen: A Critical Interpretation* (New York: Scribner, 1953), esp. pp. 170–193.

[5] See E. Wight Bakke, *The Unemployed Worker* (New Haven: Yale University Press, 1940), pp. 83–89, and by the same author, *Citizens Without Work* (New Haven: Yale University Press, 1940), pp. 66–68.

[6] Many observers contend that these traditional American beliefs did change during the New Deal. Today, most Republican spokesmen emphasize that prolonged unemployment would be intolerable and that all the instrumentalities of government should be used to prevent it. Compared with the years preceding the Depression, this view certainly signalizes a major change in conservative opinion.

has had a strong appeal for the American people, who associate with it an ideal meaning which is clear enough: a meaning that embodies their desire to have a society in which the road of economic advancement is open to any person of talent. Indeed, many believe they live in such a society. It may be difficult or even impossible to say even approximately when a society reaches this goal, for we have no way of assessing the existing distribution of talent, but the ideal as such makes good sense in a democracy. It simply reflects man's perennial quest for a life freed from the grip of such circumstances as poverty or ill-health, and aims at a way of life in which every man must take his chance like every other. Surely this is a far-off, perhaps unattainable, goal. But the legacies of American social and political history have given this goal a value that is accepted throughout the society; and the facts of social mobility may be examined in terms of the manner in which they help to sustain it.

The belief in the widespread availability of opportunities has perhaps found its most popular expression in the stories which recount the careers of prominent American industrialists who within their own lifetime climbed the social ladder from the bottom to the top. It is true that these careers have been well publicized, and that much mythology has been added in the retelling. Moreover, it is probable that in the United States the modest social origin of a prominent man is a matter of pride to him and a source of inspiration to others, while in Europe it is more likely to be hushed up or conveniently forgotten. The author of a recent study of mobility in France states that "it is precisely among those who have experienced the greatest social mobility that reticence [in the interview] may be of most significance. One interviewer, commenting on the refusal of an interview by a respondent, adds: 'I think it was a question of self-esteem; though he is an industrialist, his father was a white-collar worker, and his grandfather's origins were humble.'" Similarly, British corporation directors are less likely than American executives to report the first menial jobs of their careers. Copeman points out in his study of the background of such men that the phrase "training for executive post," often

---

[7] Marcel Bresard, "Mobilité sociale et dimension de la famille," *Population*, 5(1950):535.

given by his respondents as characterization of their original occupation, is vague and therefore misleading, while an American executive would more readily state that he began as a laborer in a mill. This interpretation is supported by another investigation of British executives, in which personnel records were studied.[8] This study found a greater proportion of top managers whose first jobs had been of low status than did Copeman's, which was based on interviews. Such evidence suggests that the mythology of the spectacular career is more vigorously cultivated in the United States than in Europe, although we have reason to doubt that there are proportionately more such careers in America. But the very existence of the mythology is significant, for it reveals the inclination to keep alive the belief in equality of opportunity—a belief that has probably been sustained by the more modest opportunities for upward social mobility, by the frequency with which the sons of manual workers and farmers have become engineers, teachers, government administrators, and businessmen. There are several indexes of such mobility which may be summarized briefly.

In 1870 a large majority of people were concerned with producing food or manufactured goods. By 1919 the 26,000,000 workers employed in mining, agriculture, manufacturing, and construction still greatly outnumbered the 14,000,000 service workers. However, in 1955, although goods-producing employment had increased only to 28,000,000, employment in service industries had more than doubled, and totaled 30,000,000 workers.[9] Thus, today, in the American economy, about 55 per cent of the labor force is engaged in trade, finance, government, transportation, communication, and service. This shift to an economy in which a majority of persons are employed in so-called tertiary industries has had an important effect on social mobility. We have a crude but simple index for this assertion. Throughout, significant differences in average *per capita* income have existed among the groups that are gainfully employed in the primary (agriculture

[8] See G. H. Copeman, *Leaders of British Industry* (London: Gee and Co., 1955), pp. 92, 137; The Acton Society Trust, *Management Succession* (London: The Acton Society Trust, 1956), pp. 25–27; and R. V. Clement, *Managers: A Study of Their Careers in Industry* (London: Allen and Unwin, 1958).

[9] United States Department of Labor, *They Are America: A Report to the American People* (Washington: Government Printing Office, 1957), p. 13.

TABLE 3.1

NUMBER AND PERCENTAGE DISTRIBUTION OF GAINFULLY EMPLOYED POPULATION, AND
PER CAPITA INCOME, BY YEAR AND BRANCH OF PRODUCTION: UNITED STATES

Year and branch of production	Gainfully employed population		Annual income per person for work on 48-hour week basis (in dollars)[a]
	Number (in millions)	Per cent	
1850			
Primary[b]	4.97	67.2	298
Secondary[c]	1.20	16.2	737
Tertiary[d]	1.23	16.6	1,561
Total	7.40	100.0	
1870			
Primary	6.90	55.6	354
Secondary	2.72	21.9	878
Tertiary	2.80	22.5	1,558
Total	12.42	100.0	
1900			
Primary	10.7	39.6	624
Secondary	7.6	28.1	1,361
Tertiary	8.7	32.2	1,780
Total	27.0	99.9	
1920			
Primary	11.1	28.0	625
Secondary	13.0	32.7	1,313
Tertiary	15.6	39.3	1.828
Total	39.7	100.0	
1935			
Primary	10.5	24.8	669
Secondary	11.9	28.1	1,683
Tertiary	19.95	47.1	2,390
Total	42.35	100.0	

SOURCE: Adapted from Colin Clark, *The Conditions of Economic Progress*, (London: Macmillan, 1940), p. 346.
[a] Income data are computed in terms of the purchasing power of the dollar in the United States over the average of the period of 1925–1934.
[b] Primary branch of production includes agriculture, forestry, and fishing industries.
[c] Secondary branch of production includes manufacturing, mining, and building industries.
[d] Tertiary branch of production includes trade ,transportation communication, and domestic, persona and professional service industries.

and mining), the secondary (manufacturing), and the tertiary branches of production. During the past hundred years average income has increased in each of them, but the average income in the tertiary industries has always been relatively higher, well in advance of the average earnings in the other two (see table 3.1). If we assess mobility solely in terms of this one index, we have to conclude that opportunities for higher earnings have expanded rapidly with the shift of the working population into tertiary production.[10] In 1957, for the first time, the number of white-collar workers in the United States was greater than the number of manual workers. These changes in occupational structure have been accelerating in the past ten years. Since 1947 "the total of professional and technical employees has increased by 60 per cent, the fastest growth of any occupational group in the post-World War II period. In the next ten years, this group is expected to increase an additional 43 per cent, or two and a half times as fast as the expected growth of the labor force."[11]

Paralleling this expansion of high-level positions has been a contraction at the bottom of the scale. The proportion of unskilled labor (farm and urban laborers and servants) dropped from 36 per cent in 1910 to 19.7 per cent in 1950.[12] A further anticipated trend is a decline in the proportion of semiskilled workers, a category which has shown relative growth from 1910 to the present.

There is one other *national* index which corroborates this evidence concerning social mobility.[13] This index is provided by dif-

[10] In the 1951 edition of his work Colin Clark has computed the relative income of the three branches of production on a somewhat different basis, though his conclusions are much the same as before. See Colin Clark, *The Conditions of Economic Progress* (London: Macmillan, 1951), pp. 440–442.

It may be that, in recent years, with the increasing opportunities for economic advances within the manual occupations there has come about a diminishing advantage of nonmanual occupations. This possibility is suggested by the evidence assembled by Kurt Mayer, "Recent Changes in the Class Structure of the United States," in *Transactions of the Third World Congress of Sociology*, Vol. III (London: International Sociological Association, 1956), pp. 66–80.

[11] "A New Social Revolution," *Fortune*, April, 1958, pp. 215–217.

[12] Conrad Taeuber and Irene B. Taeuber, *The Changing Population of the United States* (New York: John Wiley and Sons, 1958), p. 211.

[13] All other methods of analyzing social mobility are based on more or less representative samples. The data on occupational trends and on fertility rates which the Bureau of the Census supplies every ten years are the only clues to this problem that are based on nation-wide samples. Data of similar scope concerning internal migration have only recently been added.

ferential fertility rates, which are relevant in this context for the following reasons. We may assume that the number of families earning high incomes increases with the expansion of the economy. We can assume, further, that parents will make every attempt to insure good careers for their children; hence a family will have a strong tendency to perpetuate its high economic position at least over two generations. In terms of these assumptions there

TABLE 3.2

FAMILY INCOME AND NUMBER OF CHILDREN LESS THAN FIVE YEARS OLD
PER THOUSAND WOMEN IN COMPLETE FAMILIES

Total family money income	Per cent of women in specified income groups[a]	Number of children per 1,000 women[b]
Under $1,000	6.2	677
$1,000–$1,999	12.5	628
$2,000–$2,999	22.6	580
$3,000–$3,999	23.3	571
$4,000–$4,999	14.8	476
$5,000 and over	20.5	407
All groups	100.00	550

SOURCE: U. S. Department of Commerce, Bureau of the Census, *Current Population Reports*, "Population Characteristics," Series P-50, No. 27, February 3, 1950.
[a] Based on estimate of 26,204,000 women 15 to 49, married and husband present.
[b] Standardized by age.

are two factors which increase mobility: an absolute increase of the opportunities for upward social mobility (which the previous discussion shows is probable), and a declining fertility in families in the high income brackets. In the United States, as in other industrialized countries, fertility varies inversely with the level of income (see table 3.2). Families with a relatively high income have on the average fewer children than families, whose income is low. Data for 1950 issued by the Bureau of the Census indicate that the difference is still quite great, though perhaps decreasing.[14]

In a recent publication, Joseph Kahl has attempted to assess mobility rates in the United States by relating the overall increase in size of the labor force and differential fertility rates to changes in the occupational structure. As a first step he contrasted the

[14] See Clyde V. Kiser, "Fertility Trends and Differentials," *Journal of the American Statistical Association*, 47 (1952): 25–48; and Charles F. Westoff, "Differential Fertility in the United States," *American Sociological Review*, 19(1954): 549–561.

number of men in specific occupational categories in 1920 and in 1950. In order to estimate the occupational mobility that resulted from technological change during this period, he assumed that from 1920 to 1950 the number of each occupational category would increase in the same proportion as the total labor force (27 per cent). This assumption, together with the assumption that "all men in the labor force in 1920 had been replaced by their sons by 1950" yielded an "expected number" of persons in each category for 1950 which could be compared with the number actually there. The difference between the two figures would give an indication of occupational mobility as a result of technological change. Similarly, Kahl took the occupational distribution of 1920 and applied to the number in each category the net reproduction rate for 1928 (e.g., 0.87 for the professionals, etc.). On this basis he obtained a new estimate for each category, based upon the average reproductive pattern of persons in the different occupations; this estimate could be compared again with the actual number. The difference between *these* two figures would give an indication of occupational mobility as a result of *differential fertility.* Finally, Kahl took the data from the NORC study of social mobility in 1947 in order to estimate total mobility from all causes. Since the NORC study gave the proportion of sons who said that they were *not* in the occupations of their fathers, this proportion could be contrasted with the actual number of people in each occupational category in 1950. For example: there were 3,025,000 professionals in 1950; since 77 per cent of the sons of professionals said that they were not in the occupations of their fathers, 2,329,000 professionals are estimated to have been mobile. In this way Kahl estimates that 27,900,000 out of 41,000,000 men, or 67 per cent of the total labor force in 1950, were mobile. This represents *total occupational mobility from all causes,* and includes, therefore, individual or step-by-step mobility as well as mobility because of technological change and differential fertility. Kahl comes to the conclusion that in the period between 1920 and 1950, 19.7 per cent of the labor force was mobile by virtue of technological changes, 6.8 per cent was mobile because of differential fertility, and 40.5 per cent was mobile as a result of individual occupational mobility. Although it is important to note that these percentages have no absolute meaning, since they would differ greatly if another system of classifying occupations were used (the greater the number of occupational classes the greater the mobility), Kahl's ingenious method has given the best available approximation of the relative order of magnitude of different types of mobility in American society.[15]

TABLE 3.3

PERCENTAGE OF MEN IN URBAN OCCUPATIONS WITH FATHERS IN URBAN OCCUPATIONS WHO HAVE BEEN MOBILE UPWARD OR DOWNWARD

Category	Centers 1945	N.O.R.C. 1947	Survey Research Center: 1952
Upward mobile......................	17	21	19
Downward mobile.................	8	11	13
Stationary........................	75	68	67
Number in sample................	598	719	463

NOTE: Upward mobile includes men in nonmanual occupations whose fathers were in manual occupations; downward mobile includes men in manual occupations whose fathers were in nonmanual occupations. For detailed sources, see figure 2.1, p. 21, and note a to table 2.1, p. 25.

The surveys dealing with the extent of social mobility in America which are based on national samples indicate that the bulk of the mobility in the United States has been upward. That is, when we compare the occupations of men in the urban labor force with those of their fathers, we find that three national surveys agree that there has been more upward mobility than downward (see table 3.3).

It is the expansion of the nonmanual sector of the labor force that has made possible the preponderance of upward mobility over downward mobility. However, most sons of urban dwellers have not changed their class position, as defined by a shift across the manual-nonmanual line, and approximately 10 per cent of them have fallen in status. About 80 per cent of this group have either not significantly improved their class position (from manual to nonmanual status), or have declined in position as compared to their fathers. This must constantly be kept in mind in evaluating the role of social mobility in American society.

It is curious that little of the attention given to the problem of the open society in America has considered the fact, brought out

[15] Joseph A. Kahl, *The American Class Structure* (New York: Rinehart, 1957), pp. 251–262.

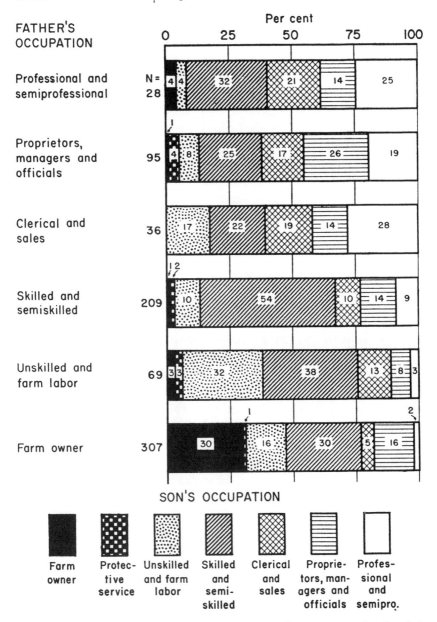

Fig. 3.1. Occupational distribution of a sample of American males, by their father's occupation. *Source.*—From data of Michigan Survey Research Center Study of 1952 presidential election. Protective Service omitted from "father's occupation" because of too few cases.

by these sample surveys, that millions of Americans regularly fall in status—that a high position of a father is no guarantee of similar position for his children. The detailed picture of the mobility of American males presented in figure 3.1 indicates that the majority of the sons of professionals, semiprofessionals, proprietors, managers, and officials— the most privileged occupations—are not able to maintain the rank of their fathers, and that about one-third of them are actually in manual employment.

In chapter ii we suggested that available European data indicate that rates of mobility comparable to present rates existed even before World War I. An excellent study which compares mobility rates in one American city before World War I with those of the late 1930's, gives similar results. Natalie Rogoff studied two samples of male applicants for marriage licenses in the city of Indianapolis, for the years 1905–1912 and 1938–1941.[16] The application forms asked for the occupation of both the applicant and his father. Her study was explicitly designed to answer the question: *has more or less occupational mobility taken place than can be accounted for by the concurrent changes in the occupational structure?* The data for both periods indicate more upward than downward mobility. Even if changes in the occupational structure are held constant, the data suggest that there was no decline in mobility: the rate of social mobility in the United States was high in both periods, even when the increased shift to tertiary occupations is taken into account; and the rate for the more recent period was higher in absolute terms.

On the level of intra-generation mobility, an investigation based on material in the city directories of Norristown, Pennsylvania, found that "the proportion of the resident population remaining in the same occupational category during each decennial period has decreased steadily from 1910–1920 to 1940–1950."[17] In other words, both upward and downward mobility increased in the period from 1910 to 1950. These results from a smaller town reinforce the conclusions derived from the Indianapolis study, since

[16] Natalie Rogoff, *Recent Trends in Occupational Mobility* (Glencoe: The Free Press, 1953).
[17] Sidney Goldstein, "Migration and Occupational Mobility in Norristown, Pennsylvania," *American Sociological Review*, 20(1955):402–408.

a high rate of *intra*-generation mobility necessarily implies a certain amount of *inter*-generation mobility.

EDUCATIONAL OPPORTUNITIES

The effect of opportunities for upward mobility on the behavior and the beliefs of Americans may be most clearly seen by an examination of education, which has become the principal avenue for upward mobility in most industrialized nations. The overall significance of education for occupational achievement is presented in table 3.4. The evidence points both to a constant increase of educational opportunities and to the compatibility between remaining restrictions and the belief in "equal opportunity."[18]

The shift of the gainfully employed population into the non-manual occupations has been accompanied by a tremendous growth in the facilities for higher education. Britain, with a third of the population of the United States (50,000,000 as against 151,-000,000 in 1950), had 102,012 university students in 1950; in the same year the United States had a fall-semester enrollment of 1,888,275 college students. To be sure, English universities are predominantly professional schools, while American universities are institutions of general education as well, but this important difference should not be permitted to obscure the discrepancy in the educational opportunities of the two countries. Between 1890 and 1950 the number of students attending American colleges and universities increased about seventeen times, and the number of persons in academic employment increased about thirteen times. Dur-

---

[18] Some idea of the significance of the American pattern of education may be obtained by comparing the two following quotations, one assessing the situation in Germany after World War I, the other in present-day America: "Differences of 'education' are today important factors in establishing caste barriers, in contrast to the *class*-forming elements which lie in the differentiation according to property and economic function. . . . Regrettable as this may be, differences of 'education' are still the strongest social barriers." Max Weber, *Gesammelte Politische Schriften* (München: Drei Masken Verlag, 1921), p. 279; "It may . . . come as a surprise to learn that schooling is one of the most equally distributed 'goods' in American society. The contrast with income distributions is marked. For the nation as a whole, the top 33 per cent of the families receive two thirds of the aggregate income. . . . Analogous national figures for education in the younger age cohort were 43 per cent . . . and in the older 50 per cent. . . . Among major items of family expenditure only that for food is today as evenly distributed as was schooling a generation ago." C. Arnold Anderson and Mary Jean Bowman, "Educational Distributions and Attainment Norms in the United States," in *Proceedings of the World Population Congress* (Rome: 1954), vol. 4, pp. 931–943.

TABLE 3.4

PERCENTAGE OF MALE WORKERS IN EACH MAJOR OCCUPATION BY SPECIFIED LEVELS
OF EDUCATION: UNITED STATES, 1950

Occupational category	Four year high school and up	One or more years college
Nonmanual		
Professional, technical and kindred...........	85.6	70.3
Managers, officials, and proprietors...........	53.1	26.1
Sales..	58.7	27.1
Clerical and kindred........................	56.4	21.6
Manual		
Craftsmen and foremen......................	28.5	6.5
Other services (except personal, house)........	22.4	5.8
Operatives.................................	20.3	3.7
Private household...........................	17.0	4.9
Laborers, except farm and mine..............	11.6	2.2
Farm		
Farmers....................................	16.0	4.6
Hired farm labor...........................	10.2	2.5
All categories...............................	34.3	14.9

SOURCE: Lawrence Thomas, *The Occupational Structure and Education* (Englewood Cliffs, New Jersey: Prentice-Hall, 1956), p. 349.

ing the same period the population of the country increased only two and a half times. Employing relative ratios rather than absolute numbers, we find that while during the years 1900 to 1950 the *proportion* of such professional groups as lawyers, physicians, dentists, and clergymen in the population declined or rose only slightly, the *proportion* of college teachers and academic personnel increased more than four-fold.[19] Figures on graduation from high schools and colleges tell the same story: in 1870, 16,000 graduated from high schools and 9,371 from colleges, while in 1950, the number of high school graduates had risen to 1,199,7000 and the number of college graduates had risen to 432,058. The percentage increase of expenditures on education by American consumers in the period from 1935 to 1948 was far higher than the percentage change in all other categories of consumer expenditures,[20] a fact

[19] George J. Stigler, *Trends in Employment in the Service Industries* (Princeton: Princeton University Press, 1956), p. 108. Stigler's table also indicates that the relative increase of military officers was even greater than that of college teachers: the bulk of this growth took place in the decade from 1940 to 1950.

[20] *Ibid.*, p. 44.

which belies the repeated recent statements that Americans do not value education.[21]

This impressive growth of opportunities for higher education cannot by itself be regarded as an index of upward social mobility.[22] We do not know whether the number of high school or college graduates has increased proportionately faster than the number of jobs for which high school or college graduation have become a prerequisite. But there is some reason to believe that this expansion of educational facilities, together with the increased social value placed on education, has aided social mobility, at least indirectly, if only because it has helped postpone the entry of teenagers into the labor market. In 1870, 57 per cent of children aged 5 to 17 were enrolled in the public schools; by 1950, that percentage had risen to 85.3. The significance of this increase is best appreciated by a comparison of these figures with related figures for England, France, New Zealand, Cuba, Japan and Portugal. Table 3.5 shows the percentage of different age-groups who were in school in the years indicated.

The dividing line between the educated and the uneducated is more blurred and the choice of career is made later in America than in European societies. Such a postponement of career choice probably reflects the fact that the parents of high school students can usually do without their supplementary earnings, and we shall see that this absence of pressure for entry into the labor market is in itself a major facilitation of upward mobility.[23]

---

[21] For further elaboration of this point see S. M. Lipset, "The Fuss about the Eggheads," *Encounter*, April, 1957, pp. 37–41, and "The Egghead Looks at Himself," *New York Times Magazine*, November 17, 1957, pp. 22, 104–107. Another index of the American concern with education may be seen in the fact that former American colonies, though poor, have been inculcated with the American belief that all men should be well educated. There are over three hundred colleges and universities in the Philippines, and more students in higher education than in any country except the United States. Similarly the proportion of college-level students in Puerto Rico is greater than that in any Latin American and West Indian nation or colony.

[22] However, the availability of college education at low tuition fees is an index of opportunities for upward mobility, even if enrollment and graduation figures are not. A large proportion of the increase in student enrollment has been due to the growth of the state universities, which are financed through appropriations of the state legislature and which charge very low tuition fees to residents of their respective states. Usually, residence in the state can be acquired within a year, and for exceptional students even this requirement can be waived.

[23] See chapter vi.

Inequities that remain in spite of the expansion of educational opportunities must also be considered. As in other countries, the overwhelming majority of American university students are children of businessmen, well-to-do farmers, or professionals. The largest study of factors affecting the admission of high-school seniors to college, based on a national sample of over 10,000 senior students in high school, indicates the extent to which the socio-

TABLE 3.5

PERCENTAGE OF AGE GROUP OF ADOLESCENTS IN SCHOOL, FOR DIFFERENT COUNTRIES

Age	United States 1950[a]	France 1951[b]	England and Wales 1951[c]	New Zealand 1950[d]	Cuba 1953[e]	Japan 1950[f]	Portugal 1950[g]
13	96	98	97	98	58	..	18
14	95	59	98	98	47	87[h]	12
15	91	40	34	60	31	..	10
16	81	29	19	33	22	..	8
17	68	17	10	15	15	31[i]	7

[a] United Nations, *Demographic Yearbook, 1956* (New York, 1956), p. 595. Includes part-time students.
[b] Approximate. These percentages were estimated by comparing the age distribution of students given in UNESCO, *World Survey of Education* (Paris, 1955), p. 246, with the age distribution of the population in *Annuaire Statistique*, 1952.
[c] United Nations, *Demographic Yearbook, 1956*, p. 604.
[d] James B. Conant, *Education and Liberty* (Cambridge: Harvard University Press, 1953), p. 3.
[e] United Nations, *Demographic Yearbook, 1956*, p. 590
[f] *Ibid.*, p. 600.
[g] *Ibid.*, p. 604.
[h] Figure for combined 13 to 15 year group.
[i] Figure for combined 16 to 18 year group.

economic status of families affects the opportunity of American youth to attend a university (see table 3.6). Only 16 per cent of the children of manual workers graduating from high school in 1947 had been admitted to a college or university, although two-thirds of the children of professional fathers had secured admission.[24]

[24] A recent study in Switzerland describes a similar pattern. Girod found that entrance into the elite strata requires a university education. Entrance into the university depends on going to secondary schools with a Latin curriculum. Almost 75 per cent of the children of leading officials, businessmen, and professionals attend such schools, as compared to only about 10 per cent of working-class children. The number of individuals in the elite groups originating in lower strata correspond closely to the number of lower-strata children in the Latin curriculum schools; the university is thus the chief vehicle of elite circulation. Roger Girod, "Ecole, université, et sélection des membres des couches dirigeantes: le cas de Genève" (Working Paper Four Submitted to the Fourth Working Conference on Social Stratification and Social Mobility, International Sociological Association, December, 1957). A similar disproportion in the social origin of students entering the humanistic middle schools which lead to the intellectual professions is reported in a Belgian study. J. Collard, "La Première orientation au sortie des écoles pri-

Since these data refer only to high school seniors, it should be noted that a large proportion of the students of poorer families never reach the senior year in high school, and these figures, therefore, still underestimate the existing inequities in the distribution of educational opportunities. An attempt to estimate the proportions of the children of various occupational groups graduating from college by a survey of the social composition of a number of colleges and a comparison of this with census materials gives the results shown in table 3.7. It is important to note that although the chances of the adolescents from lower strata to complete college are much less than the chances of those from high-status families, they still make up a large minority (31 per cent) of college graduates.[25] This fact is very important in maintaining the belief in the availability of opportunity among middle-class Americans, where such a belief already exists.

Another national study which sheds light on university attendance, the University of Michigan Survey Research Center's sample of the American population in 1952, indicates that the United States is still far from being a country in which educational opportunities are equitably distributed (see table 3.8). Only 6 per cent of the sons of manual workers and 3 per cent of the sons of farmers were college graduates, as compared with 25 per cent of the sons of men in nonmanual occupations. A majority of the sons of manual workers (64 per cent) and of farmers (81 per cent) had never completed high school, as contrasted with 30 per cent of

maires officielles," *Travaux du séminaire de sociologie de la Faculté de Droit de Liège,* 2 (1951): 90–144. A large number of European studies which agree in showing that sons of manual workers and farmers are under-represented in the high schools and the universities, while sons of professionals and salaried employees are highly over-represented, have been summarized in Sylvain de Coster and Georges Van der Elst, *Mobilité sociale et enseignement* (Brussels: Les éditions de la librairie encyclopédique, 1954), pp. 46–54. They conclude that "of the mass of children who attend primary school, only a small fraction of individuals from the less privileged classes of society succeed in reaching and pursuing the studies which permit them to raise themselves in the occupational hierarchy in particular, and in the social hierarchy in general."

[25] This may be compared with the fact that approximately 25 per cent of those admitted to English universities come from working-class families. R. K. Kelsall, *Report on an Inquiry Into Applications for Admission to Universities* (London: Association of Universities of the British Commonwealth, 1957), p. 9. A recent Canadian study reports that 29 per cent of those admitted to Ontario universities in 1956 were of manual origin. W. Woodside, "Grade xiii and the Universities," *Varsity Graduate,* 6 (1958): 62–64.

TABLE 3.6

Percentage Distribution of White High School Seniors with Fathers in Specified Occupational Groups, by Plans for Further Education: 1947

Plans for further education	Total	Father's occupational group						
		Professional and executive	Small business	White collar	Service trades worker	Factory and other worker	Farmer	Other and not reported
Applied for admission to a college..	35	73	48	45	23	20	21	32
Actually admitted to a college[a].....	30	67	41	40	20	16	21	23
Have not applied but hope to go later	22	13	19	24	25	24	27	23
Will not go to college..............	40	12	31	28	48	54	47	42
Don't know......................	3	2	2	3	4	2	5	3
Number of cases...............	10,063	1,136	1,194	1,351	1,736	2,365	1,236	1,036

SOURCE: Adapted from Elmo Roper, *Factors Affecting the Admission of High School Seniors to College* (Washington, D. C.: American Council on Education, 1949), p. 17, 143.
[a] This line has been recalculated from data in Roper's study; it should not be included in the total, since the figures are already represented in the line immediately above.

TABLE 3.7

ESTIMATED DISTRIBUTION OF COLLEGE GRADUATES, BY OCCUPATION OF FATHER

Father's occupation	Per cent of children graduating from college	Occupations of fathers of all college graduates in percentages
Professional and semiprofessional...................	43	22
Managerial.......................................	19	19
Sales, clerical and service workers..................	15	19
Manual..	8	31
Farm..	6	8

SOURCE: Estimates of Commission on Human Resources and Advanced Training, reported in Dael Wolfle, *America's Resources of Specialized Talent* (New York: Harper, 1954), p. 162.

TABLE 3.8

RELATIONSHIP BETWEEN FATHER'S OCCUPATION AND EDUCATION, AMERICAN MALES
(Percentages)

Education	Father's occupation					
	Professional and semi-professional	Proprietors	Clerical and sales	Skilled and semiskilled	Unskilled	Farm
8 years or less...	9	18	12	36	46	64
Some high school	17	20	20	26	26	17
High school graduate.....	31	26	29	24	16	10
Some college....	12	12	20	8	6	6
College graduate	31	24	19	6	6	3
Number in sample.......	35	101	41	234	73	349

SOURCE: Based on data supplied by the Survey Research Center at the University of Michigan, from their study of the 1952 Presidential election. Protective Service, included in the data as a "Father's Occupation," was not used in our calculations because there were too few cases.

the sons of middle-class fathers.[20] The effect of these differences in educational attainments on the subsequent careers of men of different social origins may be seen in table 3.9, which shows the relationship between education and the current job of men whose fathers were in different classes. The data indicate that workers'

[20] This should again not be permitted to obscure the difference between the American educational system and most European systems. Comparison of these results with data from the UNESCO survey of Germany indicates that a greater proportion of the sons of manual workers in the United States get some college education (13 per cent) than get beyond elementary school (*Volksschule*) in Germany (8 per cent).

TABLE 3.9
EDUCATION AND SOCIAL MOBILITY (MALES ONLY)
(Percentages)

Respondent's occupation	Father's occupation and education											
	Nonmanual				Manual				Farm			
	Under 12	12	Some college	College graduate	Under 12	12	Some college	College graduate	Under 12	12	Some college	College graduate
Nonmanual............	33	54	85	95	15	38	59	100	17	24	56	80
Manual..............	63	46	15	5	82	61	41	..	53	38	22	10
Farm................	4	..	..	..	3	1	..	..	30	38	22	10
Number of respondents........	49	52	20	41	153	90	22	19	223	50	19	10

SOURCE: See table 3.8.

sons who have completed college are almost certain to move into a nonmanual, presumably fairly high-status occupation. As we have seen, however, this group constitutes only 6 per cent of the children of manual workers. Among the remaining 94 per cent, who have not completed college, educational attainment is correlated with higher occupational status, but the interesting fact is that it does not compensate for coming from a working-class family. Thus, workers' sons with "some college" education are about as well off as a group as the sons of nonmanual fathers who have graduated from high school but not attended college. Similarly, high-school graduation for the sons of workers results in their being only slightly better off than the sons of nonmanual workers who have not completed high school. It is clear, therefore, that although increased educational opportunities have opened the door to mobility for many of the sons of lower-class parents, the large majority are still not able to attend college. Except for those who do attend college, educational attainment comparable to that achieved by the sons of middle-class fathers does not mean an equal chance in the labor market.

But these objective differences between classes in opportunity for schooling and in the occupational value of education are not necessarily obvious to those whose opportunities are limited. Though many high-school seniors from the working class cannot expect to attend college, the ideology of equal opportunity is supported by the fact that they might "work their way through school," even though their parents could not afford to finance their education. This ideology is also supported by the opportunities available to persons with a completed college education. In a recent study, the income and occupation of university graduates was related to whether or not they had worked their way through college. Thirty-one per cent of those who supported themselves while attending college and who were more than forty years old at the time of the study, earned over $7,500 in 1947. Thus, the chances of economic advancement were certainly considerable even for those who started with a handicap. But this should not obscure the fact that the differences in family background with which these students started had their repercussions even after their careers were well under way; for, the percentage of those earning $7,500 and over was 11 points higher among those who had earned *none* of their college expenses than among those who had earned more than 50 per cent. (See table 3.10.)

It is difficult to assess the implications of these data. Attendance at a university is indispensable today for most people who want to be considered for high positions in the government, in large businesses, in politics, and in the professions. The great majority of university students, on the other hand, never enter the graduate or professional schools; they regard their attendance at college as

TABLE 3.10

PERCENTAGE DISTRIBUTION OF UNIVERSITY GRADUATES WHO WERE 40 OR OLDER IN
1947 AND WHO EARNED SPECIFIED PROPORTIONS OF THEIR EXPENSES
WHEN IN COLLEGE, BY THEIR SALARY IN 1947

1947 Salary	Proportion of college expenses earned		
	None	1 to 50 per cent	Over 50 per cent
$7,500 and over....................	42	38	31
5,000–7,500......................	21	26	24
3,000–5,000......................	23	26	34
Less than $3,000..................	14	10	11
All groups.......................	100	100	100

SOURCE: Adapted from Eric Haveman and Patricia Salter West, *They Went to College* (New York: Harcourt, Brace, 1952), p. 171.

"the thing to do" for the children of middle-class families. Attendance at an American university does not imply a decision to enter a profession, and since the majority of students do not, the resources of the universities are primarily devoted to their general education. Hence, the intellectual demands made on the American student during his first years in college are on the whole quite moderate and he may find it possible to earn a modest living without neglecting his studies. If he shows promise in his academic work he may be able to obtain a fellowship or a position as a teaching assistant, and in this or a similar manner may be able to pursue a course of general education or professional training without financial assistance from his parents. In other words, the fact that the first four years of American university education are largely nonprofessional in character aids the student who is on his own. If his family makes no premature demands on him and if luck and talent are on his side, then he may have access to a position of high social and economic status solely on the basis of his training. Moreover, once he has graduated, his working-class background will not be much of a liability.

There are important "ifs" in this pattern of opportunities. We should add that the majority of college graduates fail to secure more than a modest income, regardless of family background. It is important to recognize that the very increase in educational opportunities of which the children of poorer families are able to take advantage is a token not only of social mobility through education, but also of the declining social prestige of higher education itself.[27] Yet the very fact that higher education is held in less esteem here than in Europe, works also in favor of the student who must make his own way. The chance to obtain a higher education is certainly not regarded as a great privilege. Indeed, the state-supported universities are another testimony to the ingrained equalitarianism of American society. Even among state legislators, who may be counted upon to take a very conservative view toward the expenditure of state funds, the booster spirit and the strong feeling that boys from the home state should have an equal chance, seems to win out more often than not. This social as well as economic accessibility of higher education, together with the related devaluation of the highly educated, has had the effect of making the American university an avenue of social mobility and an institutional bulwark of ideological equalitarianism.

BUSINESS CAREERS

Thus far we have related the social mobility of American society to the expansion of both educational opportunity and the tertiary branch of production. It is also necessary to consider it in relation

[27] The widespread practice of requiring a college education for jobs for which this was not previously a requirement has had the same effect. It is, moreover, symptomatic of the disesteem in which college education is held in the United States that skilled workers often earn a higher income than men in positions which require a four-year college education. This disesteem implies, on the other hand, that the college graduate, or even the Ph.D., is less status-conscious than his opposite number in Europe. Hence there is less danger here that the professions will be overcrowded, even apart from the monopolistic practices of several professional associations. University-trained persons are often willing as well as able to try their hand at other than "professional" jobs, partly because this does not involve as much loss of status as it appears to do in Europe.

to the declining proportion of the self-employed, especially in a country in which the ideology of economic independence and of "free enterprise" has provided so many with so much emotional satisfaction. The belief of nineteenth-century America in the possibility of going "from rags to riches" by starting a business with one's savings is too notorious to need restatement. But obsolete as it may seem in the face of the declining proportion of the self-employed, it is apparently alive enough to prompt millions of Americans to escape the dependent status of an employee by setting themselves up in a business of their own.

As we shall see in more detail in chapter vi, two-thirds of the manual workers interviewed in the Oakland labor-mobility study had thought of going into business for themselves, and over two-fifths of them had actually made efforts to start their own firm. In fact, 22 per cent of those manually employed in 1949 had previously been self-employed, and 20 per cent of those in business for themselves in 1949 had previously been manual workers.

The evidence on business turnover in the country as a whole suggests that these findings may not be idiosyncratic. Between 1900 and 1940, "15,989,000 new concerns were established and 14,013,000 closed their doors, a startling turnover."[28] This tendency has continued into the postwar period. In the four years between 1944 and 1948 a total of 1,917,000 firms opened and 1,094,000 closed. Assuming that these openings and closings involved different people, which they obviously did not always do, and ignoring the problem of the number of partners in these firms, between 1944 and 1948 about three million Americans either started or got out of a business.[29] This figure is equal to 6 per cent of the total urban work force. By extrapolating this figure to a twenty-year period, we conclude that somewhere between 20 and 30 per cent of the American urban work force have been self-employed at

[28] Temporary National Economic Committee, "Problems of Small Business," in *Investigation of Concentration of Economic Power*, Monograph No. 17 (Washington: Government Printing Office, 1941), p. 66. A more detailed analysis of this and related evidence is contained in K. Mayer, "Business Enterprise: Traditional Symbol of Opportunity," *The British Journal of Sociology*, 4 (1953): 160–180.

[29] An estimate for the prewar period which attempts to take these factors into account may be found in Alfred Oxenfeldt, *New Firms and Free Enterprise* (Washington: American Council on Public Affairs, 1943), pp. 97–101. "One person in fifteen [of the nonfarm labor force], according to a primitive estimate, goes into business for himself at some time in his life." *Ibid.*, p. 101.

some time in their work history, which checks roughly with our sample findings. However, over four-fifths of the firms which opened between 1944 and 1948 were small enterprises employing less than four workers. Clearly, many of the workers who became self-employed are little better off economically, and some of them are a great deal worse off, than those who continue as manual workers.

Yet despite such poor prospects and repeated disappointments, self-employment in a small business is a career which many Americans attempt to pursue and which many more regard as highly desirable, perhaps because of the ideal of independence associated with it. And such careers, as well as the widespread belief in them, reflect and reinforce the conviction that America is a land of expanding opportunities. With the exception of the workers at the very bottom of the occupational structure, the majority of Americans are probably either related to, or know, individuals who have become self-employed.[30]

The pattern of business careers among the economic *elite* tells a very different story. In the following chapter we review several studies of the careers of men who control large business organizations. These studies agree that since the Civil War a majority of American business leaders have come from upper- or upper-middle-class families, and that the proportion of business leaders coming from rural families has decreased. Available data do not indicate that the proportion of business leaders from working-class or lower middle-class families has declined; it has always been small. Yet, even though the evidence points to the predominant "self-recruitment" of the business elite, we cannot conclude that this elite is becoming more restrictive. A recent study by Suzanne Keller[31] has shown that the proportion of the economic elite which

---

[30] Even the workers at the bottom continue to use the language of "striving and success," although nothing in their workaday experience gives any "real" meaning to it. In his article "The Tradition of Opportunity and the Aspiration of Automobile Workers," *American Journal of Sociology*, 57 (1952): 453–459, Eli Chinoy has shown how the workers will interpret a better job assignment or the acquisition of a television set as evidence that they are "getting ahead." Much the same findings are reported in a parallel study by R. H. Guest, "Work Careers and Aspirations of Automobile Workers," *American Sociological Review*, 19(1954):155–163, though Guest rates the resulting frustrations among the workers somewhat higher than Chinoy.

[31] The study examines the backgrounds of the presidents and chairmen of the Board of Directors in leading American firms in the years 1870, 1900, 1900–1910,

is of Anglo-Saxon origin declined from 87 per cent in 1870 to 77 per cent in 1900 and to 65 per cent in 1950. The proportions of Catholics and Jews in the elite has increased from 1 per cent in 1870 to 12 per cent in 1950. These trends correspond to changes in the occupational, ethnic, and religious structure of American society; but the fact that new and originally underprivileged groups may enter the upper economic stratum is indicative of mobility where it is least expected. It should be added that upward mobility within the business elite has been facilitated because recruitment to the top positions in large-scale enterprises is much more dependent upon managerial ability than upon family influence.[32] And emphasis upon managerial abilities gives an additional chance to those who have "only" a university training and high qualifications to recommend them. It may well be that the children of working-class or lower middle-class families who attend universities are here presented with new opportunities (to the extent that the top managers of the future are recruited from the universities).

THE EFFECT OF IMMIGRATION AND MIGRATION

Both the retention of the belief in opportunity and the political conservatism of American workers have frequently been explained as results of the effect of immigration on American society. Traditionally, immigrants entered American society on the lowest rung of the occupational and status ladder. However, the native-born children of the immigrants, who generally received a better education than their parents and who were assimilated to American speech and behavior, were able to rise economically and socially as the national economy expanded.[33] Consequently, it has been

1950. See S. Keller, *The Social Origins and Career Lines of Three Generations of American Business Leaders* (Unpublished Ph.D. dissertation, Columbia University, New York, 1953). See chapter iv, for further details on this and related studies.

[32] Warner and Abegglen report that inheritance of position occurs more frequently in small than in large business firms, and, conversely, that the bureaucracy of the large firms facilitates upward mobility. See W. Lloyd Warner and James C. Abegglen, *Occupational Mobility in American Business and Industry* (Minneapolis: University of Minnesota Press, 1955), pp. 150–154, and S. Adams, "Trends in the Occupational Origins of Business Leaders," *American Sociological Review*, 16(1954): 541–548.

[33] A recent analysis of census data finds that in 1870 and 1880 "the foreign born were most typically employed in the factories, in heavy industry, as manual laborers and domestic servants. Clerical, managerial and official positions remained

argued that low status and income in American society has been the plight of groups which are "in the society but not of it." If these immigrants felt aggrieved about their position in the New World, their natural form of protest was identification with, and organization as, an ethnic group, rather than an economic-interest group. Moreover, Marcus Hanson and Oscar Handlin have suggested that most immigrants in the United States accepted the idea that America is a land of opportunity in spite of their personal economic deprivation: the lot of most European immigrants in this country was materially better than it had been in Europe, so that they could think of their situation as an improvement even though they were at the bottom of the social ladder in America.[34]

If the history of American immigration has contributed to the perpetuation of the American value system, then it may be asked why the ending of mass immigration (as a result of legislation passed after World War I) did not give rise to a native American working class which would have less faith in the "promise of America." Though it may be premature to exclude this possibility, the fact remains that the European immigration has in a sense been replaced by a new pattern of migration, which in many ways resembles the old. An expanding industrial economy resulted in a demand for labor that was met by migration from undeveloped areas to industrial centers. The migrants were, for the most part, Negroes, Puerto Ricans, Mexicans, and, in a different category, poor whites from the rural South. Now, as before, there is a close relationship between low income and membership in segregated groups. A large proportion of seasonal farm laborers and share-croppers in the South and Southwest come from them. In the cities, Negroes, Mexicans and Puerto Ricans predominate in the unskilled, dirty, and badly paid occupations. These twenty million people earn a disproportionately low share of the national income; they have little political power and no social prestige; they live

---

largely inaccessible to them." But as early as 1890 the children of the immigrants were gradually moving away from their fathers' occupations and entering business and clerical and professional work, a trend which so maintained itself that by 1950 the occupational distribution of second-generation Americans is no different than that of the nation as a whole. E. P. Hutchinson, *Immigrants and their Children* (New York: John Wiley and Sons, 1956), pp. 114, 155, 195, 216.

[34] M. L. Hanson, *The Immigrant in American History* (Cambridge: Harvard University Press, 1940), and Oscar Handlin, *The Uprooted* (Boston: Little, Brown, 1951).

in ethnic ghettos in rural and urban areas alike, and they have little social contact with white Americans. Indeed, today there are two working classes in America, a white one and a Negro, Mexican, and Puerto Rican one. A real social and economic cleavage is created by widespread discrimination against these minority groups, and this diminishes the chance for the development of solidarity along class lines. In effect, the overwhelming majority of whites, both in the working class and in the middle and upper classes, benefit economically and socially from the existence of these "lower castes" within their midst. This continued splintering of the working class is a major element in the preservation of the stability of the American social structure.

The nature of this cleavage can be seen from the following statistics. In 1939, 48.5 per cent of all Negro males who were 25 to 64 years old earned less than $500 a year. This compared with 16.7 per cent of native whites in the same age and income brackets.[35] The Federal Unemployment Census in 1937 reported that 38.9 per cent of all Negroes in the North were unemployed, compared with 18.1 per cent of the whites. In 1954, a year of full employment, the median income of nonwhite families was $2,410; that of the white was $4,339.[36] In 1958, "while one out of every fifteen white workers were unemployed, one out of every seven Negroes were jobless . . . [and] a high proportion of relief cases are Negroes and Puerto Ricans."[37] According to a sample study of college graduates, in 1947 only 5 per cent of the Negroes, as against one-third of the whites, had an annual income of over $5,000.[38]

It is important to mention these gross inequities, because the ethnic and racial minorities carrying this burden of poverty save many of their fellow white Americans from suffering the worst forms of deprivation. But after that has been said, it must be added that the position of the minorities—and especially of the Negro as

---

[35] E. F. Frazier, *The Negro in the United States* (New York: Macmillan, 1949), p. 606.

[36] In the rural sector the median income of nonwhite families was $763, compared with $2,157 for white families. See Eli Ginsberg, *et al.*, *The Negro Potential* (New York: Columbia University Press, 1956), p. 16.

[37] Daniel Bell, "The 'Invisible' Unemployed," *Fortune*, July, 1958, p. 109.

[38] Ernest Haveman and Patricia S. West, *They Went to College* (New York: Harcourt, Brace, 1952), p. 96.

the largest minority—has itself been subject to change. Recent studies have made it clear that radical ideologies have made no inroads among Negro Americans, and it may well be that their changing status is in part responsible. The large-scale migration of Negroes from the rural South to the urban centers of industry in the North during the 1920's resembled in some measure the earlier immigration of people from southeastern Europe. For, although the Negroes had to take the dirtiest and worst-paid jobs upon their arrival in the North, their incomes and living facilities, poor as they were, were better than those in the rural South. And although the impact of the depression jeopardized even this questionable gain, the shortage of manpower and the general prosperity during World War II opened up unprecedented opportunities for training and occupational advancement. These changes in economic status have been accompanied by a steady, if painfully slow, improvement in the Negro's political and legal position, culminating for the time being in the decision of the Supreme Court that racial segregation in the schools is unconstitutional. These are remarkable, even dramatic gains, coming as they do within a single generation. They have by no means overcome the discrimination and poverty which is the lot of millions of Negro Americans, but they seem to have been sufficient to give hope even to those who have not yet benefited from them. Thus the "American creed" finds many believers among the men and women who carry a disproportionate share of the heaviest burdens in American society.[39]

THE WEALTH OF THE UNITED STATES

The industrialization and advancing technology of the United States has brought about an almost unbroken increase in national wealth: between 1870 and 1950 per capita income (standardized to 1929 prices) rose from $215 to $1,043.[40] The gross national product increased five times from 1890 to 1950 as a result of a

---

[39] A detailed discussion of the modifications introduced into the ideology of equalitarianism by the tensions in the economic and social position of the Negro middle class is, E. Franklin Frazier, *Black Bourgeoisie* (Glencoe: The Free Press, 1957), part II, pp. 153–212. The disparities between the ideology and the reality are so obvious that Frazier entitles this section "The World of Make Believe."

[40] G. J. Stigler, *Trends in Employment in the Service Industries*, p. 25.

two-fold increase in population and a three-fold rise in labor productivity.[41]

Every indicator of economic productivity and consumption patterns clearly demonstrates that the United States is much wealthier than any other country in the world today. In the present context this is significant because the *distribution* of consumers' goods has tended to become more equitable as the size of national income has increased.[42] This relationship between wealth and the distribution of consumer goods has been commented on by the Swedish economist Gunnar Myrdal who writes, "It is, indeed, a regular occurrence endowed almost with the dignity of an economic law that the poorer the country, the greater the difference between poor and rich."[43] Comparing the United States with the relatively well-to-do countries of Western Europe in 1956 reveals the following more or less representative figures:

In the United States there are 32 automobiles for every 100 persons, in England and France only 8 per 100, and in West Germany only 4 per 100.

In the United States, there are 36 telephones for every 100 persons, in England only 14 per 100, and in France and West Germany only 8 per 100.

In the United States there are 89 radios for every 100 persons, in England and West Germany 28 per 100, and in France only 23 per 100.[44]

These indexes of wealth and the wide distribution of consumers' goods mean that there is a greater variation in consumption patterns and styles of life in Europe than in America. A recent Ameri-

---

[41] Frederick C. Mills, *Productivity and Economic Progress* (New York: National Bureau of Economic Research, 1952), p. 2.

[42] This is not the place to discuss the causes of more equitable distribution of income. It may be a result of economic pressures inherent in a mass-production economy, or of the redistribution of political power. In the past, national income has increased without equalizing distribution, as in nineteenth-century England, the 1920's in this country, and markedly, of course, during the 1930's in the Soviet Union.

[43] G. Myrdal, *An International Economy* (New York: Harper, 1956), p. 133. A comparative study of wealth distribution by the United Nations "suggest[s] that the richest fraction of the population [the richest tenth, fifth, etc.] generally receive a greater proportion of the total income in the less-developed than in the more developed countries." *United Nations Preliminary Report on the World Social Situation* (New York: 1952), pp. 132–133.

[44] Computed from data in United Nations, *Statistical Yearbook, 1957* (New York: United Nations, 1957), tables 1, 139, 149 and 189.

can study suggests that the emergence of mass production during the past half-century has caused such a redistribution of highly valued prestige symbols that the distinctions between social classes are much less immediately visible than they were in nineteenth-century America or are in contemporary Europe. Sjoberg states that the income of many manual occupations has increased so sharply as to reduce, if not to eliminate, the difference between incomes in some working-class and many middle-class occupations. He argues also that large occupational groups within the working class have risen socially as well. That is, the status differences between skilled workers and middle-income professionals have become less well defined, since workers, like middle-class families, have been able to purchase goods which confer prestige on the purchaser—clothing, cars, television sets.[45] Studies by economists point to similar conclusions, for they show that the proportion of income available after taxes increased much faster for family units in the lower- than in the higher-income groups. The increase in purchasing power between 1941 and 1950 was found to be 42 per cent for the lowest quintile of the income distribution, 37 per cent for the second lowest, 24 per cent for the third, 16 per cent for the fourth, and only 8 per cent for the highest quintile. The purchasing power available to family units in the top 5 per cent of the income distribution decreased by 2 per cent in the same period.[46] Moreover, the percentage of family units with incomes of $4,000 and over (cash income after taxes) increased from 21 per cent in 1929 to 45 per cent in 1953 and should reach an estimated 52 per cent in 1959.[47] Such improvements in income and style of life help to preserve the belief in equality of opportunity, especially if they occur among manual workers. A man who can buy his own house, or a new car, will feel that he has moved up in the world even if he has not changed his occupational position.

[45] Gideon Sjoberg, "Are Social Classes in America Becoming More Rigid?" *American Sociological Review*, 16(1951):775–783.

[46] S. Goldsmith, G. Jaszi, H. Kaitz, and M. Liebenberg: "Size Distribution of Income since the Mid-thirties," *The Review of Economics and Statistics*, 36 (1954): 26.

[47] See K. Mayer, "Recent Changes in the Class Structure of the United States," p. 78.

These changes in the distribution of national income imply also that the differences between classes are moderate rather than intense. To a European, different classes mean distinct ways of life, in which even the goods they own or can afford to purchase are seldom the same, even though in many European countries the rates of mobility may be comparable to those in the United States.[48] These intra-cultural class differences probably help perpetuate the belief among European workers that the existing distribution of goods and opportunities is unfair and that it must be changed; the mildness of these differences in America reinforces the belief of many Americans that they can improve their lot. In the same way, the degree of extremism of labor movements is closely related to national productivity. In poorer countries, where the contrasts between rich and poor are glaring, there is considerable discontent among workers, and this is translated into support of revolutionary political parties; in the richer countries, where the contrast in income and style of life is less striking, the lower classes support less radical reform parties. "The seven European countries in which Communist or fellow-travelling parties secured large votes in free elections had an average per capita income in 1949 of $330. The ten European countries in which the Communists have been a failure electorally had an average per capita income of $585."[49]

[48] In a detailed survey of comparative materials on changes in income distribution in Europe and America, Robert Solow points out that the more advanced countries of Western Europe, particularly Sweden and Great Britain, have roughly comparable distributions. "Our survey also suggests that the picture of America as an equalitarian mutation from the polarization of Europe will not stand up ... at least not on the income distribution figures. What facts there are seem to indicate that there has not been any great difference on this score between Great Britain and the United States in the last quarter or half century, and much the same can be said of the rest of industrial western Europe. Instead the gross outlines have been similar and the direction of change roughly the same." This finding concerning relative equality of income distribution within the industrial West may seem to contradict our assumptions that the consumption spread among the classes is greater in Europe than America. However, as Solow points out, "one may ask whether it makes sense to talk about relative income inequality independently of the absolute level of income. An income four times another income has different content according as the lower income means malnutrition on the one hand or supplies some surplus on the other." *A Survey of Income Inequality Since the War*, (Stanford: Center for Advanced Study in the Behavioral Science, 1958; mimeographed), pp. 77–78.

[49] S. M. Lipset, "Socialism—Left and Right—East and West," *Confluence*, Summer 1958, pp. 179–180, n. 16.

CONCLUSIONS

In this chapter we have pointed to those enduring elements or trends in American society which have reinforced and may have increased the belief in equalitarianism. Although we have called attention to several factors which have preserved the values of equality, we should state again that it is the American emphasis on equality as part of the democratic credo which differentiates American society from the more status-oriented cultures of Europe. This disparity between cultures is illustrated by the common but mistaken impression that in the United States the lack of recognition given to persons of intellectual attainment is simply another example of anti-intellectualism, an impression that presupposes that Americans show deference to other groups. In fact, this is not true: an American worker will show as little deference to the engineer who tries to tell him how to run his machine as his son will toward his professor. One study of the relative prestige of different occupations showed that a random sample of the American population ranked college professors higher in status than other professions or businessmen; only physicians were ranked higher than the professors.[50] Though admittedly tentative, such a result challenges the common impression of many observers, and of the American intellectuals themselves, that the status of intellectuals in the society is low. Indeed, this contrast between the self-image of the intellectuals and the fact that they are held in high esteem by the public at large illustrates the disparity between American equalitarianism and European status-orientation. Americans may esteem the attainments of a man and recognize his high position, but they will not kowtow to him.

Our survey of the relation between ideological equalitarianism and social mobility in the United States must of necessity remain preliminary. Our interpretations are consistent with available

[50] For studies which demonstrate the high prestige of intellectual occupations in America see National Opinion Research Center, "Jobs and Occupations: A Popular Evaluation," *Opinion News*, September 1, 1947, pp. 3–13 [reprinted in Bendix and Lipset, eds., *Class, Status and Power*]; and Richard Centers, "Social Class, Occupation and Imputed Belief," *American Journal of Sociology*, 58(1953):32. For a further discussion of the high status of intellectuals in America see S. M. Lipset, "The Fuss about the Eggheads."

findings, but the required comparative research still needs to be undertaken. We assume, but we do not know, that the belief in the availability of opportunities is more widespread and stronger among Americans than among Europeans; that status differences based on ascribed traits are much more common on the Continent than in the United States; that differences in wealth or occupational level appear less invidious to lower-class Americans than to their European fellows. Even the concept of *social* mobility is ambiguous. Men may change their position in the social structure in many ways; but we do not know which ways are most significant to their sense of improvement or decline. For example: was the great shift from the ranks of craftsmen or small businessmen to the ranks of factory labor, which occurred in the late nineteenth and early twentieth century, experienced as a reduction in status? What status do the sons of farmers give various kinds of urban employment? Have workers seen the increase in their standard of living (as compared with that of middle-class families) as a collective or as an individual improvement? These and many other questions await further research.

However, it is possible to strengthen our case in one area of empirical research. So far, we have considered social mobility in the twentieth century on a comparative basis. But even if our interpretation that all industrial societies show relatively high rates of social mobility be accepted, it is still an open question whether these rates have changed significantly in the course of industrialization. Offhand one would think that mobility rates increased with the advance of industrialization, but it is impossible to subject this thesis to an empirical test on the basis of representative samples as we did with regard to the studies reviewed in chapter ii. It is generally assumed, on the other hand, that rates of social mobility have declined with the decline of entrepreneurship. And this thesis is more testable because information concerning the mobility of the economic elite can be obtained over time, even if comparable information on the mass of the population cannot. There are now available five different studies which deal with the changing social origin of the American business elite. The following chapter attempts a comparative assessment of these studies in order to arrive at more specific conclusions concerning the development of social mobility in the United States. Because in this field fewer studies are available than in the study of contemporary social mobility, a comparative assessment of these few studies poses special methodological difficulties. It will therefore be necessary in the following chapter to shift from an extensive to an intensive comparison of research findings.

Chapter IV | Social Mobility and the American Business Elite

The American business elite has been studied repeatedly during the past twenty years, especially with reference to its social composition. As in studies of other "power-wielding elites," these studies have tabulated social origin, age distribution, marital status, educational background, career patterns, and so on, in order to show changes in proportion over time. The members of an elite are in this view simply indexes of excellence—for if these persons were not excellent in some way, they would not be members of an elite—and since they are, there is usually no interest to inquire further into the nature of the excellence which has made them prominent. This approach is usually associated with Vilfredo Pareto's theory of the elite, but it was given a striking formulation almost two centuries earlier by Bernard Mandeville.

Human nature is everywhere the same: Genius, Wit and Natural Parts are always sharpened by application, and may be as much improv'd in the Practice of the meanest Villany, as they can in the Exercise of Industry or the most Heroic Virtue. There is no Station of Life, where Pride, Emulation, and the Love of Glory may not be displayed. A young Pickpocket, that makes a Jest of his Angry Prosecutor, and dextrously wheedles the old Justice into an Opinion of his Innocence, is envied by his Equals and admired by all the Fraternity. Rogues have the same passions to gratify as other Men, and value themselves on their Honour and Faithfulness to one another, their Courage, Intrepidity, and other Manly Virtues, as well as People of better Profes-

This chapter was written by Reinhard Bendix and Frank W. Howton.

sions; and in daring Enterprises, the Resolution of a Robber may be as much supported by his Pride, as that of an honest Soldier, who fights for his Country.[1]

The degree of excellence, not its nature, is worthy of note, according to Mandeville, and scholars who have adopted this view have defended it on the ground that they were studying society as it really operates, unencumbered by the preferences of the observer. Heroes and Rogues get to the top, and the fact that we prefer the Heroes should not be allowed to obscure the importance of the Rogues.

Yet, this view, which does not propose to pass ethical judgments, is more easily stated than made the basis of appropriate research procedures. Studies of the American business elite have been undertaken primarily to test the hypothesis that the American social structure has become more rigid in the course of its history. This can only mean that, say, in the early nineteenth century, opportunities for upward social mobility were widely available, and that they have progressively decreased ever since. This assertion would be supported by a finding which showed that in the early period members of the business elite were more frequently recruited from families of small farmers and manual workers than in the later period. However, this proof would be conclusive only if it were based on a representative sample of the business elite, then and now, and such a sample presupposes an exhaustive and reliable compendium of biographical data on all members of the business elite. But such a compendium does not exist, partly because data for the earlier periods are deficient, and partly because judgments concerning the individuals who should be included in the elite are inevitably arbitrary.

Three types of judgments have been used in studies of the American business elite, and it is important to be aware of their respective merits and deficiencies. An early study of this kind, by Taussig and Joslyn, was based on a random sample of prominent businessmen: 85 per cent were persons listed in Poor's Register of Directors for 1928, thus insuring that they were directors of companies listed on the stock exchange and doing at least half

---

[1] B. Mandeville, "An Essay on Charity and Charity Schools," *in* F. B. Kaye, ed., *The Fable of the Bees*, Vol. I (Oxford: Clarendon Press, 1924), p. 275.

a million dollars' worth of business.[2] By comparing these business leaders of 1928 with their fathers and grandfathers an effort was made to determine whether or not the social mobility of the business elite had been declining. The advantage of this approach was that it treated the problem of elite recruitment on the basis of generations, thus emphasizing the importance of the family in the social mobility of the elite. Its disadvantage was that the membership of the "business elite" was sampled only in the present, and that the reference to social origins of fathers and grandfathers involved an analysis of family histories rather than a comparative study of the social origins of elites at different periods of American history. As a result, the data on the occupations, especially of grandfathers, were bound to show a proportion of persons coming from families of farmers and workers which was higher than the corresponding figure for the business leaders of 1928. Implicit in this study was the belief that it was sufficient to examine the social origin of the contemporary business elite in order to ascertain whether social mobility in the United States has declined or not.[3]

This belief has been questioned by scholars who have felt that more valid conclusions could be reached by selecting random samples of the business elite at different times. By selecting three independent samples from Moody's Manual of Investments for the years 1899, 1923, and 1948, Mabel Newcomer sought to avoid the difficulties inherent in the use of a progressively curtailed sample in her analysis of the changes in the social composition of the business elite.[4] Similarly, Suzanne Keller selected a total of

---

[2] F. W. Taussig and C. S. Joslyn, *American Business Leaders* (New York: Macmillan, 1932).

[3] Similar comments apply to the recent replication of the Taussig study by W. Lloyd Warner and James C. Abegglen, *Occupational Mobility in American Business and Industry* (Minneapolis: University of Minnesota Press, 1955). Besides comparing present business leaders with their fathers and grandfathers the authors make genuine comparisons between the 1952 and the 1928 elite. It may also be noted that the inclusion of vice-presidents, secretaries, treasurers, and controllers in the Warner, as in the Taussig samples gives a rather broad interpretation of the concept "business elite," as does the inclusion of medium-sized enterprises. In Taussig's 1928 samples, 56.4 per cent of the respondents held positions in companies with a gross annual income of $5,000,000 or less; in Warner's 1952 sample 43.6 per cent of the respondents held positions in companies with a gross annual income of $50,000,000 or less. Also, the fluctuation of gross annual income may be considerable without necessarily affecting the leading position of a company.

[4] M. Newcomer, "The Chief Executive of Large Business Corporations," *Explorations in Entrepreneurial History*, 5(1952):1–34, and the full report of this study

1,013 business executives who held positions in leading business firms in the years 1870, 1900–1910, and 1950.[5] Compared with the procedures used in the Taussig and Joslyn study, the merit of this procedure is that the business elite in each of the selected years or periods is sampled separately. Though appropriate as far as it goes, this approach also implies judgments concerning the nature of elites and of social mobility in modern society. Both studies relied upon objective indexes in arriving at their respective samples of the business elite, and both studies confined themselves to the *top* executives in the *largest* corporations. The men included in these samples undoubtedly belong to the elite, but it is not necessarily true that studies which restrict themselves to this meaning of the term will provide a reliable clue to the "circulation of the elite."

Such a definition assumes that the degree of upward social mobility in a society may be ascertained by determining the proportion of business leaders who have risen during their lifetime "from the dunghill to the chariot," as William Cobbett once put it.[6] That proportion is likely to be rather small at any time. American folklore has tended to overemphasize such spectacular careers as Henry Ford's. Careers of such notoriety do occur when new kinds of economic enterprise open up, and many executives from such rapidly expanding enterprises may be included if the business elite is sampled from among executives of the *largest* corporations. But in this way it is quite possible to overstate the rapidity of social mobility leading to business success, for such careers do not necessarily reflect characteristics of the business elite as a whole. It should also be noted that an emphasis upon spectacular careers definitely misrepresents the social mobility which is characteristic of the society. For such mobility consists in the social and economic advancement of *large numbers* of individuals during their lifetime, and such advancement in the aggregate is bound to be relatively slow. Moreover, there is no reason to believe that a complete hiatus exists between these gradual

in Mabel Newcomer, *The Big Business Executive* (New York: Columbia University Press, 1955).

[5] Suzanne Keller, *The Social Origins and Career Lines of Three Generations of American Business Leaders* (Unpublished Ph.D. dissertation, Columbia University, New York, 1953).

[6] G. D. H. Cole and Margaret Cole, eds., *The Opinions of William Cobbett* (London: The Cobbett Publishing Company, 1944), p. 86.

advances of the many and the more rapid advances of the few. It is *prima facie* probable that the notable business success of an individual is usually based upon and facilitated by the gradual advance of his family in preceding generations; the successful business leader is already a member of a relatively well-to-do family, and his career is, therefore, an extension or accentuation of the step-by-step advances of the many.

The typical sequence probably consists of the slow build-up of an enterprise in the first generation, the consolidation and expansion of the business by the second generation, and the successful or unsuccessful efforts of subsequent generations to maintain and strengthen the position of the family.[7] This sequence may be shortened under certain favorable conditions; for example, if the original enterprise is in a new, rapidly expanding branch of production. Yet, such developments, even if they occur as frequently as they have in American economic history, take place in the context of established economic activities. Hence the new opportunities are likely to be available only to a minority, and even if ingenuity and hard work weigh heavily in the balance, it does not follow that individuals who have these qualities but lack capital resources can take advantage of them. Studies which derive their sample of the business elite from among the *top* executives in the *largest* corporations, tend to neglect this slow build-up of "business success." Moreover, other aspects of the concept "elite" should also be considered. Since "membership" in an elite is determined by prestige as well as income, by social and political influence as well as by the assets or gross receipts of the firm, by strategic family connections as well as by the number of subordinates, by local or regional prominence as well as by national fame, by civic activities as well as by economic success, it is not as obvious as it seems that the top executives in the largest corporations are the only, or even the most representative, members of the business elite.

These other, more diverse criteria are applied, albeit with considerable uncertainty, in a third type of study, which derives its

---

[7] See J. Schumpeter, *Imperialism and Social Classes* (New York: Augustus Kelley, 1951), pp. 148–162, for an emphasis on the generational aspect of social mobility. See also F. Redlich, *History of American Business Leaders* (Ann Arbor: Edwards Brothers, 1940), I, pp. 22–30, and Warner and Abegglen, *Occupational Mobility* . . . , pp. 51–68.

sample of the business elite from biographical dictionaries. Thus, C. Wright Mills published a study which was based upon 1,464 biographical entries in the *Dictionary of American Biography* (*DAB*),[8] and in this chapter we present data from a complementary study based upon 1,097 biographies, most of them from the *National Cyclopedia of American Biography* (*NCAB*). Studies of this type leave the meaning of "business elite" as vague as the editorial policies of the compilers of the biographical source books—as vague as the *DAB* statement that persons were included who "did something notable in the field of American life." And Mills has commented that the business leaders included in his sample were above average in income, but not necessarily rich; some were founders of enterprises which became prominent only after their deaths; and many were probably prominent because of their political roles rather than because of their success in business.[9] For this reason the *NCAB* appeared to be more suitable for a study of the American business elite, because its editorial policy apparently favored the inclusion of businessmen. An editorial statement in the first volume (1898) reads in part: "It is believed that, while literary workers should be accorded ample representation, those who contribute so much to the material and physical welfare of the country deserve to command fuller recognition than has before been accorded them in the works of this character." And in a written communication the publishers declare that "special attention has been given to industrial biographies." Though in the present context such an emphasis commends the *NCAB* as a source book, it should be clear that, generally speaking, studies based on biographical dictionaries also have their drawbacks. Although they will tend to avoid giving to the concept "business elite" a clearly restricted meaning, they will only be as good as the biographical source material in the dictionaries, and that is frequently not good enough.

It is apparent, then, that a purely empirical study of the American business elite is beset with difficulties which can only be partly overcome. Moreover, each study is necessarily limited by

[8] C. W. Mills, "The American Business Elite: A Collective Portrait," *The Tasks of Economic History* (Supplementary issue of the *Journal of Economic History*, December, 1945), pp. 20–44.
[9] *Ibid.*, p. 20.

TABLE 4.1

SECULAR RELATIONSHIPS BETWEEN EXPANDING, CONSTANT, AND CONTRACTING STOCKS
OF ELITES AND THE RATES OF FLOW OF ENTRANTS AND DEPARTEES TO THE ELITE

Types of flows of entrants and departees	High turnover	Moderate turnover	Low turnover
TYPE I: STOCK OF ELITE INCREASING PROPORTION OF SOCIETY			
Entrants from nonelite..	Increasing rate	Constant rate	Decreasing rate
Departees to nonelite....	Increasing at a lower rate; or constant rate or decreasing rate	Decreasing rate	Virtually none
TYPE II: STOCK OF ELITE CONSTANT PROPORTION OF SOCIETY			
Entrants from nonelite..	Increasing rate	Constant rate	Decreasing rate
Departees to nonelite....	Increasing rate	Constant rate	Decreasing rate
TYPE III: STOCK OF ELITE DECREASING PROPORTION OF SOCIETY			
Entrants from nonelite..	Increasing rate	Constant rate	Decreasing rate
Departees to nonelite....	Increasing at faster rate	Increasing rate	Decreasing rate; or constant rate; or increasing rate

the assumptions or judgments that determine the definition of the "business elite," and hence the data included in the sample. The full measure of our uncertainty about the meaning of "business elite" is revealed if we state in schematic fashion the alternative meanings the term might have. A minority of markedly successful business leaders may be said to constitute at any one time a finite number of individuals, composed of (1) those who were already members of the elite at a previous time, (2) those who have entered it since then, and (3) minus those who have since departed from it. Because the fluctuation in the composition of the elite depends upon the last two categories, we may ignore the first group. And since we are interested in whether or not access to the elite has increased or decreased, we may consider the "flow" into and out of the elite on each of three assumptions: that its size is a constant proportion of the population; that the proportion is increasing; that it is decreasing. Table 4.1 shows the possible combinations. Since we cannot determine the changes in the proportion between business elite and population, we can only state that access to the elite increases under the conditions specified as Type I and decreases under those specified as Type III. (It should be noted that so far no study of individuals or families who have "left" the business elite, the "departees" of our chart, has been undertaken.)

The repeated studies of the American business elite and its changing composition during the past twenty years cannot be said to have solved the problems of definition and methodology discussed above. Nevertheless, certain approximate judgments can be based on their findings, and it is fortunate that we now have available two studies which relate contemporary samples of business leaders to their fathers and grandfathers, two studies based on the careers of business leaders in the largest corporations sampled for different years, and two studies based upon samples derived from biographical dictionaries. The purpose of the present chapter is, therefore, first to present our findings concerning the social composition of the American business elite, based on the data derived from the *NCAB*, and then to make a comparative analysis of the findings in the six studies.[10]

AMERICAN BUSINESS LEADERS REËXAMINED

For our study we took a random sample consisting of every ninth businessman who was born between 1771 and 1920 and whose biography was contained in the *National Cyclopedia of American Biography*: this gave us 887 usable biographies of businessmen. The *NCAB* did not, as it turned out, contain enough usable biographies for the earliest and the latest period. Consequently, supplementary data were obtained from the *Dictionary of American Biography* (100 subjects born between 1771 and 1800) and from *Current Biography* (110 subjects born between 1881 and 1920).[11]

---

[10] Comparisons between these four studies and those of Taussig and Warner are difficult because both the latter test mobility by comparing the present generation of business leaders with their fathers and grandfathers. However, Warner's 1952 and Taussig's 1928 results are comparable and will be utilized. We shall treat these two studies as one—which may then be compared with the other four studies here examined—since the Taussig-Warner data show a genuine trend only if the 1952 and the 1928 samples of business leaders are compared.

[11] The supplementary data derived from the *DAB* comprise *all* subjects born between 1771 and 1800 whose biographies did not duplicate those contained in the

TABLE 4.2

PERCENTAGE DISTRIBUTION OF THE AMERICAN BUSINESS ELITE
BORN IN SPECIFIED YEARS, BY FATHER'S OCCUPATION

Father's occupation	Year of birth				
	1771–1800	1801–1830	1831–1860	1861–1890	1891–1920
Businessmen	40	52	66	70	69
Gentry farmers	25	11	3	3	5
Subtotal	65	63	69	73	74
Master craftsmen and small entrepreneurs	9	4	3	1	..
Professionals	3	12	11	12	11
Government officials[a]	4	7	3	3	3
White collar workers (includes foremen)	7	2	2	3	6
Subtotal	23	25	19	19	20
Farmers	12	11	10	6	4
Manual workers	..	2	1	2	3
Subtotal	12	13	11	8	7
Total[b]	100	100	100	100	100
Number of subjects	125	89	360	380	143
Data on father's occupation available	91	56	225	281	106
Data on father's occupation *not* available	34	33	135	99	37
Percentage for whom information was not available	27	37	37	26	26

[a] Includes a few school officials and army officers.
[b] Details do not always add to totals because of rounding.

Table 4.2 summarizes our findings concerning the parental
background of prominent businessmen (i.e., their father's occupation) at several different periods in American history. It is notable
that since 1801 a majority of prominent businessmen have come
from families already well-established economically. Moreover, if

NCAB and were sufficiently detailed to be usable. The supplementary data derived
from *Current Biography* were obtained by selecting *all* biographies of businessmen
born after 1890, beginning with the 1952 edition and going back to the 1945
edition, provided that the subject was not already included in our original sample
from the *NCAB*.

we add the businessmen whose fathers were "gentry farmers"[12] to those coming from families of businessmen, it becomes clear that throughout the period covered, about two-thirds of each generation of successful businessmen had a very favorable family background.[13] The data show the well-known decline in the proportion of business leaders coming from a farm background, but it may be noted that the especially marked decrease in the percentage of sons of "gentry farmers" was made up by a proportionate increase in business leaders who came from families of businessmen, with the result that the overall proportion of business leaders coming from well-to-do families has remained relatively stable (between 63 and 74 per cent). The second subtotal in table 4.2, which comprises the business leaders coming from families in the middle class or lower middle class, shows a similar overall stability, though the figures give some indication of the declining importance of craftsmen and small entrepreneurs and the increasing importance of professionals. Finally, the proportion of business leaders coming from families of workers and small farmers has also remained relatively stable.

This interpretation of the data presented in table 4.2 has not placed much reliance on relatively small percentage differences. Such caution is indicated because it is difficult to determine the occupational group of the fathers, especially in the early periods, so that at best, this is an uncertain index of the family's economic position. The Remington family may be cited by way of illustration. The *NCAB* describes Eliphalet Remington, Sr. (?–1828) as " . . . a mechanic . . . who set up a [power] forge [circa 1800] . . . and carried on the manufacture of rude agricultural implements . . . and did horse-shoeing and general repair work for farmers." His son, Eliphalet Remington, Jr., as a youth " . . . forged a gun barrel for himself from some scraps of iron . . . took it to a gunsmith to be rifled . . . who thereupon praised the barrel so highly

---

[12] In classifying the biographical data of the *NCAB* an attempt was made to separate out very prosperous farmers. All cases in which such prosperity was clearly indicated were included under the category of "gentry farmers."

[13] This finding is in keeping with recent studies of entrepreneurship in the early nineteenth century. According to these studies, success in business enterprise was much more dependent upon family connections than had been assumed previously. See especially R. K. Lamb, "The Entrepreneur and the Community," *in* W. Miller, ed., *Men in Business* (Cambridge: Harvard University Press, 1952), pp. 91–119.

that young Remington was encouraged to make others. The Rem-
ingtons [i.e., Remington Sr. and Jr. as well as the latter's three
sons] soon set up a rifling machine of their own." In 1829 the
family set up a complete rifle manufactory in a new location made
favorable by the building of the Erie Canal. From then until the
end of the Civil War the enterprise prospered, largely owing to
government contracts. Remington Jr. died in 1861 and the business
was taken over by his eldest son, Philo Remington. For another
decade the enterprise prospered, even though government contracts came to an end with the close of the Civil War. However,
with the end of the Franco-Prussian War (1871) the arms business
fell off, and the effort to shift to other lines, especially agricultural
implements, typewriters, and electrical appliances, was unsuccessful. Though the name continued to be used, the main plants
of the Remington enterprises were sold at auction in the 1880's.

The relevance of this brief sketch to the present context consists in two points: the first Remington made the original steps
towards establishing a family enterprise which was an important
enabling factor for his son but which clearly did not constitute
business success in the accepted sense. His son, Remington Jr.,
was clearly a successful entrepreneur who owed part of his
achievement to the start his father had made but whose entrepreneurial achievement was for the most part his own. Moreover,
the oldest son of Remington Jr. was apparently responsible for
the decline of the family enterprise; at any rate this decline
occurred while he headed it. Now, in categorizing such a case
for statistical tabulation we will have to neglect two of its aspects:
we would treat both Remington Jr. and his son, Philo, as sons of
manufacturers, although Remington Jr. was a small manufacturer's son who enlarged his father's enterprise into a major
business, and Philo was the son of a major manufacturer who
headed the firm at the time of its dissolution. However, both
Remington Jr. and Philo Remington would be classed as prominent
businessmen.

The case illustrates the point that our findings concerning the
favorable family background of successive generations of prominent businessmen are equivocal. Remington Sr. was obviously
more than just a craftsman, but if we categorize him as a manu-

facturer we equate his position with that of his son, which is misleading. This uncertain meaning of "father's occupation" as an index of family background suggests that findings such as those cited above are at best a rough approximation. Fortunately, it is possible to check this approximation in one respect.

It will be noted that we could not obtain information on father's occupation in 338 out of 1,097, or 31 per cent, of our cases. This is hardly surprising when one considers that the major objective of the biographies is to give a résumé of the subject's career rather than information on his family. Our guess is that information on father's occupation was included when it was readily available, and that it was more readily available if the father was in a nonmanual occupation. Hence we suspected that our data overrepresented those cases in which the subject's family was relatively well-to-do. In order to check this possibility we compared all cases in which we *did not* obtain information on the occupation of the father with all those in which we did have this information. This comparison was made in terms of the first job which our subjects held and in terms of their respective educational attainment. It is admittedly tenuous to infer the family background of an individual from the fact that his first job was "manual" or "lower white collar" and from the fact that he had little education. Yet, it is probable that the person whose parents are well-to-do has more education and begins his career in a "higher" occupation than the person whose parents are poor. Accordingly we might expect that the sons of fathers whose occupations were recorded had more education and better first jobs than the sons of fathers whose occupations were not recorded. This did not prove to be true since we found only small and random differences between the two groups.

There is another index which points to the same conclusion. For 55 per cent of the 338 subjects whose father's occupation was unknown we were able to ascertain "other enabling circumstances." These circumstances were: that the family was "old" or wealthy or the father was well-established, even though his occupation was not known, or that the subject's in-laws were well-established. We found that such "enabling circumstances" were present for 61 out of 112 subjects who were born before

1845, and for 123 out of 226 subjects who were born after 1845. Hence it is apparent that a large proportion of those whose father's occupation was *unknown* came from relatively well-to-do families, even though many of them began their careers in low-status positions.

TABLE 4.3

PERCENTAGE DISTRIBUTION OF THE AMERICAN BUSINESS ELITE BORN IN
SPECIFIED YEARS, BY LEVEL OF EDUCATION ATTAINED

Level of education attained	Year of birth				
	1771–1800	1801–1830	1831–1860	1861–1890	1891–1920
College: graduated............................	22	8	15	39	67
College: did not graduate.....................	10	8	13	18	17
High school, business school, or private school...	51	51	46	26	11
Grammar school or less[a].....................	17	33	26	17	5
Total.....................................	100	100	100	100	100
Number of subjects...........................	125	89	360	380	143
Information available.........................	69	63	318	359	136
Information not available	56	26	42	21	7

[a] Includes subjects described as having had "little" education, "only a few years," etc. We are not able to correct for the cases for which we have no information concerning the education of our subjects. It is, therefore, possible that the proportion of subjects with little educational background is underrepresented in the period 1771–1830. Even then the number of subjects who have had high school or college education was 57 out of 125 in 1771–1800 and 42 out of 89 in 1801–1830, or a little less than one-half. However, it is improbable that *all* those subjects for whom we lack information had only an elementary education.

So far as these checks of the internal consistency of the data are conclusive, we can infer that the data presented in table 4.2 do *not* overrepresent the proportion of business leaders coming from well-to-do families. A similar conclusion seems to follow from our data on the educational attainment of our subjects (table 4.3). These data reveal more than the secular trend toward higher education. Before the Civil War, a majority of prominent businessmen were educated in private schools, high schools, and business or vocational schools. If it is remembered that attendance at private or high schools was then largely equivalent to attendance at college today, it becomes apparent that the education of businessmen has been more important throughout than is conventionally assumed. Indeed, more than one third of each generation received either private schooling or a college education, a fact which is clearly at variance with the common notion that businessmen were not "in need" of higher education until at least the turn of the century, if not indeed until the 1920's. And if we examine the figures for the period following the Civil War it is rather surprising to discover that in that era of the Robber Barons well over half of the prominent businessmen had gone to college, while another 26 per cent had attended private schools, high schools, or vocational schools.

The evidence cited so far points strongly to the favored social and economic background of a great majority of those whose later careers placed them in the American business elite. And since the proportion of business leaders coming from middle-class and working-class families has not changed greatly with time, our overall finding is that the recruitment of the American business elite has remained remarkably stable. We may attempt to allow for the tenuousness of the categories we have had to work with by assuming that between 10 and 20 per cent of the successful businessmen have come from families in which the father was a worker, craftsman, small entrepreneur, lower-white-collar employee, or small farmer.[14] Such a result is still at variance with the popular impression that during the early period of industrial development opportunities for spectacular upward mobility were readily available to an individual, and that these opportunities have declined markedly with the advance of industrialization. Our data allow us, therefore, to question the validity of the doctrine that the successful businessman had proved himself to be the fittest in the struggle for survival. This doctrine, an amalgamation of classic economic liberalism with a popularized Darwinism, drew its strength from the folklore of the American frontier and the thriving business civilization of the late nineteenth century, and was bolstered by selected examples of the "rags to riches" story, liberally embellished by wishful thinking. These stories were fashioned into a symbol of American society in keeping with the ideology of equalitarianism. Such a doctrine could have carried little conviction if it had been widely known that economic suc-

---

[14] In making this assumption we have considered the fact that the proportion of business leaders coming from "nonelite" families has varied between 27 and 38 per cent since the end of the eighteenth century, but that only part of these families were likely to be poor.

cess was greatly facilitated by the influence of a favorable family background.[15]

A COMPARATIVE ASSESSMENT OF RESEARCH FINDINGS

The findings of our survey call into question, though they do not disprove, the widely held hypothesis that the American social structure has become more rigid in the course of its history. This hypothesis would presumably be substantiated by a finding which showed that in the early period members of the business elite were more frequently recruited from families of small farmers or manual workers than in the later period. It is difficult to conduct a test that might give such substantiation; it is of considerable advantage that several studies of this problem have been undertaken which have used different sources of information (though broadly for similar purposes) and which may, therefore, be compared with one another.[16] Such a comparison is beset with methodological difficulties—a rough cross-checking of the several findings is the best that can be expected—but a brief comparison will be attempted and may be found useful.

The sampling procedures used in the various studies were not the same. C. Wright Mills' data from the *Dictionary of American*

---

[15] As is often true, this symbol had some relation to social fact. The data reported above have been analyzed also in terms of the changing career patterns of American business leaders. By classifying these patterns under the three headings of "entrepreneur," "bureaucrat," and "heir" it was shown that between the generation born at the end of the eighteenth century and the generation born after 1891 the proportion of "entrepreneurial" business leaders declined from 76 per cent to 18 per cent, while the proportion of "bureaucratic" business leaders increased from 5 per cent to 48 per cent. During the same period the "heirs" increased from 19 per cent to 34 per cent. Further data on career patterns and an explanation of these categories are given in Reinhard Bendix, *Work and Authority in Industry* (New York: Wiley, 1956), pp. 228–236, 251–253. It may be added that even the cultural symbol of the "entrepreneurial" career was essentially ambiguous. Richard Wohl has shown that the original Horatio Alger stories had for their heroes individuals who were frugal and hard-working, to be sure, but whose success was invariably the result of accidents, rather than of personal achievement. See R. R. Wohl, "The 'Rags to Riches Story': An Episode in Secular Idealism," *in* R. Bendix and S. M. Lipset, eds., *Class, Status and Power* (Glencoe: The Free Press, 1953), pp. 388–395.

[16] All but one of the studies used for this comparative assessment have also been examined by Bernard Barber, *Social Stratification* (New York: Harcourt, Brace, 1957), pp. 443 ff. However, Barber did not examine the definitions of the elite which are implicit in the sampling methods used in the various studies. C. Wright Mills' summary evaluation of the evidence relies primarily upon the study by Suzanne Keller and concentrates on the composition of the business elite in 1950. See his *The Power Elite* (New York: Oxford University Press, 1956), pp. 126–134.

Biography included *all* businessmen for whom sufficient biographical information was available. The total number of cases in this study was 1,464, comprising subjects born between 1570 and 1879. Although all businessmen listed in the *DAB* were included in the study, the number from the early period was necessarily small.[17] A comparison of Mills' study with our own is pertinent here, because both are based on biographical dictionaries. In contrast to Mills' study, which included *all* biographical entries for businessmen contained in the *DAB*, our own study includes a *sample* of every ninth businessman contained in the *National Cyclopedia of American Biography*. Thus, the *DAB* has an estimated total of 1,830 entries for businessmen born after 1570; the *NCAB* comprises an estimated total of 9,000 to 10,000 entries for businessmen born after 1771. This contrast confirms the statement by the editors of the *NCAB* that they placed a heavy emphasis on prominent businessmen—our reason for choosing this source for our study.[18]

The comparison of sampling procedures in the studies by Newcomer and Keller presents fewer problems. Newcomer chose the years 1899, 1923, and 1948 for her study, and included in it the top executives (president, board chairman) of the largest nonfinancial corporations—railroad, public utility, and industrial, with primary emphasis on the latter group. The corporations were chosen from the listings of *Moody's Manual of Investments* in the selected years, and included only those with the greatest financial assets. In this fashion 143 executives of 134 corporations were selected for 1899, 282 executives of 206 corporations for 1923,

---

[17] From 1570 to 1760 the number of cases was 221 and from 1760 to 1789 it was 162. The total number of cases after 1760 which we can use for comparative purposes was 1,243.

[18] The total number of businessmen in every twentieth page of the index was counted. On this basis it was estimated that nine to ten thousand out of about 49,000 entries in the *NCAB* (or about one fifth) were businessmen; we decided to select every ninth person listed by a business occupation. Very incomplete sketches were eliminated *ad hoc*. This accounts for the difference between the *anticipated* size of the sample (1,100 to 1,200) and its actual size (887). If one assumes that the proportion of usable entries is the same in both dictionaries (80 per cent of the entries appeared usable on the basis of our estimates from the *NCAB*), then one out of every five entries in the *NCAB* is a businessman, compared with one out of every thirteen entries in the *DAB*. Mills states that the *DAB* contained 1,464 *usable* entries on businessmen, which compares with an estimated 1,830 entries for businessmen.

and 274 executives of 253 corporations in 1948.[19] The total number of subjects was 799; information concerning their official position was obtained from *Moody's Manual,* and all other biographical information from a wide variety of sources. A similar procedure was followed by Suzanne Keller, whose study was based in part on earlier studies by William Miller.[20] The years chosen for this study were 1870, 1900–1910, and 1950, covering an 80-year period as compared with a 50-year period in the Newcomer study. Miss Keller also chose the top executives of the largest corporations, but included among them officials of banks and other financial enterprises (which Newcomer had not). Also, the enterprises chosen for 1950 included a number in wholesale distribution, entertainment, and mass communications. This was done on the ground that rapidly expanding branches of the economy should be represented, though wholesale distribution may not qualify in this respect. The sample of top executives comprised 401 for 1870, 190 for the decade 1900–1910, and 422 for 1950, making a total of 1,013 subjects. Biographical information on these executives was obtained from a variety of published sources and from a questionnaire which was sent to the executives included in the 1950 sample.

These details concerning the sampling procedure of four of the studies illustrate the specific judgments involved in any definition of the "business elite." The studies by Newcomer and Keller gain in rigor of selection what they lose in coverage. On the other hand, Mills' study and ours are necessarily as vague as the editorial policies of the respective biographical dictionaries. Clearly, the subjects of Newcomer and Keller are all members of the business elite in the literal sense of that term. But what is gained by eliminating from our concept of the "business elite" subjects whose prominence is, say, political rather than economic, or who have achieved success in the industries excluded by Newcomer and Keller? As in other industrial societies, there is considerable uncertainty in the United States about who belongs to the "busi-

[19] Newcomer, *The Big Business Executive,* p. 10. In this study 9 business executives were included in both the samples for 1899 and 1923 and 30 in those for 1923 and 1948.

[20] It should be remembered that the years mentioned correspond to the years in which individuals were listed as prominent businessmen in published sources. Since success is likely to occur when a man is in his forties or fifties, the average year of birth may be estimated accordingly.

ness elite." In view of that uncertainty, none of the studies can correct adequately for any bias involved in the definition of the population from which they have obtained their basic data, though it is well to keep the different "biases" in mind.

These considerations suggest that numerically comparable results may not be expected from the studies now available; but differences in magnitude should not affect the relative similarity of trends. We turn first, then, to a comparison of the studies with reference to "father's occupation," which for want of complete information we must confine to "businessmen," "farmers," and "professionals." In order to emphasize the trends, we have represented the changes in percentage of fathers in each of these three occupations on a semilogarithmic graph (figure 4.1).

The most notable discrepancy in the trends that characterize the changing social derivation of the American business elite is apparent in the period before 1800. We have only data from the *DAB* and the *NCAB* for this period, and in both information on the fathers of successful businessmen is especially difficult to evaluate. Still, assuming that the results are not wholly fortuitous, what can we make of them? Mills' data show a proportionate decrease of businessmen and a proportionate increase of farmers among the fathers of the business elite until a little after the turn of the century. Our data show exactly the reverse, a decline in the proportion of farmers and a simultaneous increase in that of the businessmen.[21] The discrepancy of the trends is unmistakable, however much allowance we may make for the distortion in time (and hence in the placing of the curve to the right or left on the graph) which the arbitrary comparison of the data entails. Further study of the problem is obviously indicated, since available historical studies give qualitative support to both propositions.

These discrepancies vanish, however, when we examine the graph for the period after 1810. Whatever the differences in the proportion of businessmen coming from one or another family background, the similarity in the *trends* shown by all of the studies is impressive. Though the proportion of businessmen among the fathers is greatest in our sample and smallest in Mills', it is striking

[21] Mills has 162 cases for 1760–1789 and we have 125 cases for 1771–1800.

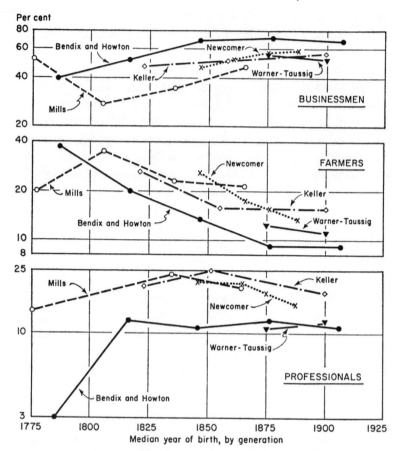

Fig. 4.1. Proportions of businessmen, farmers, and professionals among the fathers of American business leaders, by median year of birth. Mills' and our data are grouped by 25-year periods, whereas Newcomer's and Keller's consist of samples for three selected years. To make these data comparable we have listed Mills' and our data by the median year of birth for each period and we have estimated the median year of birth for the Newcomer and Keller samples. The Warner-Taussig data are also listed by the median year of birth.

that in four out of five comparisons this proportion has steadily risen, presumably at the expense of the "gentry farmers."[22] It is equally striking that aside from the obvious decline of the farmers there is evidence of some increase in the proportion of prominent businessmen coming from professional families in the period from 1775 to 1850. Four out of five studies show a stabilization or slight

[22] It may be mentioned that our data level off, beginning in the 1860's; the Taussig-Warner data show a slight decline.

decline in the proportion with this "professional family background" in the second half of the nineteenth century.[23]

As pointed out earlier, "father's occupation" is a rather unsatisfactory index of family background. Yet, in the absence of better indicators, it is necessary to utilize this information and combine it, if possible, with some corroborative evidence. Accordingly, each of the studies has attempted to combine "father's occupation" with some other classification of the data, in order to arrive at a better clue to the social recruitment of the American business elite. Thus, Mills and Newcomer utilize a variety of indexes which supplement "father's occupation": they employ categories such as "upper class" or "wealthy" and "lower class" or "poor," although admittedly these categories are tenuous also.[24] Keller draws considerable circumstantial evidence of family background from the religious affiliation, the national origin, and the "social stability" of the parental families, and in our own study an attempt is made to classify the careers of business leaders in terms of the direct or indirect aid given them by their families or through family connections. Such classifications and supplementary material are necessary in order to utilize the data in these studies for an analysis of social mobility. But such procedures add to the ambiguity of the categories and the evidence, so that conclusions with regard to the "circulation of the American business elite" still remain matters of reasonable inference. Difficulties are compounded, of course, when a comparison of different studies is attempted: but we must do what we can with the inadequate evidence that is available.

We may begin by comparing the evidence on "father's occupation," including such supplementary categories as "upper class," in each of the studies. Table 4.4 gives the relevant data from each study: the listed years being the estimated median year of birth for each generation of business leaders. In evaluating this table

---

[23] It should be added that half of our sample for the period 1771–1800 was derived from the *DAB* in order to supplement the data from the *NCAB* (see p. 121). Since all of Mills' data are derived from the *DAB* it is certainly curious that the findings of the two studies should be as inconsistent as they are for this period. As the text makes clear, this discrepancy of the trends revealed by the two studies is confined to this period; for the nineteenth century the studies corroborate each other.

[24] For explanations of these terms see Mills, "The American Business Elite," p. 31, and Newcomer, *The Big Business Executive*, p. 25.

TABLE 4.4

PERCENTAGE OF AMERICAN BUSINESS LEADERS BORN IN SPECIFIED ERAS,
BY SELECTED OCCUPATIONS OF FATHERS, FROM FIVE STUDIES

Estimated year of birth	Father's occupation	Number of subjects

KELLER

	Businessmen	Wage earners and office workers	
1820...................	47	8	254
1855...................	50	4	168
1900...................	57	12	348

BENDIX-HOWTON

	Businessmen	Gentry farmers	Combined	Farmers and manual workers	
1785...................	40	25	65	12	125
1815...................	52	11	63	13	89
1845...................	66	3	69	11	360
1875...................	70	3	73	8	380
1905...................	69	5	74	7	143

NEWCOMER

	Wealthy	Medium	Poor	
1849...................	46	42	12	118[a]
1873...................	36	48	16	253
1898...................	36	52	12	342

MILLS

	Upper	Upper middle	Combined	Lower middle and lower	
1805...................	26	37	63	37	
1835...................	20	37	57	43	...[b]
1865...................	41	29	70	29	

WARNER-TAUSSIG

	Businessmen			Skilled and unskilled laborers	
	Large firms	Medium firms	All firms		
1875...................	31	26	57	11	
1900...................	23	29	52	15	...[c]

SOURCES: S. I. Keller, *The Social Origins and Career Lines of Three Generations of American Business Leaders* (Unpublished Ph.D. dissertation, Columbia University, 1953), p. 69; Mabel Newcomer, *The Big Business Executive* (New York: Columbia University Press, 1955), p. 63; C. W. Mills, "The American Business Elite: A Collective Portrait," *The Tasks of Economic History* (Supplementary issue of the *Journal of Economic History*, December, 1945), p. 30; W. Lloyd Warner and James C. Abegglen, *Occupational Mobility in American Business and Industry* (Minneapolis: University of Minnesota Press, 1955), pp. 62, 135; R. Bendix and F. Howton. "Social Mobility and the American Business Elite," *British Journal of Sociology*, 9(1958): 6, further data are available in this article.

[a] The number of subjects for this table is taken from the corresponding data in Miss Newcomer's earlier publication, "The Chief Executive in Large Business Corporations," *Explorations in Entrepreneurial History*, 5 (1952):26.

[b] No totals are given, but Mills notes that they comprise 78.8 per cent of the "total elite" or 1,155 out of 1,464 subjects.

[c] No totals are given. The total number of cases available for comparisons between the Taussig and the Warner study is given as 7,371. See Warner and Abegglen, *Occupational Mobility* . . . , p. 234.

it should be remembered that considerable differences of magnitude must be expected in the results of these studies because of the diverse data and categories on which they are based. It is, moreover, inadvisable to attempt interpretations where the respective studies show changes of less than 10 or 15 per cent, since these may easily result from the crudity of the data or from chance. In spite of such shortcomings it is possible to derive some tentative conclusions from this comparative table. Four of the studies indicate that the proportion of business leaders who have come from families of businessmen, or of businessmen and gentry farmers, or from families classified as "wealthy" and "middle class" has remained remarkably *stable* in the course of time. Keller's study and our own show increases of 10 per cent and 8 per cent respectively, but these increases reflect only the growing importance of businessmen at the expense of farmers, which is shown by all five studies and is familiar enough. In both Newcomer's study and ours the proportion of business leaders who come from well-to-do families is substantially higher than in Keller's, but this discrepancy is only apparent, since Keller's data on professionals and farmers no doubt include many who might be either "wealthy" or "middle class." The data from the Taussig-Warner studies show similar results with regard to the upper- or middle-class background of businessmen. Thus, the proportion of business leaders coming from economically privileged families has remained more or less stable, whether the categories used lead to an estimate of one-half, two-thirds, or four-fifths.

This conclusion is at variance with the one reached in Mills' study, whose major finding is the notable *instability* of the recruitment pattern of the American business elite during the nineteenth century. Disregarding again minor changes in percentage, the data of this study show first a marked decline in the proportion of business leaders coming from upper-class families from 1715 (69 per cent) to 1835 (20 per cent) and, secondly, a marked increase of that proportion from the low of 20 per cent in 1835 to 41 per cent in 1865, with indications that this upward trend has continued since then.[25] This discrepancy between Mills' study and the four others is necessarily reflected in the related findings concern-

---

[25] Mills, *ibid.*, p. 30. The 1715 figure is omitted from table 4.4, because none of the other studies has comparable data.

ing the proportion of business leaders coming from families variously designated as "skilled and unskilled laborers," "poor," "farmers and manual workers," or "wage earners and office workers." Again we should ignore differences of magnitude and relatively small differences of proportion. Thus, neither the increase by 4 per cent in Keller's data for 1820–1900, nor the decrease by 5 per cent in our data for 1785–1905, nor the increase by 4 per cent in the Taussig-Warner data for 1875–1900, warrant any conclusions about the social mobility of "poor" or "lower class" families.[26] The notable fact is that these three studies, as well as Newcomer's, show a more or less *stable* proportion of business leaders in each generation coming from relatively underprivileged families. This result also differs from Mills' findings, which seem to indicate a decline in the upward social mobility of "lower middle" and "lower class" families (from 43 per cent in 1835 to 29 per cent in 1865).[27] On the basis of his evidence Mills concludes, tentatively, that "in the nineteenth century the business elite was composed of significantly more men from the lower classes than was the case previously or than has been the case since," thus apparently confirming the widely held belief that a significant decline has occurred in the upward social mobility of individuals from "lower class" or "lower middle class" families.

On this point Keller's study of the problem, and to some degree our own study, enable us to arrive at tentative conclusions, largely based on circumstantial evidence. If we consider Mills' data on

[26] This interpretation differs from Keller's, who sees evidence of upward mobility in the change from 4 per cent in 1855 to 12 per cent in 1900. It may be noted, however, that small as it is, this difference is in part due to the puzzling decline from 8 per cent to 4 per cent between 1820 and 1855. See Keller, *Social Origins . . .*, pp. 70, 76–77. The interpretation also differs from that of Warner and Abegglen, *Occupational Mobility of American Business Leaders*, p. 25 and *passim*, who now see evidence of increased vertical mobility on the strength of a 4 or 5 per cent difference where Warner saw evidence of decreased mobility before. See the references in S. M. Lipset and R. Bendix, "Social Status and Social Structure," *British Journal of Sociology*, 2(1951):233–241.

[27] This decline is perhaps made more striking by the fact that Mills' data also show a secular increase in the proportion of business leaders coming from "lower middle" and "lower class" families, ranging from a low of 14 per cent in 1715 to a high of 43 per cent in 1835. Furthermore, Mills adds a reference to an unpublished study of 328 subjects born during the period 1800–1839, which showed that one-third of the business elite came from "lower class" families. (See Mills, "The American Business Elite," pp. 29–31.) None of the other studies has data for the eighteenth or early nineteenth centuries which could be compared with Mills' study.

the proportion of business leaders coming from "lower class" families exclusively, we find that they show a very small and probably fortuitous increase during the nineteenth century. This increase is quite comparable with that shown by Keller; it turns into a decrease only if business leaders from "lower middle class" families are added. Keller has contributed substantially to our understanding of this equivocal evidence by examining the family background of her subjects. She found that 86 per cent of the 1870 generation of business leaders came from "colonial families" who had settled in the United States before 1777, the remaining 14 per cent being "later settlers." By 1950, 50 per cent of the business leaders came from "colonial families" and 50 per cent from "later settlers," paralleling the proportion of these two groups which was estimated for the population as whole.[28] A similar contrast exists between foreign and native birth. Native-born business leaders of native-born fathers constituted 90 per cent of the business elite in 1870, but only 76 per cent in 1950, while the proportion of native-born business leaders whose fathers had been born abroad, increased from 2 per cent in 1870 to 18 per cent in 1950.[29] In her consideration of religious affiliation Keller finds that the business elite has always been predominately Protestant. Nevertheless, the proportion of Catholics, Jews, and those without religious affiliation among American business leaders has increased from 1½ per

[28] Keller, *Social Origins* . . . , p. 37. It is rather difficult to determine the relevant population whose composition may be compared with that of the business elite at a particular time. Keller compares the composition of the elite with the composition of the U. S. population at the median year of birth for the elite. For example, the business elite was about 50 years old, on the average, in 1950; hence, she compares the 1950 sample with the population in 1900, or as near to that date as possible. This is better than nothing, but it ignores important differentials: for example, business leaders are proportionately more urban than the general population and minority groups are also concentrated in urban areas, hence comparisons between the business elite and the general population tend to underestimate the disadvantages of minority groups with regard to elite access. Such difficulties would be compounded if an attempt was made to compare the changing composition of the business elite with changes in the economic structure of American society. The data contained in the studies here under review are not good enough, in our judgment, to permit such a comparison.

[29] *Ibid.*, pp. 40–41. The rest of the business leaders were foreign-born: 8 per cent in 1870 and 6 per cent in 1950. These data compare with an estimate for the population in 1900 of 61 per cent native-born sons of native-born parents, 23 per cent native-born sons of parents one or both of whom were foreign-born, and 15 per cent who were foreign-born themselves.

cent in 1870 to 15 per cent in 1950.[30] There is also evidence of a parallel and probably related shift in the national origin of the business elite, the proportion of business leaders from southern Ireland and southeastern Europe—i.e., of people who are presumably Catholic or Jewish and, also presumably, lower or lower-middle class—having increased from 3 per cent in 1870 to 12 per cent in 1950.[31]

Admittedly, these several trends do not modify the established conclusion that the American business elite is disproportionately derived from Protestant, Anglo-Saxon, native-born, well-to-do families. But they consistently indicate that an increasing, if continuously small, proportion of business leaders come from families outside this privileged group. "Lack of privilege" is not necessarily a synonym for "lower class" in the economic sense, as Keller emphasizes, and hence this finding does not bear directly on Mills' assertion that the proportion of business leaders coming from "lower middle class" families has declined. It *suggests*, however, that an increasing proportion of those who have moved upward into the *top* echelons of the business elite during the last two generations have come from well-to-do families of high economic but *relatively* low social status. For Keller's data show a far more conspicuous and clear-cut increase in the proportion of business leaders coming from families whose social status is below that of the privileged minority than from families categorized as "wage earners and office workers." Given the great obstacles standing in the way of very rapid mobility, it is *prima facie* probable that persons who come from well-to-do families but suffer from social discrimination can overcome those obstacles more readily than can persons who come from "lower class" families, even if these are Protestant, Anglo-Saxon, and native-born. Since all five studies show that the proportion of business leaders coming from "lower class" or "poor" families has remained more or less stationary, it appears legitimate to conclude that upward mobility into the top echelons of the business elite more typically involves a successful fight against social discrimination than a "rags to riches" story.

[30] *Ibid.*, pp. 62–63. Compared with the population as a whole the 1900 sample of business leaders shows a slight overrepresentation of Catholics and Jews, while the 1950 sample shows a slight underrepresentation.

[31] *Ibid.*, p. 44. Compared with the general population they are still underrepresented in the business elite.

It is apparent, however, that this is not the whole picture, for it omits the majority of business leaders—those who belong to the business elite but are not in its "top echelon" (i.e., the executives of the largest corporations). Does the changing social composition of this American business elite give us any clue to its ability to reserve career opportunities for members of the family? Has this

TABLE 4.5

PERCENTAGE DISTRIBUTION OF THE AMERICAN BUSINESS ELITE BORN IN SPECIFIED YEARS RECEIVING VARYING DEGREES OF CAREER ASSISTANCE

Degree of career assistance	Year of birth				
	1771–1800	1801–1830	1831–1860	1861–1890	1891–1920
Received substantial assistance (direct evidence)	43	44	44	50	47
Probably received significant assistance (inferential evidence)	12	19	11	15	12
Subtotal	55	63	55	65	59
Some enabling circumstance (no evidence of direct assistance)	22	20	22	18	15
No information	23	17	23	17	26
Total	100	100	100	100	100
Number of subjects	125	89	360	380	143

ability increased or decreased? We have attempted to answer these questions on the basis of our data from the *NCAB*. The total context of each biographical entry included in the sample was judged in terms of a three-fold distinction: Was the subject's business career directly aided by his family? Is there inferential evidence to indicate that this was true? Is there general evidence of the middle-class status of the family without either direct or indirect evidence of its effect upon the subject's career? We judged a subject's career to have been "directly aided" by his family when the biographical information indicated that he inherited control of a firm or was given an important position within an enterprise in which the father or a relative occupied a dominant position. Persons were included in this category when there was evidence that they had inherited large estates. A career was also considered to be "directly aided" when subjects received substantial assistance at some time through friends of their family. The data presented in table 4.5 indicate that from 43 per cent to 50 per cent of the businessmen in our sample were directly aided in this sense.

It did not seem to us, however, that such direct evidence was quite sufficient. Since the information in a biographical dictionary is intended to provide information other than that which we have sought here, it seemed legitimate to use the information which *was* supplied as circumstantial evidence. We therefore assessed the *probable ability of a relative or a patron to lend substantial aid* in furthering a subject's career, even though there was no direct evidence that such aid had actually been given. In fitting cases into this admittedly elusive category, we have used two criteria: the economic or political "power" of a mentioned relative or sponsor which clearly put him in a position to give substantial and effective aid, and, secondly, the circumstantial evidence which makes it probable that such aid was actually given. To illustrate: One subject is recorded as having held a "minor position" in a bank. At the age of 27 he was the proprietor of a retail stationery store; a year after marrying the daughter of a manufacturer he was employed by the firm his father-in-law founded, and six years after that he was the first vice-president of this firm. It seems reasonable to infer that the subject was substantially aided in his career. On the other hand, the son of a department store executive was first employed by, then become a partner in, and finally moved up to a vice-presidency and the board-chairmanship of a cotton textile concern. It is quite possible that the father helped the son, but we did not feel it was safe to infer this from the available evidence.

Several observations may be made about these findings. They show, first of all, that the proportion of business leaders who received direct assistance has remained *stable* throughout the period covered by our study.[32] This conclusion contrasts with the findings of Keller and Newcomer, though it is not incompatible with them. Keller shows that between 1870 and 1950 the self-made and the family-made careers have declined sharply (from 68 per

---

[32] Table 4.5 indicates that this conclusion is not modified by the inferential evidence concerning career assistance.

cent to 17 per cent), while the bureaucratically made careers have increased accordingly (from 18 per cent in 1870 to 68 per cent in 1950).[33] But these findings are to a large extent preconditioned by her sample, since it is in the top echelon of the business elite that the decline in the opportunities for self-made and family-made careers in the giant corporations of today is bound to show most clearly. If our findings reveal a rather stable proportion of business leaders receiving direct assistance during their careers, they probably reflect a characteristic of elite formation outside these top echelons, for the subjects from the *NCAB* constitute a business elite in the broad rather than the restricted meaning of that term.[34] This interpretation is confirmed indirectly by Newcomer's findings, which parallel Keller's, as do the procedures by which the samples for the two studies were selected. Newcomer shows that the proportion of business leaders who received no direct aid during their careers has remained quite stable, though it increased somewhat—from 56 per cent in 1899 to 70 per cent in 1948.[35] Although Newcomer's criteria of direct aid are more stringent than ours, this hardly explains a particularly striking contrast between the findings of the two studies. Newcomer's study, based upon a sample of the top echelons of the business elite, indicates that direct career assistance by the family is of minor importance among business executives in giant enterprises; a conclusion that confirms the decline of family influence in the largest corporations. But our study, based on the *NCAB*, in which the business elite is more broadly defined, suggests that family influence has remained a very significant factor in the recruitment of that elite.

This conclusion bears on a larger theoretical issue. A century ago, Sir Henry Maine advanced the theory that modern society is a society of contract, rather than status. This distinction was defined by Maine in the following terms:

The individual is steadily substituted for the Family, as the unit of which civil laws take account. . . . Nor is it difficult to see what is the

[33] Keller, *Social Origins . . .* , p. 82. Her fourth type, the "professionally made" career, showed no significant change.

[34] Keller notes this possibility when she states that her findings on career types may not hold true for the business leaders of substantial enterprises which are not included in her study. *Ibid.*, pp. 83–84.

[35] Newcomer, "The Chief Executive . . . , p. 23.

tie between man and man which replaces by degrees those forms of reciprocity in rights and duties which have their origin in the family. It is Contract. Starting, as from one terminus of history, from a condition of society in which all the relations of Persons are summed up in the relations of Family, we seem to have steadily moved towards a phase of social order in which all these relations arise from the free agreement of Individuals."[36]

This theory has been popular among sociologists since Maine's day, but they have interpreted it in a manner which Maine studiously avoided. Their interpretation ignored the legal context of the theory, somehow posited the notion that in the course of the nineteenth century the autonomy of the individual had developed *de facto* rather than *de jure*, and then proceeded to the demonstration that modern society was on the way to develop a status society out of a contractual society.[37]

But the *de jure* autonomy of the individual never implied that the individual would willfully divest himself of the advantages which the status of his family afforded him. It would be closer to the mark to contend that the contractual autonomy of the individual has enabled him to escape many of the familial liabilities which had been his merely by virtue of his birth. The family and its individual members have always jealously guarded the rights and privileges of their social and economic status against encroachment and diminution; and on the whole, families have probably continued the practice of conferring as many advantages upon their individual members as lay within their power, even though for the individual the recognition of duties toward the family has become in some measure a discretionary act. It is consistent with such an understanding of the transition from a society of status

[36] H. Maine, *Ancient Law* (Everyman's Library) (New York: E. P. Dutton, 1931), p. 99.

[37] The most clear-cut statement of this thesis is contained in P. Drucker, "The Employee Society," *American Journal of Sociology*, 58 (1953): 258–263. Despite a clarifying footnote concerning the term "status" Mr. Drucker fails to use the term as Sir Henry Maine intended it, even though he makes specific reference to Maine's work. It may be added that Drucker's thesis would gain in clarity if it did not presuppose the earlier existence of a *de facto* contractual society and if it were made clear that the status system of modern enterprise is in part the consequence of contractual agreements among competing power groups mediated by government intervention. It is worth recalling that Maine advised against "applying the term [status] to such conditions as are the immediate or remote result of agreement." See Maine, *Ancient Law*, p. 100.

to a society of contract that the families of the American business elite have persisted in preserving for their descendants as much of their economic success and their social status as they were able to, and in passing it on to them. But although they have been able to preserve enough to assist their children substantially, they have not been able to withstand the inroads that bureaucratization of business and industry has made upon family influence, especially in the largest corporations.[38] And in view of the increasing role which large-scale organizations play in affecting, and frequently determining, the rights and duties of the individual, we seem to be moving steadily toward a social order in which the relations of persons will be summed up, neither in the "relations of Family," nor in the "free agreement of Individuals," but in the hierarchical regulation of official duties. The paradox is that this bureaucratization of economic enterprise also serves in some measure to facilitate the upward social mobility of the individual and thus to reinforce the social base of American ideological equalitarianism.

---

[38] Warner and Abegglen point out that over 40 per cent of the business elite in 1928 and 1952 were sons of owners of large business firms or of major executives, but that by 1952 the frequency of "occupational inheritance" decreased as the size of a firm increased. See Warner and Abegglen, *Occupational Mobility* . . . , pp. 164–169. But even in the large corporations major executives use their influence in favor of their sons, though there is also much self-conscious concern with the problem of nepotism. See the discussion of Perrin Stryker, "Would You Hire Your Son?" *Fortune Magazine* (March, 1957), 132–135, 220–230. Other aspects of this process are analyzed in W. H. Whyte, Jr., *The Organization Man* (New York: Simon & Schuster, 1956), and in R. Bendix, "The Bureaucratization of Economic Enterprises," *in* his *Work and Authority in Industry* (New York: Wiley, 1956), pp. 198–253.

Part Two | *Social Mobility*
in a Metropolitan
Community

Chapter V | The Oakland
Mobility Study

In this, the second part of our book, we turn from extensive analyses of comparative international data on social mobility and of materials bearing on American stratification and mobility patterns, to an intensive analysis of some aspects of social mobility in one small area of the United States: the East Bay section of metropolitan San Francisco—largely the city of Oakland. The Oakland data were collected in 1949 as part of a study of labor mobility made by the Institute of Industrial Relations of the University of California. The labor-market emphasis in the study's design led to the collection of data not usually gathered in social-mobility studies: complete job histories of all respondents from their first to their present job. The existence of these data suggested that we could make a contribution to knowledge in the field by studying the interrelationship between inter-generational and intra-generational social mobility, even though the analysis of social mobility was not a primary objective of the original study.

The analysis in this part of the book is internal—that is, it consists of comparisons among different groups in the same sample. Although the first part of our book demonstrates, we believe, that comparisons between one mobility study and another can be fruitful, such external comparisons have validity only if there are some common elements that appear in one study in forms that match, or can be transformed into, forms that appear in another. Basic

147

to any attempt to compare one study with another is a consideration of the special characteristics which differ, and the general characteristics which are uniform, among different studies of the same subject. An understanding of the methodology which lies behind an analysis is, therefore, a crucial factor in defining the degree of generality which can be attributed to the results. The report on the Oakland survey is introduced with a description of the community environment within which the study took place, a description of the sample design, and a brief discussion of the problem of analyzing a sample of job patterns.

CHARACTERISTICS OF THE OAKLAND LABOR MARKET

The city of Oakland, which at the time of the study had a population of 400,000, is one of the two cities which constitute the heart of the San Francisco-Oakland metropolitan area. This area consists of a group of six contiguous counties grouped around San Francisco Bay, and has a population of around two and a half million persons, of whom approximately one million are in the labor force. Oakland lies on the east shore of the Bay, part of a densely populated area made up of a number of communities. The East Bay section of the area, of which Oakland is the center, is continuous from Richmond on the north to Hayward on the south.

Oakland also has marked physical, economic, and community relationships with San Francisco: the San Francisco-Oakland Bay Bridge provides a physical connection for automobiles and interurban transit; most of the cultural life of the Bay Area is centered in San Francisco; the head offices of many western and national corporations are located in San Francisco; and although Oakland has an important "downtown" business section, the major department stores of the area have their main stores in San Francisco. Residents of the East Bay cities are still likely to go to the "city" for major buying trips, to attend the theater, or to seek other forms of entertainment.

The character of the labor force members in Oakland seems, however, to reflect the economic character of the whole Bay Area, as shall be indicated in more detail below. Many Oakland residents work outside of Oakland, either in other East Bay cities or in San Francisco, and conversely, many of Oakland's business establishments have employees who live outside the city. Its partial isolation from San Francisco gives it some of the characteristics of the central city of a large metropolitan area, even though in terms of the division of labor its character is determined by its position as the major industrial suburb and one of the important residential suburbs of San Francisco. Like most central cities, for example, it has a lower rate of growth than surrounding suburban areas, and its median family income is lower than that of a number of nearby smaller suburbs. Like other California central cities, however, it receives a greater number of migrants from other parts of the country than Eastern metropolitan centers. Although it is hard to estimate how the special characteristics of Oakland affect the patterns of social mobility within it, it is our guess that the only significant factor is that it is a California community, and hence a center for migrants.

This rapid expansion by migration has the effect of increasing the mobility rate in Oakland in almost all dimensions. Data from the study, *Labor Mobility in Six Cities,*[1] indicate that San Francisco labor, along with that of Los Angeles, is more mobile than labor in Chicago, Philadelphia, St. Paul, or New Haven. San Francisco is second to Los Angeles in population growth,[2] proportion of the labor force who have lived in the Standard Metropolitan Area for less than 12 years,[3] proportion having jobs with more than one employer,[4] mean number of changes in occupations held, and employer shifts per worker.[5]

An additional factor of some significance to an evaluation of the survey is the stage of the business cycle in which it took place. The interviews were collected from November, 1949, to January, 1950. This was a period of comparatively full employment. However, a minor cyclical decline in economic conditions which occurred in 1949 had local manifestations which were clearly visible, including decreased employment and a drop in business activity. The fact that the survey took place during a period of economic

---

[1] Gladys L. Palmer, *Labor Mobility in Six Cities,* (New York: Social Science Research Council, 1954).
[2] *Ibid.,* p. 22.
[3] *Ibid.,* p. 24.
[4] *Ibid.,* p. 49.
[5] *Ibid.,* p. 52.

uncertainty, which many persons thought presaged a depression, may have affected the responses of some informants. It is, however, not possible to make any good guesses as to the exact significance of this factor.

THE SAMPLE OF RESPONDENTS

It is important to distinguish between the two kinds of samples included in this survey; one, a sample of wage earners, and the second, a sample of jobs contained in the specific work histories of the respondents. The objective of this section is to describe rather than analyze the group of respondents. The sample of jobs will be described in the subsequent section.

The respondents were 935 principal wage earners in families residing in clusters selected at random within 55 of the 72 census tracts in the city of Oakland. No samples were taken in 17 tracts that were characterized either by extremes of wealth or poverty. Their omission was based on special considerations related to the original purpose of the study. At the time, the Institute of Industrial Relations was also conducting a study of the traits of the irregularly employed, and it was felt that the census tracts in which this group was concentrated could, therefore, be left out. In addition, it was believed that the labor-mobility patterns of the work-force elite would not be germane to a study primarily concerned with the job-shifting patterns of employed persons. There can be no question that these omissions seriously limit the possibility of generalizing from an analysis of social mobility based on the data, particularly so far as conclusions about the *amount* of social mobility are concerned. Whatever the reasons for the curtailment of the sampled area were, it is fortunate for our purposes that the deletion did not fulfill the intended purpose. Tract areas are large, and many of them are extremely heterogeneous in social and economic characteristics. Consequently, the sample included many persons at the top and bottom of the social structure, and a comparison of the socioeconomic characteristics of the survey sample with that reported by the 1950 census for the entire city indicates that the differences are not great.

The principal difference between the characteristics of the sample and those of the total labor force is the sex ratio. Because the sample design called for interviewing only heads of households, women and younger men are naturally underrepresented. This, however, had the positive virtue of increasing the number of persons in the sample who had had time to secure a stable position in the labor market. And, as in most other studies of social mobility, the analysis is concentrated on the males, since meaningful comparisons of the occupational status of fathers and daughters is much more difficult than comparisons of fathers and sons.

A comparison of the sex ratio of heads of families in the sample with that reported by the census indicates, however, that the sample contains fewer female heads of families (14.8 per cent) than are reported in the census (32.8 per cent). This deficiency may be a result of a number of factors, but it is most likely, however, that the difference between the definition of family head used in the survey and that used in the census caused a gap between the two. The survey design called for interviewing the principal wage earner; the census listed as head of the household that member of the family who was regarded as head by the members of the household. In some families these may not be the same person.

Survey and census data on occupational composition are not strictly comparable: the survey's "principal wage earners" have to be matched with all "employed persons" in the labor force reported by the census. Generally, in spite of this difference, the sample and the census do not differ greatly. Among males there is, in the sample, a slight underrepresentation of professionals, a substantial underrepresentation of unskilled workers, and an offsetting overrepresentation of white-collar workers; other groups appear to correspond rather closely to census figures. The differences between the census results and those of the sample may be a result of the sample design. Professionals are likely to be concentrated in the excluded high-status tracts, and unskilled workers to predominate in the omitted low-income areas. In addition, secondary workers are more likely to be in unskilled and semi-skilled positions than are the older family heads.

There were only minor variations between the census results and the sample population with regard to color or racial composition. The exclusion of a number of low-income tracts with a high concentration of nonwhites from the sample design means, however, that the nonwhites in the sample cannot be considered representative of their group. This correspondence between the sample and the census does suggest, however, that a frequent source of sample bias, the undersampling of nonwhites, was not a major factor in this study.

The proportion of homeowners and tenants in the sample corresponds, within limits that allow for sampling variability, with that reported by the census for all of Oakland. The age distribution of the survey sample was compared with that of heads of households for the Standard Metropolitan Area reported by the census. The results show close correspondence for males.

Although the sample design clearly makes it impossible to make any quantitative comparisons between the amounts of social mobility shown by this and other community studies, the comparison of the characteristics of the sample with those reported for the city of Oakland by the census does suggest that the original probability-sample design fulfilled its objectives. It must be understood that, in all the analytical sections of this study, any statements concerning differences among groups—for example, that the status of the first job has more bearing on subsequent job career than does level of education achieved—indicate the direction but not the magnitude of the relationship. The ultimate value of this study lies in its usefulness as a basis for further tests of hypotheses such as these, rather than for any estimate of the extent of mobility in California or American society. This brief description of the nature of the sample, together with the more detailed report of the sampling procedure,[6] may, however, be of some use to scholars who find discrepancies between their results and our own, since different sample design is one possible source of such variations.

THE SAMPLE OF JOBS

In much of the subsequent analysis, the unit of comparison will not be the immediate occupation or the job shifts of the individual members of the sample, but rather the aggregate of the individual jobs reported in the respondents' work histories. It is important to recognize that the distribution of jobs that are given in work

[6] See William Goldner, *The Methodology of the Oakland Labor Mobility Study* (Institute of Industrial Relations, University of California, Berkeley; mimeographed). Available on request.

histories is quite different from the distribution of jobs held by respondents at any given time. When the distribution of the respondents' occupations at time of interview is compared with that of the aggregate of jobs in the work histories, as is done in table 5.1, certain differences in the proportions in various categories give insight into the nature of the data.

TABLE 5.1

AVERAGE NUMBER OF JOBS PER RESPONDENT, BY OCCUPATIONAL GROUP

Occupational group	Jobs in work histories		Respondents' present occupation		Ratio $\frac{J}{R}$
	Number (J)	Per cent[a]	Number (R)	Per cent[a]	
Professional	300	5	68	7	4.4
Farm	193	3	...	...	...
Business owners and executives	439	8	138	15	3.2
White collar	1,245	22	252	27	4.9
Sales	462	8	66	7	7.0
Skilled	1,193	20	200	22	4.2
Semiskilled	1,372	24	143	15	9.6
Unskilled	606	10	60	7	10.1
All jobs in civilian employment	5,810	100	927	100	6.3
Other	1,135	...	8	...	...
Total	6,945	...	935	...	7.4

[a] Percentage distributions were calculated excluding the "other" categories. "Other" includes war service jobs, periods of unemployment and labor-force nonparticipation.

First, the turnover of various occupations is different. Turnover among business owners and executives, skilled workers, professionals, and white-collar workers is less than that for other occupations, such as salesmen and unskilled and semiskilled labor. These first set of positions apparently represent career goals which, once achieved, are not easily given up.

Secondly, the age distribution of the members of a sample affect the average number of job shifts reported. Clearly, the older people are, the more opportunity they have had to change jobs. The fact, therefore, that the persons included in a sample of principal wage-earners are older than those in a sample of the entire labor force serves to exaggerate the number of job shifts in the labor market. This bias is an analytic asset, since we are not concerned with reporting the amount of job shifting, but rather with analyzing different life-history patterns. Such an analysis only makes sense if based on persons who have been in the labor force for some time, and, in fact, most of the tables in subsequent chapters dealing with career patterns deal only with respondents more than thirty years old.

The work histories which were collected are life histories—respondents were asked to supply information about every job which they held after entering the labor market. Obviously, "recollection bias" will be greatest for jobs held earliest in the respondents' careers, and among respondents who had many positions. A more significant qualification is that the data for earlier dates, such as those for first jobs, are not representative of the population of Oakland, but rather of persons who have lived in many parts of the country, since the work histories of respondents who migrated to Oakland reflect the labor-market conditions in the communities from which they came. Migration may also affect the total amount of job mobility reported, since we cannot determine from the available data whether those workers who have moved out of the city were more mobile or less mobile than those who moved in.

One of the variables that will be used a great deal requires special explanation. We talk of "per cent of time spent" in an occupational category by a certain group of persons. This figure was obtained by computing the percentage of each individual's career spent in various types of occupations. That is, if a man has been in the labor market for ten years, and has spent three of them in semiskilled work, he has spent 30 per cent of his career in the semiskilled category.

CONCLUSIONS

The total effect of these qualifications on the data suggests that extreme caution should be used in comparing the *amount* of social mobility found in this study with that found in others. The imputation of rates of social mobility from this study to any general population is clearly a hazardous procedure. However, there is little evidence that the relationships among subgroups in the sampled population would be misrepresented because of sampling errors; the sample of business owners, for example, is subject to the same limitations as the sample of skilled workers. Since the analysis in the following section is largely based on comparisons of subgroups within the sample—subgroups constituted in accordance with a consistent and standardized system of classification —the limitations on the sample do not invalidate the conclusions. But it is important to keep in mind the qualifications discussed above lest inferences not intended by the authors be drawn.

Chapter VI | *Intra-generational*
Mobility

Much sociological analysis based on survey data attempts to relate occupational status to opinions, values, and behavior patterns. Thus, studies of voting behavior speak of the differences between the "blue collar" and "white collar" workers. Analyses of class identification and class consciousness relate subjective feelings about class position to occupational position.[1] The major effort to construct a scale of social-status positions in America employs occupational position as one of the principal items in the scale.[2] All of these studies are based on the frequently validated assumption that how a person thinks and acts, as well as how he is regarded by other people, is in large measure determined by his occupational experiences.[3] Marxian sociology makes such experi-

[1] Richard Centers, *The Psychology of Social Classes* (Princeton University Press, 1949).
[2] W. L. Warner, *et al.*, *Social Class in America* (Chicago: Science Research Associates, 1949), p. 124.
[3] "A man's occupation exerts a most powerful influence in assigning to him and his immediate family their place in society, in deciding their place of residence, and in determining the occupational status of the children when they enter employment. The work a man does to earn his livelihood stamps him with the form and level of his labor, use of his leisure, influences his political affiliations, limits his interests and the attainment of his aspirations, and tends to set the boundaries of his culture. In a word, except for those few persons whose way of life and future are secured by the inheritance of great wealth, occupation is the supreme determinant of human careers." H. Dewey Anderson and Percy E. Davidson, *Occupational Trends in the United States* (Stanford: Stanford University Press, 1940), p. 1. See also Raymond W. Mack, "Occupational Ideology and the Determinate Role," *Social Forces*, 36(1957):37–38, which presents a summary discussion of the literature stressing occupational position as a determinant of social role.

ences the key element in its effort to predict social behavior. Thorstein Veblen distinguished the conventional and pecuniary frame of mind of the typical businessman from the radical matter-of-factness of the engineer. The Lynds in their studies of Middletown attempted to show the great differences in ways of life and thought between those who worked with their hands and those who used their tongues.[5]

The pervasive influence of a common occupation on the mentality of all who are in it is unquestioned. And presumably, the more uniform the career of individuals, the easier it should be to predict their thoughts and actions. It is curious, however, that with all the interest in social mobility in America, and the recognition that a large proportion of the population do actually move up and down the social hierarchy and that an even larger proportion move horizontally by shifting jobs and occupations at the same social level, there has been little effort to refine the character of occupation as an interpretive variable by securing data on past occupational experiences of individuals. *As most current research is done, the man who has been a skilled worker or an independent businessman for the past twenty-five years is classified in the same category as the man who has been in the occupation for six months!*

The life-career data collected in the Oakland study enable us to indicate some of the variations in occupational background which characterize men currently in the same jobs and hence the degree to which different occupational classes vary in the heterogeneity of their collective work experience. These materials bearing on intra-generational mobility and its significance for analysis of social structure constitute the major contribution of the study. In this chapter, we shall lay out some of the characteristics of "occupational career patterns."

STABILITY AND INSTABILITY OF OCCUPATIONAL CAREERS

A person's characteristic pattern of mobility was determined by ascertaining the frequency with which he changed from one job to another, shifted from one occupation to another, or moved

---

[4] Thorstein Veblen, *The Theory of Business Enterprise* (New York: Scribner, 1921), pp. 66–91 and 302–373.

[5] Robert and Helen Lynd, *Middletown* and *Middletown in Transition* (New York: Harcourt, Brace, 1929 and 1937).

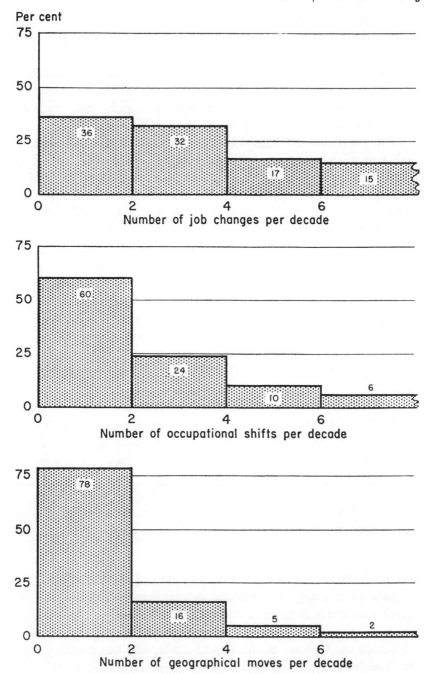

Fig. 6.1. Percentage of the 935 respondents making job changes, occupational shifts, and geographical moves, by mobility rate.

TABLE 6.1

RELATIONSHIP BETWEEN SPECIFIED TYPES OF MOBILITY RATES
(Percentages)

Range of mobility rates	Range of mobility rates		
	Low	Medium	High
OCCUPATIONAL MOBILITY RATES			
Job mobility rates			
Low..........................	22	14	..
Medium......................	6	26	7
High.........................	1	4	19
Total........................	30	45	25
GEOGRAPHICAL MOBILITY RATES			
Job mobility rates			
Low..........................	32	4	..
Medium......................	16	16	8
High.........................	7	3	14
Total........................	54	23	22
GEOGRAPHICAL MOBILITY RATES			
Occupational mobility rates			
Low..........................	23	5	2
Medium......................	23	14	8
High.........................	8	5	13
Total[a]......................	54	23	23

NOTE: Low mobility is here defined as 0 to 1.9 job changes per decade, 0 to 0.9 occupation or community changes; medium mobility as 2 to 4.9 job changes per decade, 1 to 2.9 occupational changes, and 1 to 1.9 community changes; over 5 job changes per decade, 3 occupational changes, or 2 community changes are considered high mobility. The percentages shown in each cell of this table are expressed as a proportion of the total of the 935 respondents.
[a] Details do not always add to totals because of rounding.

from one community to another. The rate of individual mobility
of each of the 935 respondents was computed by dividing the
number of changes the person has made by the number of years
he has been in the labor force. The calculated ratios were
expressed in the form of rates per decade, and the results for the
three different types of mobility are presented in figure 6.1.

It is clear from the tabulated data that men are more likely to change from one job to another than to shift occupations, and that they are more likely to change occupations than to move to another community. One obvious question about these three types of mobility concerns their interrelationship. Are the same individuals mobile on all three dimensions, or are persons who move readily from occupation to occupation resistant to moving from one community to another, while men who change communities tend to remain in the same occupation? The members of the sample were divided into three categories—high, medium, and low—for each type of mobility, and the patterns were compared. (See footnote to table 6.1 for classification system employed.) The results (see table 6.1) indicate that there is a high degree of association among mobility rates of different kinds.[6] Men who are mobile in one respect (e.g., shifting jobs) are also likely to be mobile in other respects. This finding is perhaps to be expected, but a further inference from these data suggests that resistance to geographical movement may be greater than the resistance to changing occupations, a datum which casts some interesting light on the problem of rigidities within the labor force.[7]

In order to determine the homogeneity of occupational career patterns, we have calculated intra-generational mobility by

---

[6] A paper by Gösta Carlsson based on the Swedish Mobility Study reports that for virtually all status groups geographical mobility (in terms of individuals residing outside the county of their birth) is highest for the upward mobile, intermediate for those in occupations similar to those of their fathers, and lowest for downward mobile persons. For purposes of analysis all mobility to and from agricultural occupations was eliminated. Carlsson suggests that migration is a result, not a cause, of social mobility. "Those who move to high status groups are more likely to become migrants than those who remain in a lower status group, but they show a lower incidence of migration than those who were all the time, so to speak, in these upper status groups." The main factor is therefore the marked association of high geographical mobility with high social and occupational status. Gösta Carlsson, "The Causal Connection between Migration and Social Mobility," (Working Paper Eight submitted to the Fourth Working Conference on Social Stratification and Social Mobility, International Sociological Association, December, 1957).

[7] Charles Walker in his study, *Steeltown* (New York: Harper, 1950), which attempted to find out the plans of steelworkers living in a community in which the only steel plant in town was planning to close down, found that most workers intended to change their occupations rather than move to another community and continue to work in the steel industry (pp. 169–180). Similar resistance to geographical movement when the only factory in Marienthal, Austria, closed during the depression was found by Hans Zeisel and Marie Jahoda, *Die Arbeitslosen von Marienthal* (Leipzig: S. Hirzel, 1933), p. 51.

TABLE 6.2

PERCENTAGE OF RESPONDENTS WHO SPENT DESIGNATED PROPORTIONS OF THEIR WORK
CAREERS IN THEIR PRESENT OCCUPATIONAL GROUP
(Excludes female respondents and males 30 and younger)

Occupational group of present job	Proportion of work career in present occupational group			Number of respondents
	80–100%	50–79%	Under 50%	
Professional......................	70	9	22	23
Semiprofessional..................	47	32	21	19
Own business.....................	11	31	57	105
Upper white collar................	14	21	65	72
Lower white collar................	18	33	49	67
Sales............................	26	24	50	42
Skilled..........................	22	35	43	169
Semiskilled......................	22	29	49	98
Unskilled........................	18	21	61	44
Manual..........................	65[a]	21	14	314[b]
Nonmanual.......................	58[a]	23	19	343[b]
All groups.......................	22	29	50	657

[a] The proportion of all manual or all nonmanual workers who have spent 80–100 per cent of their time in these categories is, of course, higher than the corresponding proportion for the separate occupational groups. Shifting between jobs may be frequent without entailing a cross-over from the manual to the nonmanual occupations, or vice versa.
[b] These figures include 15 business executives and 3 manual (odd-job) workers not shown separately.

determining the percentage of total job career which respondents spent in different occupational categories. When the proportion of time which the respondents spent in their present or in some other occupational group is computed, many turn out to have had relatively unstable careers, as the data in table 6.2 indicate.

Although there are members of all occupational groups who have spent the largest portion of their careers in occupations other than their present ones, there are considerable differences among the various strata of the occupational hierarchy. Occupational careers appear to be more unstable among unskilled than among skilled workers, and among white-collar workers and the self-employed than among the professionals and semiprofessionals. Perhaps most interesting of all is the fact that there are more non-manual workers who have spent a large proportion of their careers in manual employment than there are manual workers who have

TABLE 6.3

PERCENTAGE OF RESPONDENTS WHO HAVE EVER WORKED IN DESIGNATED OCCUPATIONAL GROUPS OTHER THAN THEIR PRESENT ONES

(Excludes female respondents and males 30 and younger)

Occupational group of present job	Occupational groups other than present												Number of respondents
	Professional	Semiprofessional	Own business	Upper white collar	Lower white collar	Sales	Skilled	Semiskilled	Unskilled	Farm owner	Farm labor	Odd jobs, unemployed	
Professional	..	9	9	13	26	9	9	22	17	..	..	13	23
Semiprofessional	..	..	16	5	32	10	21	21	32	5	..	10	19
Own business	3	5	..	9	41	33	48	46	20	1	10	14	105
Upper white collar	3	7	17	..	78	29	15	26	18	3	10	17	72
Lower white collar	..	3	12	9	..	27	45	54	36	6	13	36	67
Sales	..	7	38	17	64	..	26	50	29	2	14	14	42
Skilled	..	1	24	..	22	11	..	73	40	4	18	30	169
Semiskilled	..	3	24	2	28	22	42	..	56	4	24	33	98
Unskilled	..	2	14	2	31	9	39	64	..	4	30	36	44
All groups	1	4	17	4	34	19	26	45	32	3	16	25	639

NOTE: Percentages based on numbers as small as some of these are quite unreliable, but are included for their suggestive value.

TABLE 6.4

Percentage Distribution of Job Shifts to Occupations Respondents Assumed, by Occupational Group of Previous Job

(Excludes all jobs of female respondents and of males 30 and younger.)

Occupational group of previous jobs	All groups	Professional and semiprofessional	Farm	Own business and business executive	Upper white collar	Lower white collar	Sales	Skilled	Semiskilled	Unskilled	Casual labor
Professional and semiprofessional	6	68	7	2	3	4	2	2	2	3	1
Farm	3	..	21	3	1	1	2	2	4	6	5
Own business and business executive	5	2	4	22	7	2	8	5	3	3	3
White collar	16	9	8	12	62	50	16	4	6	6	9
Sales	7	2	5	12	4	7	37	2	3	3	8
Skilled	18	4	7	18	2	4	5	54	9	6	14
Semiskilled	20	2	20	12	3	10	13	14	43	20	24
Unskilled	9	2	10	5	2	4	5	4	11	32	16
Casual labor	4	1	7	1	2	2	2	3	5	6	8
Unemployed[a]	10	9	8	9	8	13	8	7	11	14	10
War service	3	2	2	3	8	3	3	4	4	2	2
All groups[b]	100	100	100	100	100	100	100	100	100	100	100
Number of job shifts	5,171	240	137	426	120	855	390	1,118	1,168	498	219

a Unemployed includes also persons who have left the labor force.
b Details do not always add to totals because of rounding.

held nonmanual positions. It is clear that unskilled manual labor in America is not the *cul-de-sac* that it is reputed to be.[8] The unskilled are the second most mobile group in the sample—if we measure mobility by the proportion of people who have spent more than half their careers in occupations other than their present one.

Thus far, we have discussed the proportion of career time which the respondents have spent in or out of their present occupation. Since we have data on every job which the sample's members can remember holding for more than three months, it is also possible to specify the variety of jobs characteristic of men currently in the various occupations. The data reported in table 6.3 reveal a variety of job experiences which is staggering. Among the unskilled, one-third or more have held white-collar and skilled positions. A fifth of those now in professional or semiprofessional employment have at some time in the past been employed in semiskilled manual work, and the majority of those in lower white-collar and sales occupations have also held such low-level jobs.

In order to obtain an overall picture of the actual shifts between occupations, which are subsumed in the percentages given in table 6.3, we have examined the 5,171 actual job changes reported by respondents (table 6.4). This reveals that as a group, persons who own or manage a business have the most heterogeneous past experience. Thirty-six per cent of the shifts into self-employment were from manual jobs of various kinds; slightly under 30 per cent were from various nonmanual occupations other than business ownership; only one-fifth shifted from the ownership of one business to another. Conversely, changes from job to job at the "same" occupational level occurred most frequently in the high-status occupations—among professionals, semiprofessionals, and upper white-collar workers. In each of these groups over 60 per cent of the changes took place within the category. Among manual workers, stable intragroup shifting has been most characteristic of the skilled workers.

---

[8] It may be easier to leave the unskilled category in California than in other parts of the country. Only 17 per cent of those whose first jobs were unskilled were still in this category at the time of the survey. For discussion of the problem in a comparative context see the Appendix.

MANUAL AND NONMANUAL OCCUPATIONS

Though there are many shifts from one occupational group to another, especially in the lower strata, these are, on the whole, shifts between groups of similar status. There is, however, relatively little shifting between manual and nonmanual groups, as figure 6.2 indicates: all those who work with their hands have spent 80 per cent of their working lives in manual occupations; all in nonmanual employment have spent 75 per cent of their careers in such positions.

The division between persons in the manual and in the nonmanual occupations has important ideological implications. Manual labor in the United States is not regarded as degrading, and the dignity of manual work is frequently stressed. Nothing has contributed more, for instance, to the popular legend of Henry Ford than the fact that this man who built an industrial empire worked on a farm as a boy.[9] But slogans cannot obliterate the great differences between the outlook and way of life of people on either side of the barrier, some of which have been documented statistically in chapter ii. Some characteristics of working-class life have been tellingly stated by Granville Hicks:

> Hunting and machinery—those are the two great topics of conversation when men get together. Sam Josephs loves to talk about both, and he is usually the central figure in any discussion. Being currently employed in a garage, he is regarded as an authority, and the session is likely to open with a question directed to him, but once the topic is launched, everyone—everyone but me—joins in. The talk grows more and more technical, but human interest is never excluded, for Sam is always being reminded of what some stupid customer said or what some incompetent mechanic did, and his anecdotes evoke others. Some of the men in our group are closely confined to things they have actually worked with, but others are interested in general principles and capable of dealing with them. Stan Cutter, for instance, though he was unable or at any rate unwilling to finish the sixth grade, has a genuinely speculative mind, and has worked out certain theories of mechanics for himself, just from handling machinery, even as he acquired some knowledge of physiology from the butchering of domestic and game animals. For all these men machinery is, among other things, a field of compe-

[9] See Keith Sward, *The Legend of Henry Ford* (New York: Rinehart, 1948), pp. 275–288.

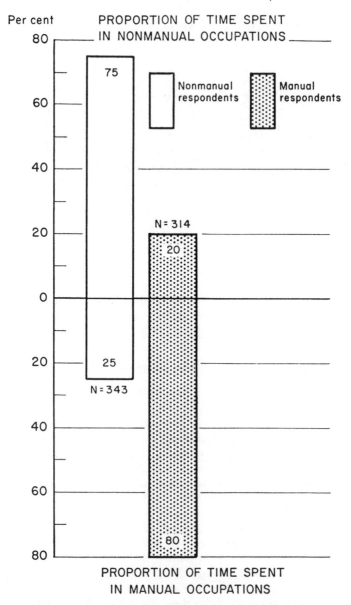

Fig. 6.2. Proportion of career time spent in manual and nonmanual positions. (Excludes female respondents and males 30 or younger.)

tence, and it is obvious that they enjoy talking about the subject simply because it is one on which they have something significant to say.[10]

Many people in the manual occupations have in common a way of life in which men are judged in terms of what they do with their hands and how they do it. The way of life of persons in the nonmanual occupations, however, is too varied, even in a small town, to permit of such generalization. In the absence of a simple interest in manual skill and the intricacies of animals and machines, their concern, as Veblen has shown, is with social prestige and material comfort, and this often overshadows the matter-of-fact aspects of daily living.

The need of subsistence and of an increase of physical comfort may for a time be the dominant motive of acquisition for those classes who are habitually employed at manual labor. . . . On the other hand, so far as regards those members and classes of the community who are chiefly concerned in the accumulation of wealth, the incentive of subsistence or of physical comfort never plays a considerable part. . . . The dominant incentive was from the outset the invidious distinction attaching to wealth, and, save temporarily and by exception, no other motive has usurped the primacy at any later stage of development.[11]

But, although the barrier is high, the same sort of occupational shifts are found on either side of it. The manual workers in our sample have spent 80 per cent of their work careers in manual occupations, but from 45 to 55 per cent of their time has been spent in occupational groups other than their present ones. Nonmanual workers have spent 75 per cent of their work careers in nonmanual occupations, but have spent from 20 to 61 per cent of their time in occupational groups other than their present ones.[12]

---

[10] Granville Hicks, *Small Town* (New York: Macmillan, 1946), p. 115.

[11] Thorstein Veblen, *The Theory of the Leisure Class* (New York: The Modern Library, 1934), p. 26.

[12] See S. M. Lipset and R. Bendix, "Social Mobility and Occupational Career Patterns," *American Journal of Sociology*, 57(1952):369, table 7. This table is not included in the present volume.

Comparative British data suggest that there also it is much more common for nonmanual workers to have manual job experience than it is for manual workers to have had employment in nonmanual occupations. Although it is hard to be precise because of problems of different classification schemes and sample compositions, the data on job shifts also indicate that the English industrial worker is much less likely to have had white collar experience than his counterpart in Oakland. See Geoffrey Thomas, *The Social Survey: Labour Mobility in Great Britain, 1945–1949,* An Inquiry carried out for the Ministry of Labour and National Service (Mimeographed; no date), p. 30.

TABLE 6.5

PERCENTAGE OF RESPONDENTS WHO HAVE WORKED IN DESIGNATED OCCUPATIONAL
GROUPS OTHER THAN THE PRESENT ONE
(Excludes female respondents and males 30 and younger)

Occupational group of present job	Occupational group other than present							Number of respond-ents
	All manual	Semi-skilled and appren-tice	Un-skilled	All non-manual	High status[a]	Lower white collar and sales	Own busi-ness	
All manual..............	..	..	..	47	26	33	23	314
Semiskilled and unskilled.	..	..	..	47	26	37	21	145
All nonmanual	62	40	24	..	..	..	..	343
High status[a]............	46	25	19	..	..	65	16	129
Lower white collar and sales................	75	52	33	..	33	..	22	109

[a] "High status" includes professionals, semiprofessionals, business executives, and upper white-collar workers.

TABLE 6.6

PERCENTAGE DISTRIBUTION OF RESPONDENTS IN OCCUPATIONAL DIVISION OF JOBS
ASSUMED, BY OCCUPATIONAL DIVISION OF PREVIOUS JOB
(Excludes all jobs of female respondents, of male respondents 30 and younger and
job shifts for which the previous job was not classifiable in an occupational division)

Occupational division of previous job	Occupational division of job assumed		
	Manual	Nonmanual	Farm
Manual..........................	80	26	50
Nonmanual......................	16	72	27
Farm............................	4	2	23
Number of jobs..................	2,607	1,792	124

Moreover, shifts between manual and nonmanual occupations occur. Table 6.5 shows the proportion of male respondents, grouped by overlapping sociological categories, who have spent some time in occupations that are socioeconomically distant from their present position. The data indicate that 47 per cent of the manual workers have held nonmanual jobs, and that 62 per cent of the nonmanual workers have worked with their hands—clear evidence of the flexibility of the American occupational structure.

Another measure of the shift between manual and nonmanual occupations is obtained when all job shifts are cross-classified, as in table 6.6. When all jobs held by the respondents are taken into account, one-sixth of the manual jobs are shown to have been filled by people from nonmanual occupations, while one-fourth of the nonmanual jobs have been filled by people who previously worked with their hands.

UPWARD AND DOWNWARD MOBILITY

The amount of social mobility involved in the interchange between manual and nonmanual occupations can most easily be shown by considering the proportion of their total careers members of different occupational groups have spent on either side of the manual-nonmanual line. Although, as we have noted, there is considerable intra-generational mobility across this line in terms of specific job experiences, the data of table 6.7[13] indicate that in terms of actual percentage of a work career such mobility is rather small. Nonmanual workers have spent 20 per cent of their occupational careers working with their hands; manual workers have spent 11 per cent of their job histories in nonmanual occupations.

These data indicate again that there is considerable variation in the stability of career patterns for different occupational groups. Among nonmanual workers, professionals who spend only 6 per

---

[13] Support for the approximate proportions of the time spent across the line may be found in Gladys L. Palmer, *Labor Mobility in Six Cities*, p. 115. A cross-classification of jobs in 1940 by jobs held in 1950 gave the following results:

JOB IN 1940 BY JOB IN 1950, FOR MALES, IN SIX CITIES
(Largely metropolitan centers)

Occupation in 1950	Occupation in 1940		
	Manual	Nonmanual	Total
Nonmanual.....................	20	80	100
Manual.......................	89	11	100

These results, based on probability samples of six major cities, correspond closely with our own data and this suggests that the Oakland findings may be representative of the normal amount of interchange between manual and nonmanual occupations. The Oakland data, for example, indicate that about a fifth of the time of those in nonmanual employment in 1949 had been spent in manual occupations, and the Six City Study, based on a much wider sample, indicates that a fifth of those in nonmanual work in 1950 had been in manual jobs in 1940.

cent of their career in manual occupations are clearly the most stable in terms of this particular indicator, while independent businessmen and lower-white-collar workers are notable for their greater career instability. Among manual groups, the skilled workers have spent the least percentage of time working in non-manual occupations.

TABLE 6.7

PERCENTAGE OF TIME SPENT IN OCCUPATIONAL DIVISIONS OTHER THAN PRESENT
(Excludes female respondents and males 30 and younger)

Present occupational group	Percentage of time spent		Number of respondents
	In manual occupations	In nonmanual occupations	
Professional.	6	. .	23
Semiprofessional.	13	. .	19
Own business.	26	. .	105
Upper white collar.	10	. .	72
Lower white collar.	30	. .	67
Sales.	21	. .	42
Skilled.	. .	9	169
Semiskilled.	. .	14	98
Unskilled.	. .	13	44
Nonmanual.	20	. .	343[a]
Manual.	. .	11	314[a]

[a] These figures include 15 business executives and 3 manual (odd-job) workers not shown separately.

An important aspect of social mobility in American society may be obscured by speaking, as we have, of *all* moves from manual to nonmanual as upward, and of the reverse shift as downward. The test of a rise or fall in the socioeconomic hierarchy is clearly the permanence of the change, and our data indicate (table 6.7) that there is relatively little *permanent* crossing between manual and nonmanual occupations among the respondents.

Table 6.8 indicates, however, that a *temporary* change from one category to the other occurs with considerable frequency. Significantly, the temporary crossings are more frequently downward than upward. Workers in the lower job echelons of American society may well feel that their chances to rise in socioeconomic status are slight. Yet those in the middle and upper strata of the occupational hierarchy may continue to insist that ready opportunities for social and economic advancement exist, because from 40 to 80 per cent of their numbers have at one time or another worked in manual occupations. Although this is not the place to explore the subjective aspects of social mobility, we want to emphasize the importance of considering the impact of casual job experiences on the subjective appraisals of opportunities and on the presence or absence of subjective class identifications.

TABLE 6.8

PERCENTAGE OF RESPONDENTS WHO EVER SPENT TIME IN OCCUPATIONAL DIVISIONS
OTHER THAN THE PRESENT ONE
(Excludes female respondents and males 30 and younger)

Present occupational group	Respondents ever spending time		Number of respondents
	In manual occupations	In nonmanual occupations	
Professional..........................	39	..	23
Semiprofessional.....................	53	..	19
Own business........................	68	..	105
Upper white collar...................	46	..	72
Lower white collar...................	82	..	67
Sales...............................	64	..	42
Skilled.............................	..	47	167
Semiskilled.........................	..	49	98
Unskilled...........................	..	41	44
Nonmanual..........................	62	..	343[a]
Manual.............................	..	47	314[a]

[a] These figures include 15 business executives and 3 manual (odd-job) workers not shown separately.

SPECIFIC AVENUES OF MOBILITY

Though 935 job histories provide a mass of information, this mass is quickly reduced to insignificance when more than two or three breakdowns are attempted. It is nevertheless possible to analyze the upward and downward mobility of respondents in greater detail than we have done so far. "Areas" of high and of low mobility may first be distinguished, using the previous tabulations of job changes. Here again (table 6.9) the pattern is similar to that found in the total job-history data. The self-employed have the greatest mobility from manual to nonmanual positions. Shifts from farm jobs are largely to manual labor, especially the unskilled and semiskilled positions. The lower white-collar and sales positions are those in which manual workers have the greatest opportunity to secure nonmanual work (if we exclude self-employment) and such positions do not usually bring about immediate upward economic mobility. The professional, semi-professional, business-executive, and upper white-collar positions are filled largely by persons from other nonmanual positions. As one would expect, skilled manual positions are seldom obtained by nonmanual workers.

TABLE 6.9

PERCENTAGE DISTRIBUTION OF JOB SHIFTS TO OCCUPATIONS ASSUMED,
BY OCCUPATIONAL DIVISION OF PREVIOUS JOB
(Excludes all jobs of female respondents and of males 30 and younger)

Occupation assumed in job shift	Occupational division of previous job				Number of job changes
	Nonmanual	Manual	Farm	Total[a]	
Professional and semipro- fessional...............	90	10	..	100	215
Own business.............	56	41	3	100	373
Upper white collar........	89	10	1	100	102
Lower white collar........	74	24	1	100	717
Sales....................	70	28	2	100	346
Skilled..................	14	84	2	100	995
Semiskilled..............	17	79	5	100	1,000
Unskilled...............	17	75	8	100	421

[a] Details do not always add to totals because of rounding.

It is difficult to estimate from the data how much genuine social mobility is reflected in these tables, since persons changing from manual work to lower white-collar and sales jobs or to owner-ship of small businesses may not actually be changing their status and income level. The fact remains, however, that a considerable amount of such shifting does occur. Table 6.9 suggests that the greatest social mobility occurs in the form of shifts into "own business," and that shifts into the white-collar occupations and sales rank next: these are the occupations of most of those who manage to pass from manual to nonmanual work. There is, how-ever, a significant difference in the mobility patterns if "own business" is compared with the white-collar occupations. The majority of persons in white-collar jobs have always been employed in such jobs, though 24 per cent of those employed in lower white-collar occupations have previously worked at manual labor. On the other hand, more than 40 per cent of the persons who own their business have come from the manual occupations.

The type of social mobility represented by persons who establish their own businesses and that represented by those in the white-collar occupations—which may be called "old" and "new" types of mobility—present rather striking contrasts in our data. To run a business of one's own is still a much-cherished ideal, and those who achieve it are felt to have moved up in the social scale. But with the growth of large-scale organizations in all parts of American society small-business ownership has lost some of its meaning, though its ideological appeal has not necessarily been weakened thereby.[14] Many persons still cherish the idea of success achieved through individual effort, though their own careers show little evidence that "private enterprise" has had much significance for them personally. Mobile persons in the white-collar occupations are mobile in a bureaucracy; the qualities which lead to the promotion of the salaried employee are radically different from those which would make him a successful independent businessman. The data reveal some significant differences between the idolized "free-enterprise" career of the businessman and the bureaucratic career of the white-collar worker.

The degree of mobility—determined by the "occupational distance" between the first and the present job—which characterizes these career patterns can be quite accurately assessed. Other data in this study reveal that the first job is a good predictor of the subsequent career. The "occupational distance" between first and present job is clearly greatest for business owners and sales people, almost as great for the lower white-collar workers, and least for persons in the upper white-collar positions.[15] A number of other variables are associated with these differences. Business owners and executives are an older group than the white-collar workers: 7 per cent of the first group, and 22 per cent of the

[14] Cf. Kurt Mayer, "Business Enterprise: Traditional Symbol of Opportunity," *The British Journal of Sociology*, 4 (1953): 160–180.

[15] These findings are compatible with the notable mobility across occupational lines which we discussed earlier. See S. M. Lipset and F. Theodore Malm, "First Jobs and Career Patterns," *American Journal of Economics and Sociology*, 14(1955): 247–261, for a discussion of the "first job" as a predictor of career patterns.

second, are thirty or under; 54 per cent of the business owners and 43 per cent of the white-collar workers are forty-six or older. The age of the business owners, together with the fact that many of them have had manual occupations, suggests that opportunities for manual workers to turn businessmen do not come to them until their middle and later years. In all other respects there is

TABLE 6.10

PERCENTAGES OF RESPONDENTS IN SELECTED PRESENT OCCUPATIONS, BY NUMBER OF OCCUPATIONS IN CAREER, AND NUMBER OF JOBS IN CAREER
(Percentages)

Number of occupations and number of jobs	Present occupation		
	Own business	Business executive and upper white collar	Lower white collar and sales
Number of occupations			
1..	13	14	19
2 or 3...........................	44	39	36
4 or more.......................	43	47	45
Total.........................	100	100	100
Number of jobs			
1 to 5...........................	47	58	60
6 to 10..........................	37	36	31
11 to 15.........................	11	3	6
16 or more.......................	5	3	3
Total.........................	100	100	100
Number of respondents..............	119	108	162

little difference between the mobility patterns of business owners or white-collar workers and those of the sample as a whole: mobility among jobs, occupations, and areas is greatest in the younger age groups and decreases with age.

The mobility of the middle-class occupational groups, considered as a whole, is, however, quite striking (see table 6.10): between 40 and 50 per cent of business owners and white-collar workers have had four or more different jobs. The similarity of the past patterns of mobility of these groups is upset when we consider the possibilities of future mobility that proprietorship

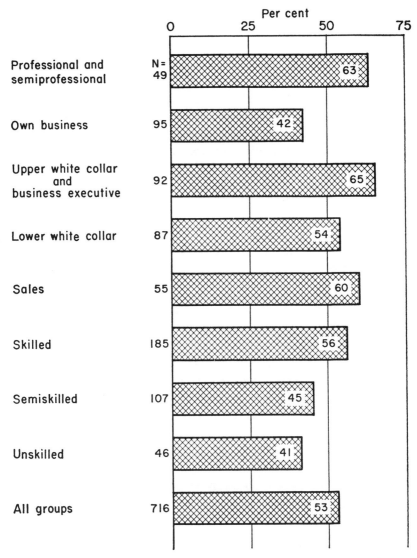

Fig. 6.3. Knowledge of other jobs by respondents' present occupational group. Based on replies to question: "Since you began this job, have you known about any other jobs which you might have been able to get?"

and bureaucratic careers afford, as reflected in whether persons have known of other available positions since they began their present jobs. Answers to this question presumably reveal something of a person's potential mobility, since his mobility depends in good part on his awareness of alternatives (see figure 6.3).

More than half of the semiskilled and unskilled workers and of the business owners state that they have not known of other jobs since starting on their present one: respondents in the other nonmanual and the skilled occupations have known of other jobs much more often. Business owners in particular are not at all concerned with other jobs but rather with how to make profitable their present, mostly small-scale, investment. Thus, although business ownership is a goal of the socially mobile, especially for persons in manual occupations, it cannot be considered a step to other jobs. A significant difference between business ownership and bureaucratic position as a goal for the socially mobile lies in the fact that in modern society the first is the final step in a person's work career, and the second is at least potentially a means to a better-paying job in the same or another large-scale organization.

Changing implications of proprietorship.—That there is a certain finality in proprietorship does not mean that persons in this group never move into other occupations. But, since a good proportion of these men come from the manual occupations, it is probable that their only choice is between manual labor and proprietorship. The self-employed businessman, so far as the data of this study represent him adequately, is today a very different person, both socially and economically, from his counterpart of two generations ago. Then he could hope and work for the real economic success which could result from the building-up of a large enterprise out of a small beginning. Then hope and work were meaningful, regardless of the individual's particular fate, because the social and economic distance between the small business and the large enterprise was nowhere near so great as it is today. Success in proprietorship today usually consists in the stabilization of an enterprise at a given social and economic level, because the opportunities for building large enterprises out of very small ones are relatively meager, though they have certainly not disappeared.[16] It is in part a by-product of the predominance of large-scale organizations that those who head them have usually had a bureaucratic career. The "industrial bureaucrat," not the small independent businessman, is the one most likely to advance to the peak of the economic structure, both socially and economically.[17] For these reasons the data on self-employed businessmen are of special interest.

The 105 individuals who were self-employed at the time of the interview had been so employed for less than half of their average working careers. Sixty-eight per cent of the group had at some time been employed in manual work, while 74 per cent of them had had jobs as lower white-collar workers or as salesmen. If one considers the lower-status occupations in American society to comprise lower white-collar workers and salesmen, as well as semiskilled, unskilled, and farm workers, then 89 per cent of the self-employed business owners have spent some part of their work careers in lower-status occupations. If their work careers are considered collectively (rather than the proportion of the group that has been in the lower-status occupations at some time), then the group is shown to have spent, on the average, 36 per cent of its work careers in these low-status jobs, which is only slightly less than the average time spent in self-employment (41.5 per cent).[18]

Although only about 10 per cent of the American population are presently self-employed businessmen, it is obvious that a much larger part of the labor force has owned a business in the past, given the large turnover in this category. It is especially noteworthy that over one-fifth of the members of the Oakland sample who are currently engaged in manual work were at some time in business for themselves. The data on business turnover in the

[16] G. F. Lewis and C. A. Anderson, for example, report that in Louisville, of the 25 business owners with less than 5 years education, 24 assumed their present position when the business grossed less than $10,000 a year. But at the time the study was made, 11 of them operated businesses grossing over $200,000, and 22 of them owned businesses grossing over $50,000. "Social Origins and Social Mobility of Businessmen in an American City," in *Transactions of the Third World Congress of Sociology*, Vol. III, (London: International Sociological Association, 1956), p. 259.

[17] See chapter iv.

[18] Percentages which are cited in this paragraph without references to tables are from tabulations of the Oakland study data not included here.

United States presented in chapter iii corroborate the implication of the Oakland materials that somewhere between 20 and 30 per cent of the urban work force have been self-employed for some time, although predominantly in very small, insecure enterprises.[19]

The conclusion suggested by the objective data on the previous jobs of those who become businessmen—that this career is preponderately a mobility path of manual workers and low-status, relatively unskilled, sales people—is reiterated by subjective

TABLE 6.11

PERCENTAGE OF RESPONDENTS WITH BUSINESS ASPIRATIONS,
BY PRESENT OCCUPATION
(Excludes female respondents and males 30 and younger)

Present occupation	Per cent with business aspiration	Number of respondents
White collar.............	56	138
Sales....................	74	42
Manual..................	67	310
Skilled...............	63	168
Semiskilled............	71	98
Unskilled..............	68	44

NOTE: Based on affirmative replies to question: "Have you ever thought of going into business for yourself?"

materials obtained by questions concerning aspirations. The majority of every employed occupational group answers "Yes" to the general question whether they had *ever* thought of going into business. This aspiration, however, is more widespread among all groups of manual workers[20] and sales people than it is among the white-collar workers, the lower echelons of the managerial hierarchy, who presumably look forward to moving up within the company (see table 6.11). Responses to the question "Have you

[19] Of course, this rate of turnover varies by industry. The entrance and discontinuance rates are higher for construction firms, for example, than for financial firms. And these differences in turnover rates are naturally reflected in the experience of self-employment among different groups in the labor force.

[20] This emphasis on business ownership in occupational aspirations has been shown to vary with class position among adolescents as well, with those from lower-income groups aspiring to business ownership, and those from higher income groups hoping for professional careers. "For most of this group [sons of lower-income families], to own a business is the outer limit of their expectations. No one fantasied about becoming a millionaire, but almost everyone was able to anticipate the possibility of owning a business." Eli Ginzberg, *et al.*, *Occupational Choice* (New York: Columbia University Press, 1951), p. 152.

ever tried to own your own business?" are similar, as table 6.12 reveals. The proportion of persons who report that they attempted to own a business show that the aspiration documented in this table has its effect on business ownership. The contrast between the proportion who try and the proportion who succeed, according to the job history data, show that the men least likely to carry through their attempts are those at the bottom of the entire occupational structure—the unskilled workers.

TABLE 6.12

PERCENTAGE OF RESPONDENTS WHO ATTEMPTED TO OWN BUSINESS,
BY PRESENT OCCUPATION

(Excludes female respondents and males 30 and younger)

Present occupation	Have been in business[a]	Attempted to own business	Did not try	No answer	Total[b]	Number of respondents
White collar.............	14	29	53	18	100	139
Sales.....................	38	64	31	5	100	42
Manual..................	23	35	49	17	100	313
Skilled.................	24	36	46	18	100	169
Semiskilled.............	24	31	53	16	100	97
Unskilled..............	14	36	50	14	100	44

NOTE: Based on replies to the question: "Have you ever tried to own your own business?"
[a] Based on job history data; although 107 respondents have owned a business, 282 indicate that they have made attempts in this direction. The percentages in the first column are not added in the figures on the right.
[b] Details do not always add to totals because of rounding.

A recent report on mobility patterns in Sweden suggests that in that country also, small business tends to be an avenue of upward mobility for manual workers, while white-collar employees, if they move up, tend to do so through the ranks of large-scale industry. C. Arnold Anderson reports that, "The bulk of the 1930 big businessmen had in 1925 been functionaries [white-collar workers] ... Small business recruited largely from urban labor groups ..."[21] These Swedish materials yield some further evidence on the way in which educational attainment affects one's choice for bureaucracy or small business as a source of mobility. Those white-collar workers who became small businessmen instead of remaining in a bureaucracy were among the least educated of the white-collar workers, while those manual

[21] C. Arnold Anderson, "Lifetime Inter-Occupational Mobility Patterns in Sweden," *Acta Sociologica*, 1 (1955): 184–185.

workers or small businessmen who shifted to white-collar employment were among the best educated in their previous occupational class.[22]

CONCLUSIONS

Certain characteristics of an urban labor market emerge from this consideration of the occupational career patterns of our respondents. The first is that our respondents have had an extraordinary variety of occupational experience. A very large proportion of them have worked in different communities, in different occupations, and in many different jobs. By implication, this challenges the picture of the class structure derived from studies of small communities, which present it and the individual's position in it as pretty much "given."

It is important to note, however, that there are major areas of stability; there are certain limits to the variety of occupational experience of the respondents. In the first place, their mobility is largely confined to mobility on either side of the dividing line between manual work and the nonmanual occupations. There is little permanent occupational movement across this basic line. This means that although many persons have experience in a wide variety of occupations, most of it will be homogenous to the extent that it will be either manual or nonmanual. The departures from this conclusion are generally of two major types.

1. Individuals whose occupational career is predominantly manual may have brief experience in nonmanual occupations, especially in small business, sales, and lower white-collar positions.

2. Individuals whose career is predominantly nonmanual quite often have spent some of their occupational career in manual positions, generally briefly and generally early in their career. This is particularly true of small businessmen. This type of mobility is somewhat more prevalent than the first.

The desire of American wage earners to become self-employed is still very strong, and the opportunity to become self-employed for at least brief periods of time is still open. Statistics on the small proportion of self-employed at any one time conceal the fact that many more than the present number have owned their own business at some time in the past, and many more will do

---

[22] *Ibid.,* pp. 187 ff.

so in the future. Self-employment is one of the few positions of higher status attainable by manual workers. That most of those who try it apparently fail does not change the fact that they do try.

We have indicated that studies of social mobility which only compare the father's occupation and the occupation of the respondent at the time of the study miss some of the most significant aspects of social mobility. What, for instance, are the characteristics of those individuals who have a highly mobile occupational career, as opposed to those who are stable? What are the consequences of the variety of occupational experience which a large proportion of American wage earners have? The next chapter deals with major turning points in the career patterns of our respondents—with their relation to the career as a whole. The considerations introduced in this chapter provide the logical basis for these studies, which emphasize the fluidity of career patterns and of the American occupational structure.

Chapter VII | Some Sources
of Inter-generational
Mobility

In the preceding chapter we have considered the occupational career patterns of individuals in terms of their mobility between jobs and occupations, *from the time that they began their work careers.* However, in the past, sociological studies of social mobility have analyzed any given group in terms of the jobs and occupations which the members of that group held at the time of inquiry. When such studies have dealt with *inter-generational mobility,* they have therefore reported the relationship between the occupations of fathers and sons, much as we have done in chapter ii. That is to say, the job which the son held at the time of the interview was compared with the major occupation which the son reported for his father, and the mobility between the generations was assessed accordingly. This conventional method of analysis presents a number of pitfalls.

One of these consists in the fact that the comparison between the generations is not specific for age, so that one cannot judge the respective stages of the careers of father and son for which the comparison is made. Thus, a father may be reported as having been an executive, or a skilled worker, at the height of his career, while his son is interviewed at the start of his career, when he may be in a lower white-collar or unskilled position. Yet, the father's position at the height of his career is frequently not the most relevant index for assessing the influence which the father's position has had on the career of his son. Some recent studies have attempted to meet this problem by asking the respondent to give his father's occupation when he was of the same age as the son is at the time of the interview. This method of inquiry represents some improvement over methods which do not have controls for age. But it, too, may result either in underestimation or over-estimation of the advantages flowing from the socioeconomic position of the parents, since the family status which is probably most relevant in affecting the son's educational and career opportunities is that which exists when he is in high school or when he is beginning his occupational career. Indeed, one major problem of social-mobility analysis is that no one period of the career of father or son is necessarily representative of occupational status, and for different types of analysis the researcher may actually need information about different points in the job history.

It is fairly obvious that this basic methodological difficulty may not be solvable in any absolute sense. Presumably, what is wanted is a complete career history of both generations, father and son, a goal which is unattainable. The best approximate solution (that of interviewing the living fathers of all sons in a sample) has never been attempted in any study. Through such a "generational panel" one could specify in considerable detail the interrelationships of *inter*-generational and *intra*-generational mobility. The job history materials obtained in the Oakland study permit an analysis of the relationship between the "principal" occupation of fathers and the career patterns of their sons, an approach which represents some advance over the customary method. The analysis of these materials constitutes the main subject matter of this chapter. In dealing with the influence of family background on occupational career patterns, we also treat its effect on educational attainment, since next to direct inheritance of occupational position, education constitutes the most important asset of an individual who begins his career in a bureaucratized society. Education can be viewed both as an index of the family's position while the respondent was of school age (given the high correlation between parental status and duration of children's education), and as a major independent determinant of occupational choice. It is important, therefore, to consider the relationship of education to career in dealing with inter-generational mobility.

FATHERS' OCCUPATIONS AND CAREER PATTERNS OF SONS

Inter-generational transmission of status and inter-generational mobility necessarily complement each other. There is a strong correlation between the occupational status of fathers and the occupational status of positions in which the sons spend the greater part of their careers. But there is also clear evidence that most men of high social origin have at some time held low-level manual positions, and that almost half the men of working-class parentage have had at least one "high-status" position.

Table 7.1 shows the proportion of sons of men in different occupational groups who, since leaving school, have worked at least three months in one or more of the four major occupational divisions. Thus, 45 per cent of the 42 sons whose fathers were professionals or semiprofessionals have held low-level manual jobs at some time, and 46 per cent of all the sons of manual workers have had at least one position in a "high-status" occupation. In reading this table, one should keep in mind that the same respondent may be counted more than once; for example, the same son of a professional father could appear first as having held a "high-status" job, then under "all nonmanual" (a classification which includes high- and low-status nonmanual positions), again under "all manual" because he has at some time worked "with his hands," and finally under "low-status working-class" because his work as a manual worker was unskilled.

This table indicates only that the respondents *have worked*, but not *how long* they have worked, in the various occupational divisions. The results are, nevertheless, suggestive. If we consider only the summary categories, we find that 66 per cent of the sons of fathers in nonmanual occupations have worked in "high-status" occupations, while 58 per cent have been in "low-status working-class" occupations. Even when we consider a high-status group such as business owners and executives, we find that 66 per cent of their sons have held "high-status" occupations, but 62 per cent have also held jobs in "working-class" occupations. It is true, of course, that the variation in this respect is less for the sons of fathers in the manual occupations. Only 46 per cent of this group worked in "high-status" occupations, while 77 per cent have been in "working-class" occupations. Although these and similar discrepancies between the careers of sons of middle-class and

TABLE 7.1

PERCENTAGE OF MALE RESPONDENTS WHOSE FATHERS WERE IN SPECIFIED
OCCUPATIONAL GROUPS AND WHO HAVE WORKED AT SOME TIME
IN SPECIFIED OCCUPATIONAL DIVISIONS

Fathers' occupational group	Occupational division in which sons have worked at some time				Number of respondents
	High status[a]	All nonmanual	All manual	Low-status working class[b]	
Professional and semiprofessional.....	69	86	57	45	42
Business owner and executives........	66	85	69	62	130
White collar and sales..............	62	87	70	59	53
Skilled...........................	48	73	84	75	158
Semiskilled and unskilled............	42	70	85	80	94
Farm owner and farm laborer........	45	63	92	88	167
Nonmanual.......................	66	85	67	58	225
Manual..........................	46	72	85	77	252
All groups........................	53	74	80	73	644

NOTE: All data on fathers' occupations are based on replies to the question: "What is or was your father's occupation during most of his life?"
[a] "High status" includes the professionals, semiprofessionals, business executives, and upper white-collar workers.
[b] "Low-status working class" includes all those in semiskilled and unskilled occupations, as well as apprentices and farm laborers.

working-class fathers are significant, it is perhaps even more significant that they are not greater. A large proportion (58 per cent) of the sons coming from a relatively privileged (nonmanual) family background have worked in the least-privileged jobs, and, conversely, a large proportion (46 per cent) of the sons coming from the least-privileged (manual) family background have worked in "high-status" occupations.

This analysis of inter-generational mobility in terms of all occupational divisions in which an individual ever held a job sheds important light on the range of experience to which many Americans have been exposed, regardless of the social stratum in which they originated. Clearly, however, this method tends to exaggerate greatly the amount of *permanent* mobility which occurs between generations because the work experience examined involved jobs of short duration. But it is possible to refine the conventional father-son comparison. Individuals may be classified as mobile or nonmobile by comparing their present position with the regular occupation of their fathers. And these mobile or nonmobile persons may then be classified according to the amount of time they have

TABLE 7.2

INDICES OF INTRA-GENERATIONAL MOBILITY

Type of inter-generational mobility by son's present job	Type of intra-generational mobility				Number of respondents
	Proportion of respondents *ever* holding job in category other than present	Per cent of total career in manual occupations	Number of respondents	Per cent of total career in category other than present among those who have *ever* held jobs in both categories	
Manual					
Father manual.....	49	90	134	21	65
Father nonmanual..	54	85	72	28	39
Nonmanual					
Father manual.....	67	26	118	39	72
Father nonmanual..	51	7	153	26	78

spent on either side of the invisible barrier between manual and nonmanual occupations. In table 7.2 we have, therefore, divided the respondents into four groups depending on the occupational division of their own present job as well as of their father's principal position. Each of these groups is then cross-tabulated using three different indices of inter-generational mobility.

The data in table 7.2 reveal different relationships between *inter*-generational and *intra*-generational mobility. If we look at the first column in the table, we see that regardless of the relationship between the fathers' occupation and the sons', from one-half to two-thirds of the men in each category have held at least one job on the opposite side of the manual-nonmanual line. The greatest amount of such intra-generation mobility is to be found among the respondents in nonmanual employment whose fathers were manual workers, while the least amount of cross-class experience is to be found among manual workers who are the sons of manual workers. However, when we examine the same groups in terms of the proportion of their total career which they have spent in manual employment, as is done in the second column, we get a very different picture. Here the range is from 90 per cent among the manual sons of manual workers, to only 7 per cent among nonmanual individuals whose fathers were in nonmanual occupations at the time of the interview. Clearly, though half of each group have held jobs across the manual-nonmanual line, these have almost all been of fairly short duration.

It is interesting to note that there is comparatively little difference betweeen manual workers whose fathers have been in the same occupational class, and those whose fathers held nonmanual positions. The former have spent 90 per cent of their work careers in manual employment, while those mobile downward have been in manual employment for 85 per cent of their job histories. Similarly, among those manual workers who have held at least one nonmanual position (see the fourth column in table 7.2), those in the same class as their fathers have spent 21 per cent of their careers in nonmanual positions, while those who have fallen in status have spent 28 per cent of their time in nonmanual jobs.

Although father's occupation does little to differentiate among the job histories of manual workers, it does make a fairly large difference among those in nonmanual employment. If the son of a nonmanual father who is over 31 holds a nonmanual job, the chances are very high that he has spent all or almost all of his work history on the upper side of the manual-nonmanual line (93 per cent). On the other hand, the nonmanual sons of manual workers have not only been mobile upward as compared with their fathers, but two-thirds of them have held at least one manual job during their own career. As a group they have spent over one-quarter of their job history working with their hands. And the two-thirds of the group who have held manual jobs, have spent almost two-fifths (39 per cent) of their work careers in manual employment. It seems clear, therefore, that the current job of an individual over 30 is most predictive of his permanent status if he is in the same occupational class as his father. Its predictive power is slightly less for those mobile downward and it is least predictive for those mobile upward, many of whom spend time on both sides of the invisible barrier in their attempt to secure higher status. Thus the middle-class sons of nonmanual fathers have a decided advantage over the sons of fathers in manual occupations, even though the latter may be successfully mobile upward. Persons in the middle class more often spend their entire careers in nonmanual occupations, and if they have done manual labor they have done it for a somewhat shorter proportion of their work careers.

All available evidence on inter-generational mobility tends to emphasize the determining effect of occupational choice, as we have pointed out. Yet, exclusive attention to this fact would lead us to underestimate the effects of intra-generational mobility which our data on total job-histories reveal. As the first column in table 7.2 indicates, half of the men who currently have the same status as their fathers have spent some time across the line, and this experience may do much to affect their attitudes about the potentialities for social mobility in America. Those who remain in the same high-status position as their fathers can nevertheless feel that they have been personally mobile because they have held low-status jobs, and those who have not been able to rise permanently above their fathers' occupational statuses may feel that they have or have had a real opportunity to improve their social position. The cross-class experience may also serve to contribute to the consensus concerning the prestige of different occupational roles, a consensus which strengthens the equalitarian ideology of American society, as discussed earlier in chapter iii.

Qualification needs to be added at this point. We have contrasted the shifts between the manual and the nonmanual occupations with the mobility of an individual among all the jobs he has held throughout his career. This can be misleading. Important job changes, as well as changes between occupations, occur *within* the manual or the nonmanual groups. Thus, the shift from unskilled to skilled labor is of major importance in the career of an individual worker, yet it would be lost sight of in our categorization of the material. At this point we understate the degree of job mobility which actually occurs, and conversely we overstate the degree of "occupational inheritance" between the generations. This distortion results from the crudeness of the categories (manual versus nonmanual) which we have used to make comparisons. It is difficult to avoid such distortions in an analysis of occupational statistics, and our data on "occupational inheritance" should be evaluated accordingly.

FATHER'S OCCUPATION AND EDUCATIONAL ATTAINMENT

Thus far in this chapter we have considered the careers of the respondents exclusively in terms of their relationship to parental status. Underlying such comparisons between the fathers and sons is the assumption that the occupation of the father will be a major help or hindrance to an individual in acquiring vocational skill and motivation for achievement before starting his career. The Oakland data do not include information bearing directly on these processes, but an analysis of the relationship between father's occupation, educational attainment, and initial job selection does shed light on the effects of interaction between generations upon occupational placement.

There is a growing link between educational attainment and occupational advancement. With over half of the gainfully employed working in tertiary industries, and with the increasing growth of industrial and governmental bureaucracies, nonmanual skills are requisite for a large proportion of the available jobs every year. And nonmanual skills are increasingly acquired through formal education.[1] Moreover, the expansion of American education reflects both the need to supply trained personnel for the positions which require considerable education and the fact that educational requirements for jobs have been increased. A generation or two ago, high school diplomas were not prerequisites for many of the jobs for which they are demanded today—store clerks, for example. That the growth of education has resulted in a downgrading of the jobs associated with a given level of education is suggested by the fact that 71 per cent of the persons in each of the groups, "high school graduates" and "some college," have held at least one manual position (table 7.3). This suggests that although education is generally a prerequisite for occupational advancement, a high school education—or for that matter a college degree,

---

[1] See Lawrence Thomas, *The Occupational Structure and Education*, (New York: Prentice-Hall, 1956), pp. 343–363.

since 36 per cent of college graduates have been manual workers—
does not automatically result in high occupational status.

Since educational attainment is strongly related to high occupational status, any examination of family influences on occupational
choice must take into account the way educational opportunities
are unequally distributed among men coming from different social
strata. These relationships have been discussed on the basis of
national data in chapter iii. While these data make it obvious

TABLE 7.3

PERCENTAGE OF RESPONDENTS WHO EVER HELD JOBS OF SPECIFIED TYPE,
BY EDUCATION ATTAINED

| Education attained | Occupational divisions of jobs respondents ever held | | | | | Number of respondents |
	High status[a]	All non-manual	All manual	Low-status working class[a]	Farm	
8 years or less..............	50	67	93	87	25	228
Some high school...........	44	68	90	83	18	147
High school graduate.......	47	77	71	64	9	160
Some college..............	66	89	71	56	11	73
College graduate..........	89	98	36	33	2	45

[a] For definitions see table 7.1.

that children of families with high status have much better chances
than do children of working-class families, it is important to bear
in mind that significant minorities of children depart from the
modal pattern of their class. Many children with a "favorable"
family background leave school at an early age, while a considerable number of workers' children manage to continue in school
despite great obstacles. This widespread variation of educational
attainment within classes suggests that one's family background
plays an enabling and motivating rather than a determining role.
Some of the sources of this variation are discussed in chapter ix.

In spite of the fact that relatively large numbers of sons of
manual workers complete high school, their chances of holding
a nonmanual position are considerably less than the chances of
children of middle-class families with the same education. The
job history data allow further specification of this relationship.

In table 7.5 the relationship between father's occupation, education, and first job is presented. If we hold educational attainment constant, we find that the sons of manual fathers predominantly *enter* the manual occupations even when they attain some high school education (70 per cent). On the other hand, only about half the sons of nonmanual fathers who have the same amount of education enter manual occupations. The children of manual workers are frequently forced out of school at an early

TABLE 7.4

PERCENTAGE OF TIME SPENT IN OCCUPATIONAL DIVISIONS, BY EDUCATION ATTAINED

Education attained	Occupational divisions in which career time was spent					Number of respondents
	High status[a]	All non-manual	All manual	Low-status working class[a]	Farm	
8 years or less..............	18	32	60	39	5	228
Some high school...........	15	35	57	34	4	147
High school graduate.......	21	51	44	29	2	160
Some college..............	33	63	31	18	1	73
College graduate...........	63	86	12	7	2	45

[a] For definitions see table 7.1.

age; but even if they are not, they seem to find it considerably harder than the children of nonmanual workers to enter the labor market in a "higher" job. Though some correction of this discrepancy between educational attainment and first job takes place after entry into the labor market, the level of entry in itself is a powerful determinant of future occupation.[2]

[2] "When the influence on present job status of education, father's occupation, and first job is held constant, the first job is clearly the most important predictor among the factors analyzed [here] as affecting present occupational position.... 59 per cent of the men who began in a nonmanual position but whose education is low [less than high school graduation] and whose fathers were manual workers, were still in a nonmanual occupation, when interviewed. On the other hand, 49 per cent of the men who are high in educational attainment and parental occupational status, but began as manual workers, are now in nonmanual positions. The combination of high school education or better and parental nonmanual status does not operate to make up for beginning in a manual occupation, as contrasted with starting in a nonmanual occupation, while not possessing the congruent attributes of high education and parental status." S. M. Lipset and F. Theodore Malm, "First Jobs and Career Patterns," *American Journal of Economics and Sociology*, 14(1955): 247–261.

Social Origin and Entry Into the Labor Market

Although the unequal distribution of educational opportunities is a major source of variation in chances for occupational advancement there are many other sources of variation. One-third of our male respondents (age 31 and over) never went beyond grammar school, and another one-fourth did not finish high school. Educational attainment did not constitute, therefore, a major step

TABLE 7.5

Percentage Distributions of First Jobs of Respondents with Specified Educational Attainment Whose Fathers Were in Specified Occupational Divisions
(Excludes female respondents)

Grade completed in school and fathers' occupational division	Occupational division of first job			Total respondents	
	Manual	Nonmanual	Farm	Per cent	Number
Completed grade 0–8.....	64	20	16	100	228
Manual...............	73	21	6	100	92
Nonmanual..........	66	32	2	100	47
Farm................	53	15	32	100	89
Completed grade 9–12....	60	35	5	100	387
Manual...............	70	28	2	100	177
Nonmanual..........	49	50	1	100	139
Farm................	55	23	22	100	71
Completed grade 13 or higher..............	29	67	4	100	157
Manual...............	34	63	3	100	41
Nonmanual..........	24	75	1	100	94
Farm................	41	41	18	100	22

in the occupational careers of more than one-half of our male respondents over 31. As we have seen earlier, a relative lack of education has an adverse effect on the occupational level at which the individual enters the labor market, as well as on his subsequent career. Since so much depends on this initial step it may be useful to analyze somewhat more closely the factors which facilitate or obstruct the individual's career at this point.

It has been suggested that young people entering the labor market are in effect floundering around in a new world for which they are ill prepared and for which they have made few plans.[3] The majority of the Oakland Mobility Survey respondents are no exception to this generalization, for 55 per cent of the sample reported that they had no specific job plans while in school.[4] As one would expect, the proportion of those without specific job plans declines as they continue their education, both because of growing personal maturity and because of the greater urgency

TABLE 7.6

RELATION OF FIRST JOB OBTAINED IN DECADE 1940–1949 TO AGE IN 1940
(Percentages)

Occupation entered	Age in 1940			
	5–9 years	10–14 years	15–19 years	20–24 years
White collar..............	19.4	21.4	26.3	36.6
Craftsmen and foremen.......	6.1	12.1	16.4	23.4
Other manual, excluding farm.	43.4	44.1	43.8	29.6
Agriculture.................	31.2	22.4	13.4	10.4

SOURCE: Based on an analysis of the 1940 and 1950 censuses in A. J. Jaffe and R. O. Carleton, *Occupational Mobility in the United States, 1930–1960*, (New York: King's Crown Press, 1954), p. 32.

of making a decision. When respondents are classified by level of education, 78 per cent of those with an eighth-grade education or less stated that they had no job plans, but among high school graduates only 47 per cent had none, and among college graduates, 13 per cent.

Because respondents were asked at the time of the survey to remember what, if any, plans they had had while in school, it may well be that the above results are not entirely accurate. Some are likely to have forgotten that they did have definite plans when they were in school, and others are perhaps prompted by the question to attribute to their school days particular plans which are in fact only a reflection of their later experience. But however inaccurate in detail, the data suggest that the prolonged availability of educational opportunities in this country enables some American youngsters to postpone the decision on occupational

[3] P. E. Davidson and H. D. Anderson, *Occupational Mobility in an American Community* (Stanford: Stanford University Press, 1937), chap. iii, "The Floundering Period."

[4] The percentages quoted here and below are based on detailed tabulations which are omitted because of space limitations.

choice which most of their European age-mates, for example, must make at the age of 14 or before.[5] Some evidence that early entry into the labor market almost necessarily means entry at a low level in the occupational structure may be seen in an analysis of the relationship between age and the first job of workers during the decade 1940–1949. These materials drawn from the census show clearly that those who entered while young began either in farm work or in other positions requiring little skill (see table 7.6).

TABLE 7.7

PERCENTAGE OF RESPONDENTS WHO HAD SPECIFIC JOB PLANS WHILE IN SCHOOL,
BY FATHERS' MAJOR OCCUPATIONAL GROUP

Occupational group of fathers	Had specific job plans	Did not have specific job plans	Number of respondents
High status[a]	55	45	249
White collar and sales	46	54	90
Skilled	46	54	213
Semiskilled, unskilled, and miscellaneous	40	60	168
Farm	35	65	211
Nonmanual	53	47	339
Manual	44	56	381
All groups	45	55	931

[a] In this table, "High-status" includes professionals, semiprofessionals, business owners, and business executives.

This postponement of decisions about a career by most Americans has other causes which are related to the educational system. In part, job plans crystallize only in the later years of high school and college because not until then do most students receive advice concerning their future careers. Among those in the sample with an eighth-grade education or less, 67 per cent had *not* received vocational advice from their parents, teachers, or any other persons; among high school graduates this proportion fell to 45 per cent, and for college students to 31 per cent.

The disadvantages which beset the careers of individuals with little education tend to be cumulative. Such persons receive little

[5] See chapter iii, p. 93 f., and A. Kaehler and E. Hamburger, *Education for an Industrial Age* (Ithaca: Cornell University Press, 1948), pp. 5–6.

vocational guidance in school. Specifically, 87 per cent of those who did not go beyond grammar school reported that they received no vocational advice from their teachers. It is true that 63 per cent of the college students and even 53 per cent of the college graduates did not receive vocational advice from their teachers either, but this does not alter the fact that such advice is given least to those whose lack of education presumably makes them need it most. It is also true that most of those who *do* receive advice in school are ill-advised. Of those who were advised by their teachers, between 60 and 75 per cent say that they were advised to choose a professional career: advice apparently given as often to those who later went no farther than grammar school or high school as to those who went to college. The comments of our respondents indicate, in short, that few teachers took the trouble to advise their students about their careers, and that those few who did made no attempt to base their advice on the real labor market.[6]

A student does not receive advice concerning his future plans only from his teachers. He is even more likely to receive advice from his parents, particularly if they are well-to-do. Advice is given somewhat more frequently when the father is a professional man or a business executive than when he is a manual laborer; however, the percentages (57 per cent as against 42 per cent) do not differ as much as one might expect. Probably there are few fathers who do not advise their sons in some fashion or other. The question was not clear enough to ascertain whether or not the father had given *specific* advice concerning job plans for the future.

Respondents were also asked whether they had planned on a particular job which they would attempt to get once they left school. Their answers to this question are clearly differentiated by fathers' occupation (table 7.7). Whatever distortions of memory may enter into the retrospective answers to this question, the data

---

[6] It should be noted that selecting the sample from *principal wage earners* resulted in the overwhelming majority of respondents being males 31 or over, men who would have been likely to have completed their education in the 1930's or even earlier. The analysis would have been strengthened if there had been enough cases in the sample under 31 to permit holding the age factor constant at that level. The improved vocational-guidance systems of some larger communities presumably result in more and better advice being given to students today.

suggest that the family background of an individual has considerable bearing on his job-orientation during his formative years. The sons of families in the high-status occupations more frequently develop specific job plans during their school years than the sons of manual workers and farmers. Though the advice given by both teachers and parents is often unrealistic, these job plans are not, as far as the evidence allows us to judge. At any rate, there is less emphasis on a professional career as the goal, regardless of family background. And those who do plan on a professional career come from families which may be able to provide the necessary additional years in school.[7]

It is of interest that a greater proportion of those who were advised by parents, teachers, or friends than of those who lacked such advice said that they had developed specific job plans for themselves. The data on job plans for the manual or the nonmanual occupations are included in order to show that those who received advice *and* had fairly clear vocational plans were also those who more often desired to go into the nonmanual occupations. This is an interesting illustration of the cumulative effect of family background as a stimulus for "high" occupational achievement.

The cumulation of advantages or disadvantages is also reflected in the manner in which knowledge of job opportunities was distributed among our respondents at the time they left school to enter the labor market. Of the children of families in the professions and in business (owners and executives) 48 per cent indicated that they knew of other jobs available to them at the time they began work. For the other occupational groups, an average of 30 per cent knew of such alternatives.

---

[7] In the "Elmtown" study, the job aspirations of children were reported to be closely related to the vocational levels of their families. A. B. Hollingshead, *Elmtown's Youth* (New York: Wiley, 1949), pp. 286–287. See also D. C. Miller and W. H. Form, *Industrial Sociology* (New York: Harper, 1951), pp. 604, 651–652; H. H. Hyman, "The Value Systems of Different Classes," *in* R. Bendix and S. M. Lipset, ed., *Class, Status and Power: A Reader in Social Stratification* (Glencoe, Ill.: The Free Press, 1953), pp. 426–442. Materials suggesting that the lack of occupational plans to enter low-status occupations is *not* due to lesser aspiration (at least in early high school) is given by Richard M. Stephenson, "Mobility Orientation and Stratification of 1,000 Ninth Graders," *American Sociological Review*, 22 (1957): 204–212.

CONCLUSIONS

Much of the data presented in this and other studies of social mobility has dealt with the effect of family background on the occupational and social placement of individuals. The evidence indicates that educational attainment is a major determinant of career patterns, a fact which provides the strongest and most direct statistical link between family background and the assets and liabilities with which individuals enter the labor market. The nature of this link may be shown by a summary of the most relevant findings:

1. Behind differences in educational attainment lies the fact that children from low-status families do not have as much chance to stay in school as those from high-status families.

2. Our data show that Americans who have only graduated from high school spend the greater part of their careers in manual occupations, and that persons with at least some higher education spend more time in nonmanual occupations.

3. When we compare respondents whose educational attainments were the same, but whose family backgrounds differ, we find that the sons of manual workers most often enter the labor market in manual jobs, while the sons of nonmanual workers usually enter the labor market in nonmanual jobs. Only college education enables manual-workers' sons to enter the labor market in a middle-class occupation.

4. The importance of family background for the education and the careers of our respondents is seen in the characteristic cumulation of advantages or disadvantages. Vocational advice from many sources is more often given to those individuals whose families can afford to keep them in school. It also seems to be more realistic and helpful than the advice given to the children of working-class parents. The effect of these and other background factors may be discerned in an individual's choice of his first job.

5. If an individual comes from a working-class family, he will typically receive little education or vocational advice; while he attends school his job plans for the future will be vague and when he leaves school he is likely to take the first available job

which he can find.[8] Thus, the poverty, lack of education, absence of personal "contacts," lack of planning, and failure to explore fully the available job opportunities that characterize the working-class family are handed down from generation to generation. The same cumulation of factors, which in the working class creates a series of mounting disadvantages, works to the advantage of a child coming from a well-to-do family. The social status of parents and the education of their children is, therefore, closely related both to the nature of the latter's first jobs and to the pattern of their later careers. And our analysis of career predictors published elsewhere[9] tends to confirm the generalization of Davidson and Anderson that "early jobs ... [are] prophetic of the subsequent careers of respondents."[10]

Occupational and social status are to an important extent self-perpetuating. They are associated with many factors which make it difficult for individuals to modify their status. Position in the social structure is usually associated with a certain level of income, education, family structure, community reputation, and so forth. These become a part of a vicious circle in which each factor acts on the other in such a way as to preserve the social structure in its present form, as well as the individual family's position in that structure. This cumulation of advantages or disadvantages is evident also in the choice of the first job. We know that the choice of the first job is for many a largely fortuitous decision.[11] Those in the lower socioeconomic groups tend to take "the only job they know about" at the time they enter the labor market. This choice of the first job is made with more deliberation by individuals with more education and a family higher up the occupational ladder.

Almost identical conclusions were reached by Paul Lazarsfeld

---

[8] S. M. Lipset, Reinhard Bendix and F. Theodore Malm, "Job Plans and Entry into the Labor Market," *Social Forces*, 33(1955):229 ff. See also L. G. Reynolds, *The Structure of Labor Markets* (New York: Harper & Bros., 1951), p. 108.

[9] S. M. Lipset and F. Theodore Malm, "First Jobs and Career Patterns." See Appendix to this volume for discussion of studies of first jobs in other countries.

[10] The importance of the first job as a predictor of career patterns has been analyzed by P. E. Davidson and H. D. Anderson, *Occupational Mobility in an American Community*, p. 94. See also Miller and Form, *Industrial Sociology*, pp. 675–676; and L. G. Reynolds, *The Structure of Labor Markets*, pp. 136–137.

[11] S. M. Lipset, Reinhard Bendix and F. Theodore Malm, "Job Plans and Entry Into the Labor Market."

in summing up the results of the rather extensive studies of determinants of vocational choice in pre-Hitler Austria and Germany: "The more socially oppressed a group is, the more restricted in advance is the range of occupational choice of its children.... The effect of the material limitations acts in part so as to narrow the perspective of those faced with the occupational choice. The socially underprivileged adolescent has seen less, read less, heard about less, has experienced less variety in his environment in general, and is simply aware of fewer opportunities than the socially privileged young person."[12] Thus, the cumulation of disadvantages (or of advantages) affects the individual's entry into the labor market as well as his later opportunities for social mobility. In the next section of the book, we turn to an examination of some of the findings which account for the fact that in spite of this, a significant minority do move up (or down) the class structure.

---

[12] P. F. Lazarsfeld, *Jugend und Beruf*, Vol. 8 of *Quellen und Studien zur Jugendkunde* (Jena: G. Fischer, 1931), p. 19. This summary and analysis of the research on occupational choice by adolescents remains the best single work on the subject, although it is over twenty-five years old. It is an interesting commentary on the discontinuities introduced into scientific research by linguistic barriers that American research in this area has developed in almost complete ignorance of the elaborate and sophisticated empirical researches conducted in Germany and Austria before the Nazis destroyed free social science in these countries. American research on the cumulation of disadvantages is analyzed in Genevieve Knupfer, "Portrait of the Underdog," *Public Opinion Quarterly*, 11 (1947): 103–114.

Part Three | *Causes, Consequences and Dimensions of Social Mobility*

Chapter VIII	Community Structure

The discussion of occupational "inheritance" and career patterns presented in the previous section has, like most sociological studies of this subject, emphasized that the advantages and disadvantages of family background tend to be cumulative. But tendencies are reversible, and correlations should not tacitly be transformed into stone walls—we have made evident that there is a considerable amount of social mobility in all complex societies. In chapter ii, we suggested that inherent in the very existence of a stratification order, of higher and lower valuations of social positions, is the motivation to move up in the social structure if one's position is low, or to retain one's position if it is high. A number of structural factors that made it possible for men to move up were also cited in that chapter. In this, the concluding section of the book, we continue the discussion of the sources of mobility and give a more detailed analysis of determinants than was presented earlier. This discussion is not intended to be a thorough investigation of everything which is known about the subject. Rather, we here present examples of two different approaches to the problem: in this chapter, a consideration of the urbanization process as a source of increased motivation and aptitude for upward mobility, and in the next, an examination of the way in which individual differences in intelligence and personality determine social and occupational placement.

URBANIZATION

Evidence derived from a number of studies in different countries suggests that the related processes of urbanization and migration are major sources of social mobility. These data indicate that today, in some countries, migration from rural areas and smaller communities to metropolitan centers influences the placement of people in the occupational structure in the same way that large scale immigration once did.[1] That is, at one time, in the United States and other immigrant-accepting countries, large numbers of immigrants entered the economic structure at its lowest level. The native-born, often children of immigrants themselves, were, presumably, able to secure the jobs which an expanding economy created on the next higher level.[2] And though mass immigration into many countries has ended, high rates of internal migration now characterize their societies. In the United States, for example, such migration has the size of a major population movement. Between April, 1940, and April, 1947, 20.8 per cent of the total population changed their county of residence—a total of almost thirty million persons.[3] In the relatively "normal" postwar year of 1953–1954, nearly ten million persons, or 6.4 per cent of the population, migrated across county lines.[4] The Census of 1950 reports that in that year, thirty-five million persons, or 25.2 per cent of all United States residents, were living in states other than the one in which they were born.

Analysis of the Oakland study and of relevant materials from the University of Michigan's Survey Research Study of the 1952 elections shows the way in which this process operates. The Oakland data show, for example, that the larger a man's community of orientation (the community in which he spent his teens), the higher the status of the job he holds is likely to be[5] (see table 8.1).

---

[1] See chapter iii.

[2] See the data in chapters ii and iii on the occupational distribution of immigrants and their sons as compared with native-born sons of native-born fathers.

[3] U. S. Bureau of the Census, *Statistical Abstract of the United States, 1949* (Washington: 1949), p. 17.

[4] U. S. Bureau of the Census, *Statistical Abstract of the United States, 1955* (Washington: 1955), p. 42.

[5] The community of orientation was obtained by asking the respondents: "Where did you live most of the time between the ages of 13 and 19? Did you live inside the city limits? Did you live on a farm?" Each community was then classified ac-

Of those who spent their formative years on farms, only 41 per cent achieved nonmanual positions; of those who spent them in small urban places, 53 per cent; and of those who grew up in large cities, 65 per cent.[6]

The deviations from the above trend lie mainly in two largely nonbureaucratic or entrepreneurial groups, the self-employed and the professionals. In Oakland, the proportion of professionals of

TABLE 8.1

PERCENTAGE OF RESPONDENTS WITH PRESENT JOBS IN SPECIFIED OCCUPATIONAL GROUP,
BY TYPE OF COMMUNITY OF ORIENTATION

Present job	Community of orientation		
	Farm	Rural nonfarm and urban to 250,000	Urban over 250,000
Professional...................	5	11	6
Self-employed..................	16	12	16
Upper white collar.............	4	8	13
Lower white collar.............	11	15	22
Skilled........................	28	21	20
Semiskilled....................	19	17	12
Unskilled......................	12	9	3
Nonmanual[a]..................	41	53	65
Manual........................	59	47	35
Number of respondents.........	168	300	434

[a] Total of nonmanual includes categories not separately listed.

small-city origin is greater than the proportion from large cities, but nearly equal proportions of self-employed come from each type of community. As shall be shown later, the Research Center's national survey indicates that men of middle-class origin reared

cording to the population reported by the Census. The analysis revealed that size of community of orientation rather than migration *per se* was most crucial in affecting subsequent career patterns. That is, there is little difference between natives of metropolitan San Francisco and other large urban centers. The data indicate that the breaking points in terms of influence of community or orientation on job careers are those between farm, urban under 250,000, and urban over 250,000.

[6] If we compute the percentages of each occupation from various-sized communities, we find that 67 per cent of the business executives and upper white-collar workers grew up in large cities, 60 per cent of the lower white-collar workers, 51 per cent of the sales personnel, 44 per cent of the skilled, 39 per cent of the semiskilled, and 23 per cent of the unskilled.

in small communities actually do as well or better than those reared in large cities: a finding particularly related to the fact that the male offspring of small-town middle-class families usually obtain a higher education than their large city compeers. It is probable that many natives of small communities who secure higher educations leave their home towns to go to the large cities, where greater opportunity exists.[7] Thus, we find that size of community of orientation is most closely related to occupational position within the ranks of industry and large-scale organization. The smaller the community of orientation the less likely a lower-class individual is to be upwardly mobile within bureaucratic structures.

The inferences about the relationship between size of community of orientation and social mobility which have been drawn from our data may be tested directly by comparing the occupations of respondents with those of their fathers. It is clear from the data in table 8.2 that working-class youth growing up in large cities are much more likely to reach high occupational status than those coming from smaller communities. This suggests anew that migration from rural areas and small cities to metropolitan areas serves to facilitate upward mobility by those native to urban life. It is important to note, however, that the advantage is concentrated in the sons of the working class. The data bearing on intragenerational mobility indicate a definite pattern. Those from smaller communities are more likely to fall from a nonmanual

---

[7] In the year 1949–1950, the professionals and semiprofessionals had the highest rate of geographical mobility of any occupational group: 9 per cent of the males in this category changed their county of residence during this year, as compared with 5 per cent of the total labor force. See U. S. Bureau of the Census, *Statistical Abstract of the United States, 1952* (Washington: 1952), p. 40. It may well be that children from smaller towns who seek higher education are more oriented to professional careers, since they are less exposed to opportunities for bureaucratic careers. Sorokin reports that of the graduates of the University of Minnesota from 1910 to 1915 who came from small towns or the country, "55.8 per cent became lawyers, ministers, physicians, and teachers as compared with 39.5 per cent of the whole group of college graduates." P. Sorokin, *et al.*, *A Systematic Source Book in Rural Sociology* (Minneapolis: The University of Minnesota Press, 1932), p. 528. Similarly, Archie O. Haller and William H. Sewell report that although a comparatively small proportion of residents of farms have high educational aspirations, a large proportion of those who do aspire to professional positions; among urban children, even though more of them want to go to college, fewer aspire to professional positions. See "Farm Residence and Levels of Educational and Occupational Aspiration," *American Journal of Sociology*, 62(1957): 407–411.

first job, and less likely to rise from a manual first job, than are those coming from larger communities[8] (see table 8.3). The factors which underlie these relationships are discussed below.

Table 8.4 makes clear that, holding the level of achieved education constant, large-city natives are more likely to reach a high position within the bureaucracy of industry than are those from

TABLE 8.2

INTER-GENERATIONAL SOCIAL MOBILITY, BY SIZE OF COMMUNITY OF ORIENTATION
(Percentages)

Occupational division of respondent's present job	Occupational group of father				
	Professional, business owner, and executive	White collar and sales	Skilled	Semiskilled and unskilled	Farmer
COMMUNITIES OVER 250,000					
Nonmanual..............	31	37	65	54	61
Manual..................	69	63	35	46	39
Number of respondents.....	115	30	97	55	147
COMMUNITIES UNDER 250,000					
Nonmanual..............	28	21	43	50	52
Manual..................	72	79	57	50	48
Number of respondents.....	106	52	106	70	33

smaller communities. Nearly twice as many men from communities over 250,000 who have some higher education occupy high-status white-collar and executive positions as do educated men from small communities and farms (27 per cent, as against 18 and 15). The difference among those with less than high school education is even more striking: 13 per cent from large communities hold high bureaucratic positions, as against 2 per cent from small communities and 5 per cent from farms. Further evidence of the effect of urban environment on occupational success in business

---

[8] Although the differences in some of the internal comparisons are slight and the number of cases in some of the cells is small, the fact that in each of the ten possible comparisons the difference is in the direction indicated by the hypotheses suggests that the results have some validity.

TABLE 8.3

RELATIONSHIP BETWEEN FIRST JOB AND PRESENT JOB
BY TYPE OF COMMUNITY OF ORIENTATION
(Excludes female respondents and males 30 and younger)

Occupational division of present job	Occupational division of first job		
	Nonmanual	Manual	Farm
COMMUNITY OF ORIENTATION: FARM			
Nonmanual........................	60	29	40
Manual...........................	40	71	60
Number of respondents.............	20	62	48
COMMUNITY OF ORIENTATION: UNDER 250,000			
Nonmanual........................	73	31	44
Manual...........................	27	69	56
Number of respondents.............	94	120	9
COMMUNITY OF ORIENTATION: OVER 250,000			
Nonmanual........................	88	42	..
Manual...........................	12	58	..
Number of respondents.............	129	158	..

bureaucracies may be found in studies of the business elite. Warner and Abegglen note that men born in big cities are more likely to obtain positions at the top of the business world.[9] The same result was obtained by Suzanne Keller, who found that although only 39.7 per cent of the population in 1890 lived in cities of 2,500 or more, the majority of the members of the business elite born about that time (65 per cent) were born in larger communities.[10] Since both these studies selected their samples in such a way as to emphasize bureaucratic mobility, their findings support the hypothesis that urban residence during childhood facilitates bureaucratic careers.

[9] W. Lloyd Warner and James C. Abegglen, *Occupational Mobility in American Business and Industry* (Minneapolis: University of Minnesota Press, 1955), p. 87.

[10] Suzanne Keller, *Social Origins and Career Lines of American Business Leaders* (Unpublished Ph.D. dissertation, Columbia University, 1953), p. 61.

TABLE 8.4

RELATIONSHIP BETWEEN COMMUNITY OF ORIENTATION AND OCCUPATION,
WITH EDUCATION HELD CONSTANT

Occupational group of present job	Community of orientation and years of education								
	Farm			Under 250,000			Over 250,000		
	0–11	12	13+	0–11	12	13+	0–11	12	13+
Professional.........	2	2	35	0	10	35	2	3	20
Own business........	13	11	12	12	12	10	16	15	7
Business executive and upper white collar............	5	5	15	2	12	18	13	14	27
Lower white collar...	7	24	15	17	22	10	15	30	22
Sales...............	9	7	3	6	8	5	5	11	7
Skilled..............	27	22	21	29	22	16	27	18	10
Semiskilled..........	22	20	0	22	14	4	18	7	7
Unskilled...........	14	9	0	13	2	2	5	2	0
Nonmanual.........	36	49	79	36	63	79	50	72	82
Manual.............	64	51	21	64	37	21	50	28	18
Number of respondents..............	157	55	34	108	51	57	185	151	97

Another interesting internal difference revealed in our study
is the pattern for professionals (see table 8.4). More of the college-
trained persons from smaller communities are professionals than
those who originated in metropolitan centers. This finding is
probably related to the fact, pointed out earlier, that many professionals who grow up in smaller communities migrate to big
cities. Many from small communities who do well in the educational system have to leave their home towns to secure employment or remuneration commensurate with their training. Large
cities attract two types of migrants from rural areas and smaller
urban centers: a large majority who fill the lower rungs of the
occupational ladder, and thus create a base upon which the
dweller native to the metropolis may climb; and a minority of
well-educated migrants who compete with the natives for positions at the top.

The effect of community size on occupational careers may be
specified further by a consideration of data collected by the Survey

Research Center of the University of Michigan in the course of their survey of a sample of the American population during the 1952 election (table 8.5). If we compare the rates of mobility in cities having more than 50,000 population with those of cities having less, the pattern suggested by the Oakland material is repeated; inhabitants of large cities have a higher rate of upward mobility, and a lower rate of downward movement, than those living in small ones.[11]

TABLE 8.5

RELATIONSHIP OF FATHER'S OCCUPATION AND SIZE OF COMMUNITY OF
PRESENT RESIDENCE TO OCCUPATION OF SON
(Percentages)

Son's occupation	Community of present residence and father's occupation					
	Over 50,000			Under 50,000[a]		
	Nonmanual	Manual	Farm	Nonmanual	Manual	Farm
Nonmanual..........	64	36	30	60	29	30
Manual..............	36	64	67	40	71	53
Farm................	..	..	3	..	..	17
Number of respondents	100	143	73	57	113	127

SOURCE: Analysis of the University of Michigan's Survey Research Center's Study of the 1952 Presidential Elections.
[a] Excludes rural areas.

The Survey Research Center also asked respondents to report the type of community in which they grew up: "Were you brought up mostly on a farm, mostly in a small town, or mostly in a big city?" Although there is undoubtedly a great deal of unreliability in the responses to this question, they do permit a further test of the relationship between size of community of orientation and rates of social mobility, an analysis of which is given in table 8.6.

[11] Actually, the data indicate greater upward mobility in communities over 50,-000 that are not parts of metropolitan areas, than in metropolitan areas. There were, however, fewer respondents from the 50,000-plus nonmetropolitan communities in the sample and the differences reported could be an artifact of chance variation. It is important to note this datum, however, since middle-sized cities are currently the most rapidly growing areas in America, and it is probable that they do, in fact, have higher rates of mobility than metropolitan regions. Between 1940 and 1950, cities with populations over 1,000,000 grew about 9 per cent, and cities from 50,000 to 1,000,000 grew 23 per cent. See U. S. Bureau of the Census, *1950 Census of Population*, Vol. II, "Characteristics of the Population, Part 1, U. S. Summary" (Washington: 1953), table 5b.

TABLE 8.6

SOCIAL MOBILITY RELATED TO COMMUNITY OF ORIENTATION
(Percentages)

Son's occupation	Community of orientation		
	Rural	Small town	Big city
FATHER NONMANUAL			
Nonmanual.......................	.. a	65	60
Manual...........................	.. a	34	39
Farm.............................	.. a	1	1
Number of respondents.............	.. a	74	79
FATHER MANUAL			
Nonmanual.......................	20	30	37
Manual...........................	71	69	63
Farm.............................	9	1	..
Number of respondents.............	45	119	116

SOURCE: Analysis of the University of Michigan's Survey Research Center's Study of the 1952 Presidential Elections.
a Too few cases.

Among men of working-class parentage, size of community of
orientation is positively related to their opportunities for *upward*
social mobility. Larger size of community of orientation is, however, related to *downward* mobility among those with a nonmanual
family background. Although the differences are small, the data
suggest that manual-workers' sons growing up in big cities have
a better chance to move up than those reared in small towns,
but that sons of middle-class families from small towns are less
likely to fall in occupational status than those who grow up in
large cities. The number of cases in the sample is unfortunately
too small to permit any reliable comparison of the amount of social
mobility related to both community of orientation and community
of current residence. This four-variable breakdown suggests,
however, that the mobility advantage held by the sons of manual
workers raised in large cities as contrasted with those raised in
small towns occurs only *within* large cities, since those who grew
up in large cities but who now live in small cities or towns do very

little better than those who grew up in small towns and still reside in small communities. Among current inhabitants of metropolitan areas whose fathers were manual workers, almost twice as many of those who also grew up in big cities have been upward mobile (38 per cent) as have those who grew up in small towns

TABLE 8.7

RELATIONSHIP BETWEEN SOCIAL MOBILITY, COMMUNITY OF ORIENTATION, AND EDUCATIONAL ATTAINMENT

(Percentages)

Son's occupation	Father nonmanual		Father manual		
	Small town	Big city	Farm	Small town	Big city
LESS THAN HIGH SCHOOL GRADUATION (0–11)					
Nonmanual.............	33	38	7	12	22
Manual.................	62	58	83	86	78
Farm...................	5	4	10	2	.. a
Number of respondents.....	21	24	30	65	58
HIGH SCHOOL GRADUATION OR HIGHER EDUCATION (12+)					
Nonmanual.............	77	69	47	52	52
Manual.................	23	31	47	48	48
Farm...................	.. a	.. a	6	.. a	.. a
Number of respondents.....	53	55	15	54	58

a Too few cases.

(22 per cent).[12] There is no apparent sharp difference among the sons of nonmanuals when we classify their current jobs by communities of orientation and present residence.

The relationship between social origins and community of orientation may be further specified by studying the effect of educational attainments on occupational achievement. If the amount of education is held constant a pattern which emerged in the analysis of the Oakland materials is also suggested by the Center's national survey: that is, growing up in a big city constitutes a definite advantage for those who are handicapped educationally (less than four years of high school); but being reared in a

[12] These data are not reported in any table.

large urban community is not a mobility asset for the better educated (high school graduation or more). See table 8.7.

The analysis of the national survey data both reinforces and suggests some need to modify the conclusions based on the study of Oakland. The following patterns are suggested by the data cited above:

1. There is more upward and less downward mobility in large cities than in small towns.

2. The larger the community in which the son of a worker grew up, the better his chances for upward mobility, a relationship that does not hold for the sons of nonmanual fathers.

3. The positive effect of being reared in a large city on occupational opportunities is found among those with less than a high school education. Among those who have a high school education or better, size of community of orientation is not positively related to greater opportunity.

COMPARATIVE DATA

Earlier, in chapter ii, the analysis of mobility rates in different countries suggested that the same structural factors were at work in all industrial societies. The increase in the tertiary sector of the economy and the bureaucratization of industry contribute to an increasing proportion of nonmanual and higher-paid workers in the labor force. This proportionate increase has largely been at the expense of the agricultural sector of the economy. Different class fertility rates also serve to open positions for upward mobility.

Since the pattern of disproportionate growth of urban areas and of the concentration of bureaucratic enterprise in large cities is an international phenomenon, we should expect to find that the rates of upward social mobility are higher in the large cities of any industrial country, and this hypothesis is validated by data available from a few. A study which presents materials somewhat comparable to those from Oakland is one of social mobility in Stockholm, Sweden.[13]

---

[13] G. Boalt, "Social Mobility in Stockholm: A Pilot Investigation," in *Transactions of the Second World Congress of Sociology*, Vol. II (London: International Sociological Association, 1954), pp. 67–73.

The author of the Stockholm study (Boalt) followed up the careers of every man who had been in the fourth-form class in the Stockholm public schools in 1936. In 1949, there were 2,286 of these men, 94 per cent of the class, still living in Stockholm, and it was possible to secure information concerning their current occupations from the electoral register. In the course of an earlier study, information had been obtained concerning the occupations of the fathers of this class. Grouping the reported occupations of the fathers and sons into three socioeconomic classes, the lowest of which, Class III, was primarily composed of manual workers, the study found that the majority (55 per cent) of the former Stockholm schoolboys whose fathers were manual workers had moved up to Class II, the lower middle class, with a small minority in Class I, the upper middle class. Only a comparatively small minority (13 per cent) of those whose fathers were in the upper two classes (nonmanual) had become manual workers.

The problem which was naturally raised by these data was that of explaining where the present working class of the Swedish metropolis came from, if the majority of the sons of manual workers in Stockholm moved out of that class. Fortunately this question could be partly answered empirically by examining the Stockholm electoral register, which gives both the occupations and ages of all adults in the city. Boalt therefore classified the occupations of all men born in 1925, which was the birth year of the men who had been in the fourth grade in 1936, and thus was able to compare the occupations of all Stockholm *natives* who had been in the fourth grade in 1936, with those of *migrants* of the same age who had come to Stockholm after 1936. The results are presented in figure 8.1.

It is clear that in Stockholm, as in the San Francisco Bay Area, the majority of the manual working class is recruited from smaller urban communities and rural areas. Boalt sums up his findings as follows: "If we assume that our figures show a traditional pattern, then social mobility in Stockholm seems to display the following trend: that mostly workers immigrate into the city. Only some of them give their sons higher education, but nevertheless the majority of the latter advance to social class II (lower middle class)."[14]

---

[14] *Ibid.*, p. 72.

One of the earliest German mobility studies also reported comparable data. Otto Ammon states: "In the city of Karlsruhe, I was able to calculate that approximately 82 per cent of the migrants belong to the lower class, as contrasted with only 41 per cent of the sons of migrants, and 40 per cent of the grandsons of migrants. Only 14 per cent of the migrants are in the middle class as compared with 40 per cent of the sons of migrants and 35 per cent

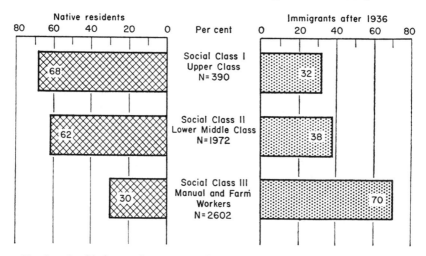

Fig. 8.1. Stockholm residents in specified social classes, by community of origin. *Source.*—Adapted and computed from G. Boalt, "Social Mobility in Stockholm . . . ," p. 72.

of their grandsons. Among the learned professions (*Studierten*), only four per cent were migrants, 10 per cent were sons of migrants, while 25 per cent were grandsons of migrants."[15]

A similar process is hinted at by a summary report of a study of recruitment to the Philips works at Eindhoven in the Netherlands.[16]

---

[15] O. Ammon, *Die Gesellschaftsordnung und ihre natürlichen Grundlagen* (Jena: Verlag Gustav Fischer, 1895), p. 145. The text does not indicate how these data were compiled, or whether Ammon is discussing three contemporaneous generations, or the sons and grandsons of the same individuals. It is clear, however, that Ammon also saw a cycle in which migrants came to the city from smaller communities and rural areas, and took the lowest-level jobs while the sons and grandsons of earlier migrants, native to the city, moved up in the occupational structure.

[16] Ida E. van Hulten, "Summary of a Study of Social Stratification and Social Mobility at the Philips Works, Eindhoven (Netherlands)," in *Transactions of the Second World Congress of Sociology*, Vol. II, p. 87.

THE PATTERNS OF OPPORTUNITY IN LARGE CITIES

The cycle in which lower-class immigrants or migrants into large cities take over the lower-status positions while native urbanites from similar class backgrounds move up in the occupational structure has been one of the more important processes underlying social mobility ever since cities began to expand rapidly. It is this cycle which gives to cities their characteristic aspect of great mobility and ever-present change. Persons born and raised in cities seldom move to small towns or the country—although they often move to other cities—and consequently, if they are socially mobile, they are mobile in a city. On the other hand, persons from rural areas and small towns who rise above their parents' status are most likely to do so in a large city—while their less mobile neighbors remain in the small communities.[17] Thus, more mobility takes place in the cities than in the country or small towns.[18] But this conclusion still leaves unexplained the

[17] It may, indeed, be suggested that the more ambitious small-town lower-class youth leaves his home community for greener pastures in large cities. Oscar Handlin has pointed out that one such small community, Newburyport (Yankee City), although not increasing its population over the past hundred years, has nevertheless always had a large immigration of foreign-born. This indicates that many natives must leave the city for other areas, although the children of the more privileged families remain. See O. Handlin, review of W. L. Warner, *et al.*, "The Social Life of a Modern Community," *New England Quarterly*, 15 (1942): 550. This hypothesis was in part validated by Scudder and Anderson, who compared the patterns of social mobility of "migrant" sons and those who remained at home in a small Kentucky community. They found that "sons who migrate out of small or moderate-sized communities are more likely to rise above their parents' occupational status than sons who remain in the home town." Richard Scudder and C. Arnold Anderson, "Migration and Vertical Occupational Mobility," *American Sociological Review*, 19(1954):329–334. A similar point is made in Harry Beilin and Kay V. Bergin, "The Social Mobility of a Limited Urban Group and Some Implications for Counseling," *Personnel and Guidance Journal*, 34 (1956): 551.

[18] The hypotheses of this chapter may seem to be challenged by the data given in chapter ii on the mobility of the farm population which migrates to the cities. In all countries except the United States for which comparable sample data were available (see table 2.1), the sons of farmers engaged in nonfarm occupations had a better chance of obtaining nonmanual positions than did the sons of manual workers. Several hypotheses may serve to explain these data: (1) The sons of farmers come from families of various socioeconomic levels; their occupational classification is not as closely correlated with socioeconomic status as is the occupational classification of the urban population. Consequently some of the sons of farmers who hold nonfarm positions come from high-status rural families. (2) The sons of farmers in nonfarm occupations are necessarily mobile geographically. As has been pointed out, there is a relatively strong relation between various types of mobility, those more geographically mobile being more mobile in number of jobs

factors which facilitate the upward social mobility of lower-class native urbanites. Although little research has been done which bears directly on this problem, it is possible to suggest a number of factors which seem significant.

1. The greater social mobility in large urban centers is inherent in the simple fact that metropolitan areas are characterized by a greater degree of specialization and a more complex division of labor than smaller communities. The economies that flow from specialization of function are able to take effect primarily in metropolitan centers, so that increased size of community is related to the existence of a greater variety of positions. This means that there is a greater likelihood, on a chance or random basis alone, that people in large cities will move occupationally than there is that small community dwellers will do so.

2. In addition to greater specialization and a wider variety of positions in large cities, there is clear evidence that the larger the city, the greater the number of nonmanual positions in the labor force. This fact may be seen from the census data in figure 8.2. The larger the city, therefore, the greater the opportunity to move into a nonmanual position.

3. Since the beginning of the great trends toward urbanization and industrialization in the nineteenth century, cities have had tremendous population and economic growth: they have far *more* than matched the growth of the countries in which they are

---

held and number of occupations. To some extent, we are comparing this mobile category of farmers' sons with all manual workers, including those who stayed in small communities, which have a low concentration of opportunities. (3) Those countries in which the urban sons of farmers have the least advantage, namely the United States, Sweden, and Russia, are also those which have the highest rate of movement off the farm into urban occupations. On the other hand, Switzerland and France, where urban sons of farmers have a definite advantage over urban sons of manual workers, have a much higher proportion of farmers' sons who remain in farming. This suggests that where the rate of rural-urban migration is slower, it is more selective, and that a greater proportion of the sons of high-status farmers move to the city than do the sons of poorer farmers. In the United States and Sweden, on the other hand, almost two-thirds of the sons of farmers are engaged in urban occupations, which means that migration cannot be highly selective. The samples that come from Germany give results which contradict each other. (4) In countries which do not have free public education, the class differences in education may be so great as to cancel out the geographical variation so important in the United States and Sweden. In other words, in the United States, the son of a manual worker in an urban area may get a better education than even a moderately well-to-do farmer's son. This may not be true where there are less "democratic" systems of education.

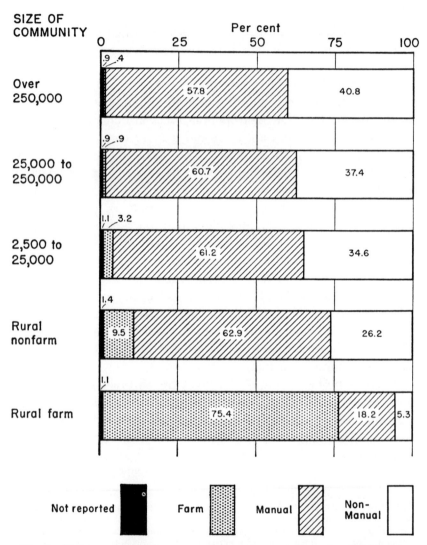

Fig. 8.2. Relation of size of city to occupational composition of male labor force in two national surveys of the United States population. *Source.*—Urban: Computed from U. S. Department of Commerce, Bureau of the Census, *1950 Census of Population*, Series P-E, No. 5A "Characteristics by Size of Place," table 5. Rural: *1950 Census of Population*, Vol. II, Part I, "Characteristics of the population, U. S. Summary," table 53.

found.[19] This pattern of urban growth necessarily means there are more new (and higher level) positions to be filled in metropolitan centers than in smaller and demographically stable communities. In a small city like Newburyport (Yankee City), which has not increased in population for a century, the chances for a lower-class individual to rise must necessarily be less than in a large city in which new positions of higher status are constantly being created.

4. In spite of their rapid rate of growth, large cities have a lower birth rate than smaller communities and rural areas. Except for a brief period after World War II, cities over 100,000 did not reproduce their population. Thus, migration to metropolitan areas not only accounts for the expansion of urban population, but also fills in the gap created by low birth rates. Since it is also true that within urban society, the wealthier and higher-status socio-economic strata have the lowest reproduction rates, it is clear that variations in fertility rates help account for the maximization of social mobility in the city.

THE ADVANTAGES OF NATIVE URBANITES

The processes cited above clearly indicate why metropolitan areas have a higher rate of social mobility than smaller communities. They do not, however, suggest why native lower-class urbanites should be more successful than low-status migrants from smaller communities and rural areas. A few hypotheses may be suggested.

As was indicated earlier, lower-class individuals growing up in a large city are likely to secure more education than their counterparts in smaller communities.[20] Almost every major city in the

---

[19] Between 1870 and 1950, the proportion of the population living in cities over 100,000 jumped from 11 per cent to 30 per cent in the United States, from 5 per cent to 27 per cent in Germany, from 26 per cent to 38 per cent in Great Britain, and from 9 per cent to 17 per cent (1946) in France.

[20] Indeed this differential shows up at a very early stage in schooling. C. Arnold Anderson reports the following percentages of white 17-year-old boys completing 8 years or less of schooling in the United States in 1940:

Region	Large cities	Rural nonfarm
North	15.2	24.5
South	23.4	42.9
West	6.9	22.9

Western world has one or more universities, and natives of such communities can attend college or university while living at home. In addition, the simple fact that a child lives in a community which has a college or university within it should mean that he will be more aware of the possibilities and advantages of attending an institution of higher learning than will one who grows up some distance from a college. Metropolitan lower-class youth also benefit from the fact that the teaching staffs in their high schools are usually better paid and trained than those in smaller communities, and hence are likely to give their students greater incentive to attend college.[21] Evidence that these assumptions are valid is contained in the Survey Research Center data, which show that 18 per cent of the sons of manual workers reared in big cities have some college education, compared with 12.5 per cent for those who grew up in small towns.

As well as having a better opportunity to obtain higher education, urban working-class youth are more likely to be acquainted with the occupational possibilities which exist in such communi-

---

In other words, from a quarter to a half of residents of villages failed to enter high school, while except in the South at least five-sixths of the residents of large cities entered high school. In the West, about 15 out of every 16 boys in large cities entered high school.

According to a national survey in France, the larger the community, the smaller the proportion of children who leave school before the end of the official compulsory education period. And after this period, the larger the community, the more likely children are to continue in higher studies and the less likely to go to work. Alain Girard, "Enquête national sur l'orientation et la sélection des enfants d'âge scolaire," *Population*, 9(1954):607–621.

[21] See R. Clyde White, *These Will Go to College* (Cleveland: Press of Western Reserve University, 1952), p. 50. He reports that in Cleveland lower-class students were more likely to attend local institutions; upper-class students to attend schools out of town. This is an implicit demonstration of the importance of the location of a college near by. Urban residents consistently score higher on intelligence tests than do rural residents. See the summary of a large number of studies in P. Sorokin, *et al.*, *A Systematic Source Book in Rural Sociology*, pp. 266–281; Charles P. Loomis and J. Allan Beegle, *Rural Social Systems* (New York: Prentice-Hall, 1950), pp. 352–353; and C. T. Philblad and C. L. Gregory, "Selective Aspects of Migration among Missouri High School Graduates," *American Sociological Review*, 19 (1954): 314–324; this difference is probably an effect of the poorer education received in rural areas. Indirect evidence of this is the rise of the intelligence scores of Southern Negroes after they had resided in New York for some time, as reported in Otto Klineberg, *Negro Intelligence and Selective Migration* (New York: Columbia University Press, 1935), and the fact reported in William H. Sewell and B. L. Ellenbogen, "Social Status and the Measured Intelligence of Small City and Rural Children," *American Sociological Review*, 17 (1952): 615, that if one controls for the education of parents, in all comparisons the children of the more rural group have the higher mean intelligence test scores.

ties than those who are raised in a less heterogeneous (occupationally) smaller community.[22] In reanalyzing the occupational choices of school youth in a number of German and Austrian cities, Paul Lazarsfeld reported that "local variations in occupational choice are parallel to differences in the economic structure."[23] Thus, the larger the proportion of persons working in a particular kind of job in a city, the greater the number of 14-year-old school youths who desired to go into that occupation. Lazarsfeld interpreted this finding as follows: "The nature of occupational choice is not determined primarily as an individual decision, but rather is a result of external influences. For the occupational impressions offered by daily life are proportional to the actual occupational distribution. The greater the number of metal workers, the more frequently will young people hear about that occupation, and the greater will they be stimulated to choose it."[24]

Further evidence of the influence of social environment on an individual's perception and awareness of occupational careers is given by recent data from Belgium. Upwardly mobile sons of farmers tend to study agronomy and veterinary medicine; architectural students are likely to be sons of construction workers.[25]

There are no corresponding American studies which attempt to relate the occupational structure of different communities to the frames of reference of school youth in making choices of occupation. Data collected by the National Opinion Research Center in 1947, however, do permit a partial test of the hypothesis that occupational goals are related to the occupational structure of the community. A national sample of youth between the ages of 14 and 20 were asked: "Exactly what occupation do you plan to

[22] See Leo F. Schnore and David W. Varley, "Some Concomitants of Metropolitan Size," *American Sociological Review*, 20 (1955): 408–414. They show that larger metropolitan areas are both more heterogeneous economically and rank higher on a number of status variables such as median family income, median school years completed, proportion of the labor force in professional occupations, and median gross rental. The importance of childhood residence in the mobility process is confirmed by research in Belgian villages which found that the chief factors determining whether lower-strata youth would be oriented toward intellectual rather than manual pursuits were degree of urbanization, nearness to educational centers, and class heterogeneity. P. Minon, "Choix d'une profession et mobilité sociale," in *Transactions of the Second World Congress of Sociology*, p. 211.

[23] P. F. Lazarsfeld, *Jugend und Beruf*, Vol. 8 of *Quellen und Studien zur Jugendkunde* (Jena: G. Fischer, 1931), p. 13.

[24] *Loc. cit.*

[25] Minon, "Choix d'une profession . . . ," p. 210.

go into?" By comparing the occupational choices of youth living in large cities with those of adolescents living in smaller communities, we can test the hypothesis that the more varied and bureaucratic occupational structure of large cities will result in higher aspirations among its youth, as compared with those in smaller communities (see table 8.8). The data of the NORC study

TABLE 8.8

PERCENTAGE DISTRIBUTION OF JOB ASPIRATIONS OF RESPONDENTS WHOSE FATHERS
ARE IN MANUAL OR NONMANUAL OCCUPATIONS, BY SIZE OF COMMUNITY

Occupational group of job aspiration	Occupational division of father and community size			
	Nonmanual		Manual	
	Communities over 500,000	Communities under 500,000	Communities over 500,000	Communities under 500,000
Professional.................	72	74	55	31
Proprietor or executive.......	14	4	11	7
White collar or sales..........	10	14	20	25
Manual work................	3	7	15	34
Farm......................	..	..	..	2
Number of respondents.......	69	69	47	67

SOURCE: The data in the above table are derived from a study of the National Opinion Research Center. As a part of a study of social mobility and the prestige of occupations, a national random sample of youth between the ages 14 and 20 were interviewed in 1947. Only those youths not in the labor force when interviewed are reported in the above table. The authors would like to express their thanks to Clyde Hart and Albert Reiss, Jr., for permission to use this table. A detailed analysis of the aspiration level of adolescents will appear in a forthcoming publication by Reiss.

suggest that relative size of community is much more influential in affecting the occupational aspirations of the *children of manual workers* than those of children of men in nonmanual occupations. This finding, of course, is compatible with the assumption that aspirations are related to perceived opportunity. Middle-class youth, even those living in smaller communities, will receive the stimulus to obtain a high-status occupation from their families and from other aspects of their environment which are related to middle-class status. It is among the working-class youth that size of community makes a major difference. Those living in smaller communities will not be as stimulated by their environment to aspire to higher goals. Opportunity within the occupational structure is, in fact, more limited than it is in the large city, for there are fewer bureaucratic or professional jobs in these communities than in metropolitan centers; and consequently the frame of reference of such small-community working-class youth is different.

Because these youths derive lower levels of aspiration from their immediate class and community environment than do lower-class city youths, they will probably be less likely to try to obtain the education or skills which will permit them to be successfully upward mobile. These lower goals, plus the greater difficulty in securing training, mean that a lower-class youth not raised in a metropolitan center enters the labor market with greater handicaps than his big-city cousin. And, in the labor market of the metropolitan centers, we find that working-class youth who are native urbanites are, in fact, more successful than migrants with similar class backgrounds.[26]

A recent study of California suburbanites does suggest that the advantage that the sons of urban workers have may occur among adults on the white-collar occupational level. Stephen Boggs found that white-collar workers of metropolitan origin had higher levels of aspiration for further occupational advance than those of nonmetropolitan origin. He postulates that men who grow up in cities have more experience in successful adjustment to the types of changes required for upward occupational mobility: changes in the job and its social relations, in primary group relations, and in residence. "Men from nonmetropolitan communities may lack such experience or have found it more disturbing."[27]

The finding of the NORC study that there is relatively little difference in the level of aspiration of *middle-class youth* living

---

[26] The fact that urban origins are conducive to upward social mobility may help account for a phenomenon that has long puzzled students in this field: the success of the Jews in moving out of lower-class occupations. As compared with any other *visible* social group, the Jews are the urbanites *par excellence*. The mobility patterns of the Jews, therefore, may in some part be a consequence of the fact that they have been urban dwellers, both in Europe and America. However, perceptive analyses of Jewish mobility stress other factors that are probably even more important: historical-cultural traditions of the group with their emphases on learning, education, and middle-class achievement values. See the articles in Marshall Sklare, ed., *The Jews, Social Patterns of an American Group* (Glencoe: The Free Press, 1958) esp. Nathan Glazer, "The American Jew and the Attainment of Middle-Class Rank: Some Trends and Explanations," pp. 138–146; Fred L. Strodtbeck, "Family Interaction, Values, and Achievement," pp. 147–165; and S. Joseph Fauman, "Occupational Selection among Detroit Jews," pp. 119–137. These are discussed further in chapter ix.

[27] Stephen T. Boggs, "Family Size and Social Mobility in a California Suburb," *Eugenics Quarterly*, 4 (1957): 208–213.

in larger or smaller communities is comparable to the findings reported earlier from the Survey Research Center study, which indicated that being brought up in a large city was not a mobility asset for those whose fathers were in nonmanual occupations. These findings indicate, as was suggested above, that middle-class youth reared in small communities are motivated to retain their social position. It may even be posited that the lower rate of downward social mobility among them, suggested by the Survey Research Center data, reflects the fact that the status structure of smaller communities is more rigid and visible than that of larger cities. In a study which compares the intercorrelations of the status indicators which make up W. L. Warner's "Index of Status Characteristics" in a large city with their inter-correlations in a small one there is some empirical evidence for this. The authors found that the correlations among variables related to social-class position were much lower in the city of Minneapolis than in the small city of Jonesville.[28] The more fluid status structure of large cities indicated by this study should mean that being in a nonmanual occupation, or possessing some other single attribute of higher status, will be less likely to mean that a given individual actually is part of a higher social class. Hence, it may be suggested that the sons of persons in nonmanual positions in smaller communities will be more likely to be exposed to more imperatives for middle-class behavior and motivation than will the sons of fathers in comparable occupations in larger cities. One bit of evidence that this is so may be found in the fact that sons of nonmanual parents who grew up in small towns are better educated than their class compeers reared in big cities. The Survey Research Center data indicate that 32 per cent of those from small towns completed college, as compared with 19 per cent of those who grew up in big cities, a fact which goes far to account for the lower rate of downward mobility among the sons of nonmanual workers who are reared in smaller communities.

Another factor which may help explain the greater motivation of the sons of nonmanual workers from small towns to retain their

[28] Godfrey Hochbaum, *et al.*, "Socio-Economic Variables in a Large City," *American Journal of Sociology*, 61 (1955): 31–38.

class status, and their apparent success in doing so, is the smaller absolute size of the middle class in smaller communities. The smaller the community, the greater the possibility that as a *social* class it will include all those who have some claim to middle-class status. This is particularly true for children who are members of age-sex groupings in the one high school of a small city. The number of middle-class children is small enough so that a tight peer-group control along class lines is possible. For example, if the 106 cliques found by Hollingshead in the "Elmtown" high school were equally distributed among the four age groups or school grades, two sex groups, and five "social class" groups that he used in his analysis of the stratification system, there would be an average of two and one-half cliques in each subclass.[29] Not many school youth could escape being involved in such a close network, and hence being directly under primary-group controls within their social class. In a large city, on the other hand, many middle-class youth can and do escape the confines of continuous participation in social-class-linked primary groups.

The implication of these analyses of the situation of middle-class youth is that the motivational advantages and objective opportunities of those who grow up in a large city are counter-balanced by the motivational pressures induced by the rigidities of the status system of smaller communities. On the other hand, among working-class youth, the rigidities of small-town structures will probably operate to reinforce the liabilities flowing from the working-class status of their families.

CONCLUSIONS

This chapter has focused primarily on the ways in which the relative size of the community of orientation affect an individual's training, opportunity, perception of the occupational structure, and aspiration, thus increasing or decreasing his chance to obtain a good position in the occupational structure. It should be recognized, however, that variation in the size of community of orienta-

---

[29] A. Hollingshead, *Elmtown's Youth* (New York: Wiley, 1949), pp. 204–242. A detailed analysis of the relation between cliques and educational motivation in "Elmtown" is R. Havighurst and R. Rodgers, "The Role of Motivation in Attendance at Post-High-School Educational Institutions," *in* Byron S. Hollinshead, *Who Should Go to College?* (New York: Columbia University Press, 1952), pp. 135–165.

tion is only a single example of the variables which determine the horizons and opportunities of individuals. The sociological and psychological mechanisms involved are little different from those set by socioeconomic origin, family patterns, education, or ethnic background. When documenting the effect of each variable on a given behavior pattern, the sociologist is calling attention to the way in which an individual's potential behavior is limited by, or responsive to, factors derivative from his location in society.

In the following chapter, we present the results of another approach to distinguishing factors conducive to mobility: that which focuses on individual differences, particularly in motivation and intelligence.

Chapter IX | *Intelligence*
and Motivation

In the preceding chapter we have demonstrated how structural analysis may help account for varying propensities for mobility. In this chapter, however, we shall deal with those basically psychological approaches which stress the effect of variations in ability and achievement motivation. Often unable to find structural determinants of deviation from group norms, many students of social mobility have dismissed or ignored the latter type of research, which, because it deals with individual differences, is presumed to be outside their legitimate sphere of interest.

THE ROLE OF INTELLIGENCE

Intelligence, as measured by various pen-and-paper intelligence-quotient examinations, has relevance for social mobility because, as we have seen, educational achievement is the main source of occupational achievement in a bureaucratized industrial society. The subculture of the school is almost everywhere defined largely in intellectual terms. High status within a school's social system is given to those who are best in their school work (although non-intellectual factors such as athletic prowess and social-class background also affect status within schools). It may be expected that educational achievement will vary with intelligence, and that continuation in the educational system will depend, therefore, upon "above average" intelligence, especially when the student has a low-status background. However, students with middle- or upper-class backgrounds frequently continue in school despite their lack of scholastic aptitude.

It has proved exceedingly difficult to go much beyond this general conclusion, because the part played by "native ability" cannot be readily differentiated from that played by various environmental factors.[1] For example, educational achievement not only depends upon intelligence and the financial resources of the family, but also upon a strong motivation to succeed in the school

TABLE 9.1

PERCENTAGE OF BOYS WHO EXPECTED TO GO TO COLLEGE,
BY I.Q. AND FATHER'S OCCUPATION

(3,348 second- and third-year male students in Boston area high schools: 1950)

Father's occupation	I.Q. Quintile					
	I (Low)	2	3	4	5 (High)	All quintiles
Major white collar...........	56	72	79	82	89	80
Middle white collar..........	28	36	47	53	76	52
Minor white collar...........	12	20	22	29	55	26
Skilled labor and service......	4	15	19	22	40	19
Other labor and service......	9	6	10	14	29	12
All occupations..............	11	17	24	30	52	27

SOURCE: Joseph A. Kahl, "Educational and Occupational Aspirations of 'Common Man' Boys," *Harvard Educational Review*, 23 (1953):188.

system. Students who come from well-to-do families will identify quite closely with the prevailing values of the school culture, partly because of parental urging and partly because parents, students, and teachers share the same middle-class values, and such sharing facilitates teacher-student communication. Students who come from lower-class families do not possess this cultural advantage and the question is, therefore, how they may overcome this handicap, provided that they have high intelligence. On a hypothetical basis this complicated relationship among intelligence, motivation, and social mobility may be formulated as follows:

[1] For example, intelligence tests which purport to measure *ability* for educational achievement cannot be constructed in the absence of an adequate theory connecting intelligence with inherited, and hence nonenvironmental, characteristics. Studies of intelligence tests reveal the influence of social bias. Allison Davis reports that by changing the vocabulary of test questions while retaining the logical operations which the question is supposed to test, the class differential in performance could be markedly reduced. See his "Education for the Conservation of Human Resources," *Progressive Education*, 27(1950):221–224.

1. High intelligence will tend to increase the capacity of lower-status children to recognize the norms held by the high-status groups and the teachers in the school, and such capacity frequently goes together with an interest in adopting these norms.

2. Parental urging will help lower-status children of high intelligence to identify with the goals of educational and occupational achievement as well as with the groups which represent these goals in the school. Such identification may also lead these

TABLE 9.2

CLEVELAND STUDENTS WHO INTENDED TO GO TO COLLEGE WHO ACTUALLY ENROLLED,
BY SOCIAL CLASS AND I.Q.

	I.Q.							
Parental social class	Under 101		101–115		115+		All	
	Per cent	Number	Per cent	Number	Per cent	Number	Per cent	Number
Upper and upper middle.	83	35	79	62	89	99	85	196
Lower middle..........	61	23	50	56	63	64	57	143
Upper lower and lower lower..............	37	46	57	67	47	76	48	189
All classes.............	58	104	62	185	69	239	63	528

SOURCE: Computed from R. C. White, *These Will Go to College* (Cleveland: Western Reserve University Press, 1952), p. 45. Classes are based on W. L. Warner's Index of Status Characteristics.

children to adopt those nonintellectual aspects of a middle-class way of life that the children of middle-class families acquire as part of their upbringing.[2]

3. The students from lower-class families who, for whatever reason, are not accepted by the status group composed of their class peers will seek to identify themselves with the school culture.[3]

As long as intelligence tests do not clearly differentiate between

[2] See Joseph A. Kahl, "Educational and Occupational Aspirations of 'Common Man' Boys," *Harvard Educational Review*, 23 (1953): 186–203.

[3] This may help explain Durkheim's interesting observation that the smaller the proportion of a religious group in the population of an area, the greater the educational attainment of its members. Presumably, by being excluded from normal peer-group identification to a greater degree when they are in a small minority, the members of a minority religious group will welcome the opportunities to identify with the "universalistic-achievement" criteria of the school system more than a majority group. See E. Durkheim, *Suicide* (Glencoe: The Free Press, 1951), pp. 167–168. The same phenomenon has been observed in another context by W. F. Whyte in reporting that the "college boys" living in an Italian slum tend to be unpopular among their peers in the neighborhood. One does not know from Whyte's

native ability and environmentally induced aptitude, it is clearly impossible to test such hypotheses in a conclusive manner. Yet it is possible to show the general character of the interrelationship between parental social class, intelligence, and orientation towards educational achievement. Boston high school students were asked to indicate whether or not they expected to go to college, and their answers to this question were then related to their fathers' occupations and their own I.Q.'s. The results of this study are presented in table 9.1. These data suggest that, although intelligence is important, parental social status provides more motivation for high school students to attend a university.[4] Most sons of high-status families declare their intention to go to college, and thus appear motivated—even those whose intelligence is quite low. On the other hand, only 29 per cent of the sons of unskilled and semi-skilled workers and 40 per cent of skilled workers' sons who ranked in the highest fifth on the intelligence test were planning to go to college. It is rather among those whose fathers are in the middle range of the class structure that intelligence appears to be particularly important as a factor affecting the intention of going to college.

But intention is one thing, action another. When one compares

data which came first, the college orientation or the peer-group rejection. See W. F. Whyte, *Street Corner Society* (University of Chicago Press, 1943), pp. 52–93.

On the other hand, a study of high school boys of low status found that those youths who were upward mobile in terms of plans to attend college received emotional support for this move from peer groups of similarly oriented pupils. And we can assume that many of Whyte's "college boys," though rejected by the "corner boys," mutually supported each other as a peer group. See Harry Beilin, "The Pattern of Postponability and its Relation to Social Class Mobility," *The Journal of Social Psychology*, 44(1956):33–48.

[4] Another study of the problem is William H. Sewell, *et al.*, "Social Status and Educational and Occupational Aspiration," *American Sociological Review*, 22 (1957): 67–73. They found that in Wisconsin, the educational aspirations of high school seniors whose fathers' occupations were in the lower three quintiles in occupational prestige were about the same, while the top two quintiles were more highly motivated. On the other hand, both educational aspirations and aspirations for professional positions were directly and strongly related to intelligence quotients. The considerable difference between Sewell's and Kahl's results may be due to the fact that the Wisconsin study tested high school seniors, so that many with low aspirations may have been eliminated, while the Kahl study tested students earlier in high school. C. T. Philblad and C. L. Gregory, "Occupational Selection and Intelligence in Rural Communities and Small Towns in Missouri," *American Sociological Review*, 21 (1956): 63–71, give data on both the relationship between I.Q. and present job, and I.Q. and father's occupation; but they have not yet analyzed the direct relationship between I.Q. and social mobility.

parental background, motivation, and I.Q., with the actual enrollment in college, it appears that intelligence does not necessarily determine who, among those motivated to do so, will actually go to college. Data from a study of the Cleveland area indicate that parental social class is much more significant than I.Q., although the latter seems to have some slight significance (table 9.2). However, after adolescents get into college their educational achievement does not seem to be affected by their family background. The records of different colleges show, according to the Commission on Human Resources and Advanced Training, that, "after students get to college . . . the influence of socioeconomic differences disappears almost entirely. When college entrants are classified by the occupations of their fathers the percentages getting degrees are fairly constant . . . unless [the father] be a farmer."[5]

In contemporary Britain, where a great emphasis is placed on intelligence-testing, I.Q. is a prime determinant of educational achievement, and presumably of consequent social mobility. At age 10 or 11, all students in state schools are divided into two groups: one, those who are admitted to "grammar school," which prepares students for higher-status occupations and continuation in the school system as far as the university, and the other, those who will continue in schools designed to prepare them for lesser pursuits. A recent study of admission to these various schools reports that admission to the grammar schools is so highly correlated with I.Q. that, when intelligence of students is held constant, there is no difference in the proportion admitted from the different social classes.[6] That is, the intelligent child from a middle-class family has the same opportunity of continuing on in grammar school as an equally intelligent working-class youth. Similar findings were reported in an earlier study, which indicated "very little overlap"

---

[5] Dael Wolfe, *America's Resources of Specialized Talent* (New York: Harper's, 1954), pp. 160–161.

[6] Jean Floud, *et al.*, *Social Class and Educational Opportunity* (London: Heinemann, 1956), pp. 42–61. T. H. Marshall has described in somewhat greater detail how the English educational system attempts to eliminate social class discrimination by segregating pupils on the basis of performance in intelligence tests: "Equality of opportunity is offered to all children entering the primary schools, but at an early age they are usually divided into three streams—the best, the average and the backward. Already opportunity is becoming unequal, and the children's range of chances limited. About the age of eleven they are tested again, probably by a team of teachers, examiners and psychologists. None of these is infallible, but perhaps

in intelligence level between grammar and other schools.[7] There were few students not in grammar schools who were intelligent enough to qualify for it.

This is not to suggest that the classes have equal representation in English higher education. In fact sons of manual workers accounted for only 26 per cent of English males admitted to universities in 1955–56 although manual workers made up 72 per cent of the population at large.[8] This discrepancy can be accounted for only in part by the fact that both intelligence and achievement aspirations are differentially distributed among the social strata.

Though much of our discussion is necessarily tentative and although the data come from a variety of studies dealing with different populations, the evidence available suggests a number of hypotheses concerning the interrelationships among social origins, intelligence, and educational achievement in America:

1. To the extent that the school system constitutes a distinctive subculture, intelligence will be strongly correlated with motivation for educational achievement; the actual decision to go to col-

---

sometimes three wrongs may make a right. Classification follows for distribution into the three types of secondary school. Opportunity becomes still more unequal, and the chance of further education has already been limited to a select few. Some of these, after being tested again, will go on to receive it. In the end the jumble of mixed seed originally put into the machine emerges in neatly labelled packets ready to be sown in the appropriate gardens."

"I have deliberately couched this description in the language of cynicism in order to bring out the point that, however genuine may be the desire of the educational authorities to offer enough variety to satisfy all individual needs, they must, in a mass service of this kind, proceed by repeated classification into groups, and this is followed at each stage by assimilation within each group and differentiation between groups. That is precisely the way in which social classes in a fluid society have always taken shape. Differences within each class are ignored as irrelevant; differences between classes are given exaggerated significance. Thus qualities which are in reality strung out along a continuous scale are made to create a hierarchy of groups, each with its special character and status. The main features of the system are inevitable, and its advantages, in particular the elimination of inherited privilege, far outweigh its incidental defects. The latter can be attacked and kept within bounds by giving as much opportunity as possible for second thoughts about classification, both in the educational system itself and in afterlife." T. H. Marshall, *Citizenship and Social Class* (Cambridge: Cambridge University Press, 1950), pp. 66–67.

[7] H. T. Himmelweit, A. H. Halsey, and A. N. Oppenheim, "The View of Adolescents on Some Aspects of the Social Class Structure," *British Journal of Sociology*, 3 (1952): 149 n.

[8] R. K. Kelsall, *Report on an Inquiry into Applications for Admission to Universities* (London: Association of Universities of the British Commonwealth, 1957), p. 9.

lege, however, is made outside of the school system, and hence class position seems to be the most significant determinant of this decision.

2. Since, in American high schools, educational achievement is mixed inextricably with noneducational values and structures, and since in the colleges and universities it is more isolated from such values, it is to be expected that intelligence rather than class origins will be most important in college, and that the reverse should be true in high school.

TABLE 9.3

RELATIONSHIP BETWEEN I.Q. AND SOCIAL MOBILITY AMONG
STOCKHOLM MEN AGED 24 IN 1949
(Percentages)

Son's occupation	Father's social class and son's I.Q.								
	Upper-class father			Middle-class father			Lower-class father		
	Under 105	105–118	119+	Under 105	105–118	119+	Under 105	105–118	119+
Upper..............	6	17	68	2	4	35	..	1	10
Middle.............	89	79	31	55	76	59	37	55	70
Lower..............	6	3	1	43	21	6	63	44	20
Number of respond- ents..............	18	70	164	112	222	288	395	445	183

SOURCE: Computed from data in G. Boalt, "Social Mobility in Stockholm . . ."

These conclusions are of interest in the present context because educational achievement (and the factors associated with it) may be taken as an indirect index of social mobility. Ideally, it would be desirable to relate intelligence and social mobility directly, and to do so on the basis of tests which isolate native ability. So far, no studies known to us meet these requirements; but three recent studies—in the United States, Sweden, and Scotland—do show that discrepancies between the I.Q.'s of the individuals and the social status of their fathers (i.e., high I.Q. related to low status or vice versa) account for a considerable amount of social mobility.

The American study attempted to estimate the proportion of social mobility in the United States that is a result of the fact that some children are born into families on an occupational level for which their intelligence is either "too high" or "too low." The authors took the data on "the relations between occupation and intelligence of one generation . . . from the Harrell and Harrell study of an army sample [and] the mobility data from Centers' study of father-son pairs."[9] They compared the actual mobility reported by Centers with a model of equal opportunity that was constructed by assuming that "an 'ideal' association between intelligence and occupational status was to be attained in the generation of sons. The proportion of actual mobility that may be imputed to disparities between the intelligence of the sons and the occupational status of their fathers was estimated to be 40 per cent."[10] The conclusions of this study are necessarily tentative because the authors were forced to work with inferential data and had no direct evidence bearing on the relationship between inter-generational mobility and I.Q.

Another study of this problem was made in Sweden by Gunnar Boalt. In it the social mobility of all Stockholm men, aged 24 in 1949, who had grown up in Stockholm, was related to their I.Q.'s. Boalt found that among those of working-class origin with I.Q.'s of 119 or more (approximately the upper third in intelligence), about 80 per cent had moved upward from the social-class position of their fathers. Among those of upper-class parentage (owners of large businesses, professionals, etc.), who were below the upper third (I.Q.'s of 118 or less), only 16 per cent remained in the upper class. Of those with middle-class fathers (artisans, shopkeepers, clerical workers, sea captains, etc.) and low I.Q.'s, 43 per cent had fallen to manual positions.[11] The results of this survey are presented in table 9.3.

Instructive as these data are, they are vitiated in part by the high correlation between I.Q. and educational achievement (.82) and between educational achievement and mobility.[12] Since the intelligence tests were made after the completion of education—in the course of the process of registering for the military draft—and since we know that education itself may result in some im-

[9] C. A. Anderson, J. C. Brown, and M. J. Bowman, "Intelligence and Occupational Mobility," *The Journal of Political Economy*, 40 (1952): 218–239.

[10] *Ibid.*, p. 235.

[11] Gunnar Boalt, "Social Mobility in Stockholm: A Pilot Investigation," in *Transactions of the Second World Congress of Sociology* (London: International Sociological Association, 1954), Vol. II, pp. 67–69.

[12] *Ibid.*, p. 68.

provement of a person's I.Q., the problem of causal imputation is not resolved. Nevertheless, I.Q. tests do measure (even if they do not isolate) native ability, and to this extent Boalt's data give clear-cut evidence for the considerable effect of intelligence on social mobility.

Additional data indicating the relation of intelligence to social mobility is provided by the Aberdeen, Scotland, study of the factors affecting women's change of social class at marriage. A greater proportion of the women who move up the social scale at marriage receive higher intelligence-test scores than those who marry within their class, who, in turn, tend to be more intelligent than those who move down the social scale at marriage. For example, approximately 70 per cent of the daughters of manual workers who marry nonmanual husbands score *above* average on the Wechsler-Bellevue intelligence test. This almost equals the percentage who are above average among the upper strata daughters who remain in the same class at marriage (75 per cent), and far surpasses the percentage among upper-strata daughters who marry down (40 per cent). On the other hand, only about 20 to 25 per cent of the daughters of manual workers who married manual husbands score above average.

The Aberdeen study again underscores the interrelations of high intelligence, educational achievement, and occupational mobility: the highly intelligent daughters of lower-strata fathers had more education than the class average and tended to be working in white-collar occupations at the time of marriage to a nonmanual husband.[13]

The evidence does not permit any definite conclusion about the precise effect of intelligence as a factor in social mobility, largely because of the difficulties in isolating "native intelligence" from the effects of social class and educational environment. There

---

[13] Eileen M. Scott, R. Illsley, and A. M. Thomson, "A Psychological Investigation of Primigravidae. II: Maternal Social Class, Age, Physique and Intelligence," *The Journal of Obstetrics and Gynaecology of the British Empire*, 63 (1956): 340. R. Illsley, "Social Class Selection and Class Differences in Relation to Stillbirth and Infant Deaths," *British Medical Journal*, December 24, 1955, pp. 1520–1524. The latter study also found that lower-strata women who married men with higher status were superior in height, physique, and health and had lower rates of prematurity, stillbirths, and infant deaths than both their nonmobile counterparts and the daughters of upper-strata fathers who fell in social status on marriage.

can be no doubt, however, that the discrepancy between the distribution of intelligence in a given generation of youth and the distribution of social positions in the parental generation is a major dynamic factor affecting mobility in all societies in which educational achievement or other qualities associated with intelligence play an important role in status placement. That is to say, the correlation between high family status and the intelligence level of children, although strong,[14] is still compatible with the fact that a considerable number of lower-class youth have high I.Q.'s. According to Himmelweit, "previous research has shown that, except for the extremes of the occupational ladder, variations in I.Q. *within* occupation groups are generally greater than those *between* the groups. Very large occupational groups like those to which semiskilled and unskilled manual workers belong should, therefore, contain a larger absolute number of individuals of the requisite ability than some of the numerically much smaller middle-class occupational groups, despite the higher average intelligence level to be found among the latter."[15] Whatever the distribution of intelligence by class among the youth of a country may be it remains true that considerable upward and downward mobility will result from the discrepancies involved when children of lower-class parents are high in intelligence, and offspring of middle-class families are low.

DIFFERENTIAL MOTIVATION

Studies of the influence of social background and intelligence on social mobility must deal with two related phenomena: the structure of opportunities to which the individuals are exposed, and their capacity to take advantage of these opportunities. Capacity consists of motivation or drive as much as it consists of intelligence. In a middle-class society the "bohemian" is, among other things, a person who has the intelligence but lacks the motivation to

[14] A comprehensive summary of the literature and bibliography on the relation of intelligence to the variable "socioeconomic status," as well as to the variables "size of family and order of birth," is found in Jean Sutter, "La Valeur de l'intelligence suivant le milieu: état présent des connaissances," *in* Institut National d'études Démographiques, *Le Niveau intellectuel des enfants d'âge scolaire*, No. 13 (Paris: Presses Universitaires de France, 1950), pp. 41–62.

[15] H. T. Himmelweit, "Social Status and Secondary Education Since the 1944 Act: Some Data for London," *in* D. V. Glass, ed., *Social Mobility in Britain* (Routledge and Kegan Paul, 1954), p. 145 (emphasis in original). Similar conclusions have been recently presented in an analysis of a mathematical genetic model of

achieve. We have already called attention to this motivational aspect.

There can be little doubt, for example, that directly urging children to achieve plays a determining role. In the Boston area, among boys from the lower middle class and the skilled working class who had I.Q.'s in the top quintile, urging by the family to get further education for the sake of occupational advancement clearly differentiated those who intended to go to college from those who did not.[16] In England the same relationship was found between parental attitude and the admission of working-class children to grammar (preuniversity) schools, with the reservation that the parents' attitudes make the difference only among those who have real opportunities,[17] that is, live in a good working-class district. (Among those sons of workers who lived in slum areas, it was found that the income level of a working-class family made more difference in gaining admission to grammar school than did parental attitudes.)

One would expect that the higher the education of the parents, the more likely they would be to instill motivation for upward movement in their children. This is confirmed by a number of studies. In the Boston area, approximately 40 per cent of working-class high school pupils with high I.Q.'s whose fathers graduated from high school went on to college, compared to only 25 per cent of those high-I.Q. students whose fathers had less education.[18] In Denmark, if fathers in lower strata have more education than the

---

the distribution of high intelligence. Even when high intelligence is assumed to be completely inherited and of greater frequency in the high social stratum, it will exist in greater absolute numbers in the lower orders. A. H. Halsey, "Genetics, Social Structure and Intelligence," *The British Journal of Sociology*, 9(1958):15–28.

[16] J. A. Kahl, "Educational and Occupational Aspirations . . . ," pp. 186–203. This has also been confirmed by Elizabeth Cohen's study of working-class boys which found that "parents of mobile sons reported more deliberate encouragement of upward mobility through educational channels, starting in the boy's childhood," and that "parents of mobile sons were more likely to have a middle-class occupational aspiration for their sons." However, a surprising finding of this research was that there were no differences between parents of mobile and nonmobile sons in their concern with their children's high school performance. Elizabeth G. Cohen, *Parental Factors in Educational Mobility* (Unpublished Ph.D. dissertation, Harvard University, 1958), pp. 136–137.

[17] Jean E. Floud, *et al.*, *Social Class* . . . , pp. 93–95, 107–108.

[18] Samuel Stouffer, "First Rough Draft of Summary Report on Some Statistics Collected in the Harvard Mobility Study" (Unpublished manuscript, Harvard University, 1958).

class mean, their sons are likely to be upwardly mobile. Similarly, in England, working-class children who reach the grammar school are likely to have parents whose education is higher than the average for their class. A report on Belgian studies states that the cultural level of lower-status families, rather than their material situation, determines the tendency toward upward mobility.[19]

One would expect further that parents who are themselves downward mobile would attempt to compensate by encouraging their children to rise. Elizabeth Cohen confirmed this relationship in her study of 100 working-class high school boys. She matched the boys by I.Q., ethnicity, and school, into two groups of 50 boys who were going to college, and 50 who were not. Of those fathers who had been downward mobile, 64 per cent had sons planning college compared to only 45 per cent of the sons of stationary fathers. Downward mobility of the mother proved to be even more highly associated with a son's mobility potential. Eighty per cent of those sons whose mother had a white-collar family background were going to college, compared to only 42 per cent with mothers of a working-class background. In addition, mothers who held white-collar jobs at the time of the study were much more likely to have a mobile son (74 per cent) than mothers who were employed in factory jobs (38 per cent), or were not employed (48 per cent).[20]

Increased amounts of stimulation for achievement may also result from especially early and long-continued association with adults and their values, rather than with other children.[21] This may help explain the findings that the most successful persons in many

[19] K. Svalastoga, "An Empirical Analysis of Intrasocietary Mobility Determinants" (Working Paper Nine submitted to the Fourth Working Conference on Social Stratification and Social Mobility, International Sociological Association, December, 1957); J. E. Floud, F. M. Martin, and A. H. Halsey, "Educational Opportunity and Social Selection in England," in *Transactions of the Second World Congress of Sociology*, Vol. II, pp. 194–208; Paul Minon, "Choix d'une profession et mobilité sociale," *ibid.*, pp. 209–213.

[20] Elizabeth G. Cohen, *Parental Factors in Educational Mobility*, pp. 67–70.

[21] This does not imply, of course, that the attitudes of peer groups may not in some situations stimulate mobility aspirations. The lower-class youth of "Elmtown" whose sociometric choices showed high educational expectations were much more likely to attend college. R. J. Havighurst and R. R. Rodgers, "The Role of Motivation in Attendance at Post-High-School Educational Institutions," in Byron S. Hollinshead, *Who Should Go to College?* (New York: Columbia University Press, 1952), pp. 135–165.

fields occupied sibling positions which intensified their relations with their parents and weakened those with other children. The more successful among Methodist ministers,[22] top scientists,[23] and a sample of extremely gifted children in New York,[24] were all more likely to be only children, oldest children, or children with longer than average distance between themselves and the next older child, than could be explained by chance.[25] Studies of the determinants of intelligence-test scores consistently show that those from larger families do less well than children from small families.[26] Both the study of scientists and the study of gifted children show that the families of those who become exceptional have kept them isolated from other children,[27] and Robert E. L. Faris found that isolation in childhood was a very common experience of the "geniuses" he studied.[28] Available evidence also indicates that the degree of adult contact may be the most important single factor in linguistic development.[29] One might summarize the implications of these studies for social mobility by saying that all factors which intensify the involvement of a child with his parents or other

---

[22] Phillip J. Allen, "Childhood Backgrounds of Success in a Profession," *American Sociological Review*, 20 (1955): 186–190.

[23] Anne Roe, *The Making of a Scientist* (New York: Dodd-Mead, 1953), pp. 70–74; and Francis Bello, "The Young Scientists," *Fortune*, June, 1954, pp. 142–148 ff.

[24] Paul M. Sheldon, "The Families of Highly Gifted Children," *Marriage and Family Living*, 16(1954):59 ff.

[25] The Scottish Intelligence Survey showed that in each size of family the *first-born* and the *last-born* had higher I.Q. scores than middle-born siblings. A plausible explanation is that both the oldest child and the "baby of the family" receive disproportionate amounts of parental attention. Sir Godfrey Thomson, "Intelligence and Fertility: The Scottish 1947 Survey," *The Eugenics Review*, 41 (1950): 168. Similarly, a British study found that a working-class boy had a greater chance of entering an upper school if he were an elder or eldest child. See A. H. Halsey and L. Gardner, "Selection for Secondary Education and Achievement in Four Grammar Schools," *British Journal of Sociology*, 4 (1953): 60–75, cited in Floud, Martin, and Halsey, "Educational Opportunity . . . ," p. 208. More evidence that the middle sibling position is a handicap comes from the Harvard mobility study, which found that with occupation and size of family held constant, middle children are considerably less likely to go to college. See S. Stouffer, "First Rough Draft . . . ," p. 21.

[26] See J. Nisbet, *Family Environment* (London: Eugenics Society, 1953), for a review of the relevant literature.

[27] Anne Roe, *The Making of a Scientist*, pp. 88–93 and Paul Sheldon, "The Families of Highly Gifted Children," pp. 59–60.

[28] R. E. L. Faris, "Sociological Causes of Genius," *American Sociological Review*, 15 (1950): 689–699.

[29] Anne Anastasi and John P. Foley, Jr., *Differential Psychology*, rev. ed. (New York: Macmillan, 1949), p. 338 f.

adults, and reduce his involvement with other children, increase the likelihood that he will be upwardly mobile.

These findings which indicate a relationship between "isolation from contact with other children" and upward mobility tie in with the historic association between social advancement and a small family of orientation: restricted fertility has recently been discussed as a factor in the long-term process which enabled certain French bourgeois families to enter the nobility in the *ancien regime*.[30]

Modern studies of social mobility from six Western European countries—England, France, Belgium, Denmark, Sweden, and Italy—all indicate that the upwardly mobile and better-educated children from lower-status groups are likely to come from small families.[31] Evidence from Italy and England suggests that a restricted family may be an important factor in enabling children of the upper classes to *maintain* the high position of their parents: children of large families in the upper strata are more likely to be downwardly mobile.[32]

A striking illustration of the relationship between mobility and restricted family size is found in a Swedish study. Using matriculation in secondary schools as an indicator of probable mobility, Moberg found that the educationally successful sons of craftsmen, workers, and minor officials came from smaller families and had fewer children themselves than the matriculated sons of higher-

[30] J. G. C. Blacker, "Social Ambitions of the Bourgeoisie in 18th Century France and their Relation to Family Limitation," *Population Studies*, 11 (1957): 46–63. In twentieth century America also, mobile entrants into the upper class have fewer children than the old-family sector of the social elite. See E. Digby Baltzell, "Social Mobility and Fertility Within an Elite Group," *The Milbank Memorial Fund Quarterly*, 31 (1953): 411–420.

[31] Floud, Martin, and Halsey, "Educational Opportunity . . ."; Marcel Bresard, "Mobilité sociale et dimension de la famille," *Population*, 5 (1950): 533–566; Alain Girard, "Mobilité sociale et dimension de la famille," *Population*, 6 (1951): 103–124; Paul Minon, "Choix d'une profession et mobilité sociale"; K. Svalastoga, "An Empirical Analysis of Intrasocietary Mobility Determinants"; Sven Moberg, "Marital Status and Family Size among Matriculated Persons in Sweden," *Population Studies*, 4 (1950): 115–127; and Alessandro Lehner, "Mobilité sociale par rapport à la dimension de la famille," *Proceedings of the World Population Conference, 1954* (New York: United Nations, 1954), pp. 911–931.

[32] A. Lehner, "Mobilité sociale . . ." In England upper-middle-class parents have been severely limiting their family size in order to afford public school education for their sons. *Royal Commission on Population*, (London: His Majesty's Stationery Office), p. 145, cited in E. Digby Baltzell, *Philadelphia Gentlemen*, (Glencoe: The Free Press, 1958), p. 318.

status and better-educated families: it would seem, from his study, that in order to rise, lower-class families must be even smaller than upper-strata families.[33]

It can be argued that "small family" is simply a spurious variable which "intervenes" between the motivation and education of the parents and the motivation and education of the offspring: that it is the better-educated and mobility-motivated parents from the lower strata who tend to restrict the number of their children, and that these are also the parents who motivate their children to advance and would do so whatever the size of their family. Although there is an element of truth in this, research data indicate that the size of family itself has a number of dynamic consequences which affect social mobility, and should therefore be considered as an "independent variable."

The first consequence is obvious and corresponds to the conscious, manifest intent of parents who restrict fertility. For people of limited income, the fewer the children the better they can be fed, clothed, and educated. Thus one of the French studies found that although size of family had no effect on the ability of wealthy parents to provide higher education for their children, only those in "modest" circumstances who restricted the size of their families could afford secondary education for their children.[34] Two other French studies also show an inverse relationship between size of family and length of education for children of low-status parentage, but indicate that size of family bears no relationship to continuation in school for those with a high-status background.[35] Table 9.4, which presents the relevant findings from one of these studies, clearly illustrates the influence of family size on the educational opportunities of Parisian school children. Upon the completion of compulsory school at the age of fourteen, 40 per cent of the children of workers coming from small families continued their education, compared to only 29 per cent of working-class children from large families. Forty-nine per cent of the children of minor officials with small families undertook further studies, compared to only 26 per cent of those from large families. However, the influence of size of family on educational opportunity for the chil-

[33] S. Moberg, "Marital status ..."
[34] A. Girard, "Mobilité sociale ... "
[35] M. Bresard, "Mobilité sociale ... ," p. 554, and data in table 9.4.

TABLE 9.4

<small>PARISIAN PUPILS' ACTIVITY AT COMPLETION OF PERIOD OF COMPULSORY SCHOOLING, BY FATHER'S OCCUPATION AND SIZE OF FAMILY: BOYS AND GIRLS.</small>

(Percentages)

Father's occupation and size of family	Further studies	Appren- ticeship	Work	No activity	Total	Number of children
Laborers and workers						
1 and 2 children..........	40	42	14	4	100	274
3 children and more......	29	43	20	8	100	288
Lower officials						
1 and 2 children..........	49	43	8	..	100	50
3 children and more......	26	58	13	3	100	69
Employees and foremen						
1 and 2 children..........	48	38	12	2	100	111
3 children and more......	39	38	15	8	100	98
Small business and artisans						
1 and 2 children..........	45	25	28	2	100	91
3 children and more......	40	25	28	7	100	61
Other middle-class occupa- tions						
1 and 2 children..........	58	16	21	5	100	20
3 children and more......	53	41	..	6	100	21
Retired and no answers						
1 and 2 children..........	42	43	12	3	100	163
3 children and more......	23	50	21	6	100	100

<small>SOURCE: Alain Girard, "L'orientation et la sélection des enfants d'âge scolaire dans le département de la Seine," *Population*, 8(1953):665.</small>

dren of white-collar workers, small businessmen, and those in other middle-class occupations, although present, is much less important than among the lowest-income groups.

In England, grammar school education is a key factor in determining whether an individual will attain a higher middle-class position. Whether a working-class child attends a grammar school rather than a modern secondary school seems to be largely decided by the size of his family. Himmelweit found that 62.9 per cent of the children of workers attending grammar school came from small families, 37.1 per cent from large families. In the modern school, 36.7 per cent were from small families and 63.3 per cent from large families. Again, for middle-class children size of family was an almost inconsequential factor, producing a difference of only three percentage points.[36]

[36] H. T. Himmelweit, "Social Status and Secondary Education Since the 1944 Act," p. 145. A recent study of high school students in the Boston area found that

A second consequence of a small family is perhaps more unintended and latent. Interaction in the smaller family unit, by increasing the involvement of the children with adults, seems to lead to higher intelligence and greater motivation, which, in turn, means greater likelihood of educational and occupational success. In addition to the evidence for this presented earlier, the findings of two national surveys are striking.

Although the Scottish Intelligence Survey found the usual associations between (1) high-status occupation and high intelligence-test scores, (2) high-status occupation and small family size, and (3) high intelligence-test scores and small family size, the finding that is significant in the present context is that *within each occupational class, the children from smaller families consistently had higher intelligence test scores.*[37]

Similarly, a French national survey found that performance on intelligence tests varies with rural-urban residence, father's occupation, and size of family. But, except for the children of professionals, there was an inverse relationship between size of family and test performance within each occupational group (residence held constant).[38]

These research findings on the relation of restricted fertility to possibilities for social advancement agree with modern population theory and research, which in recent years has given increasing consideration to the desire for upward mobility as one of the significant factors in the secular trend toward smaller family size.[39]

the average number of children per family was 3.0 for working-class boys who were going to college and 3.6 for working-class boys who were not college-bound. E. G. Cohen, *Parental Factors . . .*, p. 74. The Harvard mobility study reported that the probability of going to college for children from families of five or more was considerably less than for children from smaller families. S. Stouffer, "First Rough Draft . . . ," pp. 19–21.

[37] James Maxwell, "Intelligence, Fertility and the Future: A Report on the 1947 Scottish Mental Survey," *Proceedings of the World Population Conference, 1954* (New York: United Nations, 1954), p. 738.

[38] Institut National d'études Démographiques, *Le Niveau intellectuel . . .*, pp. 187–193. Thus while the overall performance of the children of white-collar workers in a given age group is six to eight points higher than that of the children of manual workers, an "only" child from a working-class family tends to have a score equal to or a little higher than that of children from large white-collar families (three or four children).

[39] See Charles F. Westoff, "The Changing Focus of Differential Fertility Research: The Social Mobility Hypothesis," *Milbank Memorial Fund Quarterly*, 31 (1953): 24–38. John F. Kantner and Clyde V. Kiser, "The Interrelation of Fertility, Fertility Planning and Inter-Generational Social Mobility: Social and Psychological

The recent efforts of sociologists to locate the sources of motivation towards achievement in the cultural values of different groups, and to explain which individuals secure high status by being urged toward education, hard work, proper dress, etc., have been paralleled by the work of psychologists who have sought to find in personality the sources of varying motivations to achieve. The work of David McClelland and his associates has been particularly important in this area. They have developed a number of projective and content analysis techniques that make it possible to analyze the strength of the "need for achievement." The core of this method is a coding of fictional and fantasy materials according to criteria which are measures of the extent to which the described action is interpreted by the respondent as an attempt to "achieve," either relative to some standard or to some other person.[40] Once the strength of the motivation to achieve is measured, it may be related to such other variables as religious affiliation, family structure, child-rearing practices of various cultures, and so on.[41]

Factors Affecting Fertility," *Milbank Memorial Fund Quarterly*, 32 (1954): 76–78; Jerzy Berent, "Fertility and Social Mobility," *Population Studies*, 5 (1952): 244–260. The European studies cited in the text indicate that a small lower-class family is more likely to facilitate upward mobility for its children than a large lower-class family. Here the emphasis is on small size of "family of orientation" as a condition or determinant of upward mobility. The American and English population studies cited above stress the restriction of the size of the "family of procreation" by upwardly mobile parents: here family size restriction is both a condition and consequence of upward mobility.

A recent study suggests that the hypothesis that social mobility has a restrictive effect on fertility may no longer be applicable in such environs as metropolitan suburbs. Boggs found that, on an average, upwardly mobile men did *not* have fewer children than nonmobile men: in fact he reports a slight opposite tendency. In addition, the white-collar men with several children had higher levels of aspiration than those with few children. This "changed attitude" toward the effects of children on personal advancement was especially characteristic of the younger men who grew up in metropolitan areas. Stephen T. Boggs, "Family Size and Social Mobility in a California Suburb," *Eugenics Quarterly*, 4 (1957): 208–213. Similarly a study of 2,205 salesmen, engineers, and bank employees found that there were no differences between mobile and nonmobile men in such indices of "familism" as number of offspring, housing status, age at marriage, and childless time span. In other words, the men who had risen from humble origins were just as family oriented as the men from white-collar backgrounds. The writer suggests that the social-mobility-familism thesis might be valid for the entrepreneurial, but not for the bureaucratic era. Seymour Yellin, *Social Mobility and Familism* (Unpublished Ph.D. dissertation, Northwestern University, 1955; microfilm number 15,172).

[40] An exposition of the techniques of this method and some validating materials, along with some preliminary empirical results, are presented in David C. McClelland, *et al.*, *The Achievement Motive* (New York: Appleton-Century-Crofts, 1953).

[41] M. Winterbottom, "The Sources of Achievement Motivation in Mother's Attitudes toward Independence Training," in McClelland, *et al.*, *The Achievement*

There is evidence that this achievement motive is a true personality component that stems in large part from early childhood experiences, much like the propensity to anxiety.[42] Early training for independence is related to high achievement motivation; that is, children who are weaned earlier, who are treated as independent individuals earlier, who are forced to take care of many personal functions at an early age, are much more likely to have an orientation to high achievement than those who are protected in this early period. Early training for independence is, moreover, much more characteristic of middle-class than working-class families. We would therefore expect that middle-class children would possess higher achievement motivation than working-class children, and that this fairly common-sense notion could be substantiated by empirical research. This has been done by one of McClelland's associates who found that 83 per cent of New Haven high school boys from the two highest social classes scored high on an achievement scale, compared to only 32 per cent of the boys from the three lowest strata.[43]

The few empirical findings which are available not only substantiate the notion that the middle class is more oriented to achievement than the lower class, but also that it is superior to the *upper class* in these traits of drive and ambition. Charles McArthur's study of the personality characteristics of upper- and middle-class men at Harvard shows that the latter are much more

Motive, pp. 297–304; D. C. McClelland and G. A. Friedman, "A Cross Cultural Study of the Relationship between Child-training Practices and Achievement Motivation Appearing in Folk Tales," *in* G. Swanson, *et al.*, eds., *Readings in Social Psychology* (New York: Henry Holt, 1952), pp. 243–249; and McClelland, *et al.*, "Religious and Other Sources of Parental Attitudes toward Independence Training," *in* McClelland, ed., *Studies in Motivation* (New York: Appleton-Century-Crofts, 1955), pp. 389–397.

[42] Havighurst found that upwardly mobile persons do not find relaxation in leisure-time pursuits but "play" in much the same striving, energetic manner in which they approach work and other areas of life. Robert J. Havighurst, "The Leisure Activities of the Middle-Aged," *American Journal of Sociology*, 63 (1957): 158.

[43] Bernard C. Rosen, "The Achievement Syndrome: A Psychocultural Dimension of Social Stratification," *American Sociological Review*, 21 (1956): 206. The most comprehensive summary of the results of the many psychological studies of socialization during the past twenty-five years concludes: "Though more tolerant of expressed impulses and desires, the middle class parent . . . has higher expectations for the child. The middle class youngster is expected to learn to take care of himself earlier, to accept more responsibilities about the home, and—above all—to progress further in school." Urie Bronfenbrenner, "Socialization and Social Class Through Time and Space," in E. E. Maccoby, *et al.*, eds., *Readings in Social Psychology* (New York: Henry Holt, 1958), p. 424.

likely to be work oriented and to reject both strong family ties in general and in particular their father, whom they desire to surpass in status. The men from upper-class families, on the other hand, will tell stories in response to the unstructured pictures of the TAT (Thematic Apperception Test) that suggest they are less oriented toward work as a field of accomplishment, that they respect their father, and that they have strong positive family feelings." Two other studies by Rosen also found that the "need achievement" scores of middle-class respondents are higher than those of the upper class though the differences in each study are very small." According to McArthur these findings on achievement motivation help explain why at elite colleges such as Harvard, "public school boys consistently achieve higher grades than do boys with a private school background." A number of investigations agree that "intelligence held constant, college grades showed a constant inverse relation to economic advantage." The scions of the upper class at private schools and Harvard get a "gentleman's C" and are presumably gentlemen first and achievers second in later life, while those from middle-class families are more likely to "make an A," worry about marks, take a pretechnical major, and presumably put achievement first after leaving Harvard." Perhaps this superiority in achievement and drive of a rising middle class over established elites is endemic in stratified societies which are economically progressive. In his analysis of the repeated rise of "new men" into the leading positions in the economy from the Middle Ages down to the nineteenth century, Henri Pirenne has pointed to the fact that descendants of the new rich always lose interest in achievement, and ultimately "withdraw from the struggle. . . . In their place arise new men, courageous and enterprising."[47]

[44] Charles McArthur, "Personality Differences Between Middle and Upper Classes," *The Journal of Abnormal and Social Psychology*, 50 (1955): 247–258.

[45] B. Rosen, "The Achievement Syndrome . . . ," p. 206; and David C. McClelland, "Community Development and the Nature of Human Motivation; Some Implications of Recent Research," (Unpublished manuscript, 1957), table 1.

[46] Charles McArthur, "Personalities of Public and Private School Boys," *Harvard Educational Review*, 24 (1954): 256–261; quote about intelligence is taken by McArthur from A. B. Crawford, *Incentives to Study* (New Haven: Yale University Press, 1929).

[47] Henri Pirenne, "Stages in the Social History of Capitalism," *in* R. Bendix and S. M. Lipset, eds., *Class, Status and Power* (Glencoe: The Free Press, 1953), p. 502. The entire article is pertinent.

Thus class differences in personality must be considered a factor in the perennial "circulation of the elites."

Unfortunately, granted the exciting implications for social analysis suggested by the work of these psychologists, they have not yet provided us with actual evidence that high achievement motivation is actually related to occupational success.

There is no evidence that motivation (of the sort measured by the techniques mentioned above) results in higher occupational achievement among those with equal opportunity. We do not know whether those who have achieved the transition from a working-class background into the middle class have stronger motivations than those who only maintain the positions of their families. We also do not know whether motivation for achievement which cannot be fulfilled by a high-status occupation can be easily satisfied, for example, by athletic achievement, or by doing a good job at a lower level.

However there is evidence that achievement *motivation* is related to concrete achievement *behavior* among students. Rosen in his study of New Haven high school boys found that within both upper and lower social strata, boys with high achievement motivation scores received high grades and boys with low achievement scores received low grades.[48]

The practical test of the achievement motive comes when its satisfaction requires that gratifications of other kinds be deferred in favor of occupational achievement. The Kinsey data on the deferral of heterosexual experience in adolescence on the part of those who later obtain high position in the social structure have led to a renewed recognition of Freud's insights into this phe-

---

[48] Bernard C. Rosen, "The Achievement Syndrome . . . ," p. 210. The most recent knowledge available on how achievement motivation is related to differential behavior has been summarized by McClelland: "The 'highs' work harder at laboratory tasks, learn faster, do somewhat better school work in high school even with IQ partialled out, and seem to do their best work when it counts for their record and not when other special incentives are introduced such as pressure from the outside to do well, money prizes, or time off from work. They are more resistant to social pressure, choose experts over friends as work partners, and tend to be more active in college or community activities, like risky occupations, perform better under longer odds, and choose moderate risks over either safe or speculative ones." David C. McClelland, "Community Development . . . ," pp. 4–5. This paper contains the references which document each of the above listed findings. See also David C. McClelland, *et al., Talent and Society* (Princeton: Van Nostrand, 1958).

nomenon.[49] Results similar in their implication to Kinsey's were obtained in a Danish study which indicates that postponement of marriage is a mobility asset. The author, Kaare Svalastoga, found that the upwardly mobile tended to defer marriage until they were about thirty, and that "those who marry before 25 have poorer chances of an ascending career and face increased risks of social descent."[50] An English study shows that those who marry into a higher social class are likely to marry late, while early marriage is associated with marrying into a lower-status group.[51] It is possible, of course, that such patterns undergo secular changes; in some European countries as well as in the United States early marriages appear to have become more frequent in middle-class groups, perhaps in response to economic prosperity, greater educational opportunities, and other factors.

Outside the realm of sexual behavior and marriage the idea of deferred gratification has been applied most directly to achievement motivation in a study by Leonard Reissman.[52] He asked his respondents to specify whether the fact that a better job might entail spending less time with their families, risks to health, moving to another community, etc., would interfere with their taking it. This approach may measure more accurately than any other the practical effect of achievement motivation in the occupational structure. The inclination to defer gratifications is usually inculcated in middle-class families.[53] The middle-class combination of

[49] See Alfred C. Kinsey, *et al.*, "Social Level and Sexual Outlet," *in* R. Bendix and S. M. Lipset, eds., *Class, Status and Power*, pp. 300–308.

[50] K. Svalastoga, "An Empirical Analysis of Intrasocietary Mobility Determinants," p. 17. This relationship between age of marriage and upward and downward mobility may help in part to account for the similarities between the mobility rates of the United States and Western Europe, documented in chapter ii. Though there may be greater emphasis on "planned mobility" in the United States as a result of the "open class" value system, the later age of marriage in much of Europe may facilitate considerable "unplanned" mobility in these countries. A European who marries much later and has his children at a later age than an American will have a longer period without family responsibilities in which to take risks or advance his skills.

[51] Ramkrishna Mukherjee, "Social Mobility and Age at Marriage," *in* D. V. Glass, ed., *Social Mobility in Britain*, p. 343.

[52] Leonard Reissman, "Levels of Aspiration and Social Class," *American Sociological Review*, 18 (1953): 233–242.

[53] Louis Schneider and Sverre Lysgaard, "The Deferred Gratification Pattern: A Preliminary Study," *American Sociological Review*, 18 (1953): 142–149. The concept of "deferred gratification" has recently been criticized by Beilin, who, after a study of the factors which differentiate mobile from nonmobile lower-class boys, concludes that "postponing is a phenomenon the observer introduces to explain ap-

earlier training for independence with the stronger development of the "self-control" to defer gratifications probably contributes to the advantage which the offspring of the middle class have over those from lower strata. Hence, if these hypotheses are right, some aspects of class behavior which are not explicitly related to norms urging achievement nevertheless do contribute to the incidence of mobility. These findings suggest some clues for research on the deviant cases (the socially mobile), since persons who are mobile upward should come disproportionately from families which begin training for independence early and teach the deferral of gratifications. Conversely, it may be suggested that those who are downward mobile should be found to come disproportionately from well-to-do families which for some reason have not done this.

The process of social mobility requires, beyond the motivation to achieve, the capacity to leave behind an early environment and to adapt to a new one.[54] This capacity to form social relationships at a higher level and to give up those at a lower level is probably related to personality. Thus, the socially mobile among business leaders show an unusual capacity to break away from those who are liabilities and form relationships with those who can help them.[55] The childhood experiences of lower-status men who later become business leaders often show a pattern of strong mothers and weak fathers, and an emotionally unsatisfying family life.[56] If it is assumed that a situation in which the mother has

parent differences in behavior although the actors themselves do not perceive they are behaving in this manner. To the college going youth from the lower socioeconomic classes going to college involves the *gratification* of values he has developed rather than a relinquishing of valued behavior." Harry Beilin, "The Pattern of Postponability . . ."

[54] See W. Lloyd Warner and James C. Abegglen, *Big Business Leaders in America* (New York: Harper, 1955), pp. 59–64; W. Foote Whyte, *Street Corner Society*, pp. 94–108; and Peter M. Blau, "Social Mobility and Interpersonal Relations," *American Sociological Review*, 21 (1956): 290–295.

[55] A study which contrasted the socialization patterns in Jewish- and Italian-American families found that certain beliefs, values, and personality traits conducive to high achievement and upward mobility were inculcated in Jewish, but not in Italian families. These included: "a belief that the world is orderly and amenable to rational mastery, and that therefore, a person can and should make plans which will control his destiny; . . . a willingness to leave home to make one's way in life; . . . and a preference for individualistic rather than collective credit for work done." Fred L. Strodtbeck, "Family Interaction, Values, and Achievement," *in* Marshall Sklare, ed., *The Jews: Social Patterns of an American Group* (Glencoe: The Free Press, 1958), pp. 162–163.

[56] Warner and Abegglen, *Big Business Leaders . . .*, pp. 64–107.

higher social status than the father is likely to result in this pattern of intrafamily relations, then families in which the mother had a higher occupational status than the father before marriage should result in higher social mobility. Two interesting British studies support this hypothesis. The study cited above of the relationship between social class and educational opportunity in England also found that "the mothers of successful [in getting into the highly selective grammar school at the age of 10–11] working class children moreover had frequently followed an occupation 'superior' to that of their husbands."[57] A second study reports that working-class parents are more likely to prefer grammar school education for their children when the mother's occupation, before marriage to a manual worker, was nonmanual rather than manual.[58] A similar pattern has been observed in America by Allison Davis, who writes that "many parents who push children toward social mobility are members of mixed-class marriages . . . A lower-middle class woman who marries a man from the upper part of the working class usually begins to try and recoup her original social class status either by reforming and elevating her husband's behavior to meet lower-middle class standards or by seeking to train and propel her children toward the status she once had."[59]

The characteristic family experiences in childhood of the upward mobile and his typical personality structure remain still a relatively unexplored area. The contrast among the findings of the studies on these subjects is striking. Douvan and Adelson, who investigated the occupational aspirations of 1,000 high school boys, found that those whose aspirations were upward tended to come from warm, permissive family *milieux* which encouraged the development of achievement and autonomy and of realistic attitudes toward parents and the self. The upward-aspiring boys were more likely to share leisure activities with parents than the boys with-

---

[57] Floud, *et al., Social Class* . . .

[58] F. M. Martin, "An Inquiry into Parents' Preferences in Secondary Education," in D. V. Glass, ed., *Social Mobility in Britain*, p. 169.

[59] Allison Davis, "Personality and Social Mobility," *The School Review*, 65 (1957): 137. American data which give empirical support to this hypothesis are provided by Cohen, who found that 80 per cent of the boys whose fathers were manual workers, but whose mothers had white-collar family backgrounds were going to college, compared to only 42 per cent of those working-class boys whose mother's background too was working-class. E. G. Cohen, *Parental Factors in Educational Mobility*, p. 70.

out higher aspirations.[60] On the other hand, a number of studies of which the one of business leaders by Warner and Abegglen is the most comprehensive, found that the upwardly mobile tended to be escaping from an impoverished home pervaded by a "spiritually bleak and physically depressed family atmosphere," in which quite often the father was an inadequate and unreliable figure. Although these men also show strong traits of independence, they are characterized by an inability to form intimate relations and are consequently often socially isolated men.[61]

Warner and Abegglen's negative picture of family environment and personality structure is supported by a number of more limited studies. Ellis studied 60 middle-class unmarried career women in Montgomery, Alabama and found that "larger proportions of mobile women had experienced both rejection by the general community and at least partial rejection by parents who had showed favoritism toward a sibling or siblings. Marked preference for a sibling or siblings was reported by 56 per cent of the mobile respondents, but by only 27 per cent of the nonmobile."[62] Even in adulthood these mobile women were more likely to have few friends and to be more isolated socially than the nonmobile. Additional support for the belief that unsatisfactory interpersonal relationships in the family of orientation are related to high aspiration levels is found in a study of midwestern college students. Those who had high aspirations reported that they had had feelings of rejection more frequently than did those in the group with "lower" aspirations and more often felt that another child was favored by their parents. Furthermore, a significantly greater proportion of them indicated less attachment to their parents and reported only "average" happiness in childhood.[63]

Mental illness rates would seem to provide additional data for the notion that the upwardly mobile tend to be deprived psychodynamically. People who are upward mobile, but *not* those who

---

[60] Elizabeth Douvan and Joseph Adelson, "The Psychodynamics of Social Mobility in Adolescent Boys," *The Journal of Abnormal and Social Psychology*, 56 (1958): 31–44.

[61] Warner and Abegglen, *Big Business Leaders . . .* , pp. 59–83.

[62] Evelyn Ellis, "Social Psychological Correlates of Upward Social Mobility Among Unmarried Career Women," *American Sociological Review*, 17 (1952): 553–563.

[63] Russell R. Dynes, Alfred C. Clarke, and Simon Dinitz, "Levels of Occupational Aspiration: Some Aspects of Family Experience as a Variable," *American Sociological Review*, 21 (1956): 212–215.

are downward mobile or geographically mobile, have higher rates of mental disorder than those who are stationary.[64] This suggests that it is not the anomic situation associated with mobility that is responsible for the greater vulnerability, because one would expect downward mobility to be at least as threatening to psychic equilibrium as upward mobility. It is therefore probable that a particular type of ego structure which results from a characteristic family environment is both favorable for upward mobility and vulnerable to mental illness.[65] The various researches in this area all suggest that the downward mobile have been overprotected and loved as young children, and hence are perhaps better able to cope with stress. They also have much less of a need for achievement and therefore should feel less frustrated by failure.

It seems quite likely that the personality determinants and consequences of upward mobility would differ according to the extent and character of the mobility process. Perhaps it is *extreme mobility*, especially mobility into and within elites such as the professions and the higher positions in business, that attracts per-

[64] A. B. Hollingshead, R. Ellis, and E. Kirby, "Social Mobility and Mental Illness," *American Sociological Review*, 19 (1954): 577–584 and A. B. Hollingshead and F. C. Redlich, "Schizophrenia and Social Structure," *American Journal of Psychiatry*, 110 (1954): 695–701. In their most recent publication, Hollingshead and Redlich report that within the upper class of New Haven the families of *arrivistes* (upwardly mobile) as compared with those of the "core group" (inherited wealth) are more prone to exhibit "conspicuous consumption, insecurity and family instability. Thus, we find divorces, broken homes, and other symptoms of disorganization in a significantly large number of new [upper class] families." *Social Class and Mental Illness* (New York: John Wiley, 1958), p. 79. Data drawn from Class IV (largely skilled workers) also indicate that the upwardly mobile, or those who originate in Class V (the lowest) are more unhappy and maladjusted than those who have remained in their class position. *Ibid.*, pp. 104–105. The research of Jurgen Ruesch and his associates lends supporting weight to these results. They suggest that "delayed recovery and psychosomatic diseases are conditions affecting middle class people and climbers, as contrasted with the conduct disorders affecting primarily the lower class and decliners." In a later investigation social mobility was found to be an important factor in the etiology of duodenal ulcers. Jurgen Ruesch and associates, *Chronic Disease and Psychological Invalidism: A Psychosomatic Study* (New York: Paul Hoeber, 1946), p. 161; and *Duodenal Ulcer* (Berkeley: University of California Press, 1948), p. 91.

[65] Some of the case-study materials on the adjustment of families to the Depression suggest that those families whose members were motivated to be socially mobile were more rigid in their response than were families less concerned with economic success. See Ruth S. Cavan and Catherine H. Ranck, *The Family and the Depression* (Chicago: University of Chicago Press, 1938), p. 90; Mirra Komarovsky, *The Unemployed Man and His Family* (New York: Dryden Press, 1940), pp. 78–83, 116–122; and Robert Angell, *The Family Meets the Depression* (New York: Scribners, 1936), pp. 17–18, 192–193.

sonality configurations which are a result of childhood deprivation. The businessmen studied by Warner and the career women in Ellis' research had experienced a great deal of mobility, while the college students with high aspirations in Dynes' study were presumably orienting themselves for elite positions. Psychoanalysts, such as Adler and Horney, who advance the theory that upward striving represents compensation for an unhappy childhood probably developed their ideas from their work with patients who had experienced extreme upward movement. Many recent books (*The Exurbanites* for example) portray the damaging psychological consequences of mobility and competition within elite professions. On the other hand, the most prevalent form of social mobility in our society involves not extreme but only moderate improvements in status, such as result from the shift from manual to lower nonmanual occupations. Such mobility might be facilitated by the secure family environments and ego structures described in the study by Douvan and Adelson. By defining upward mobility in terms of aspiration to *any* occupational level higher than that of one's father, these authors were clearly dealing with moderate mass mobility or perhaps just with conformity to the American value of getting ahead, rather than with the drives reflected in extreme movement into elite groups. As they put it:

> In a society which holds upward mobility to be a central value, which provides opportunity for it, and in which it is, apparently, a very common occurrence, we can expect that the dominant motivational pattern informing upward *aspiration* is not a defensive one—does not necessitate a personally damaging flight from one's past; rather, we would expect it to accompany effective ego functioning and successful socialization by a family which is transmitting a cultural value of which it approves.[66]

These studies suggest that upward mobility selects people who are distinctive in psychodynamic terms. They also indicate that a crucial variable in the motivation for social mobility is the structure of the family, perhaps independently of direct urging toward social mobility.

The relations between motivation for achievement deriving

---

[66] E. Douvan and J. Adelson, "The Psychodynamics of Social Mobility in Adolescent Boys," p. 32. (Our emphasis.) Aspiration and upward mobility are not the same thing, a fact that may account for variations in factors related to each.

from personality structure and motivation deriving directly from the social structure remain to be investigated, but recent explorations in psychology constitute the most promising line of research yet developed to supplement the sociological analysis of the relation of mobility to structural factors such as class or ethnic background. Such studies may enable us to specify how different positions in the social structure may affect family behavior, and child-rearing practices in particular.

Conclusions

To explain the "deviant" behavior of men who rise above their social origins or fall below them, a variety of studies in different countries have dealt with mobility in individual terms and have looked at such characteristics as intelligence and personality. Although intelligence is correlated with the socioeconomic status of families, many individuals have a level of intelligence which is not commensurate with the occupational achievement of their parents. This discrepancy is a major source of both upward and downward movement. Even though we know that intelligence tests seem to measure culturally learned traits as well as genetically determined ones, psychological and sociological research in this area has so far not been able to account for much of the variation between status and intelligence. Regardless of how small genetic variation may be, as long as genetic differences contribute something to variations in intelligence, discrepancies between the status of one generation and the intelligence of the next will continue to exist, and provide some of the dynamics of social mobility.

To account further for mobility psychologists have also focussed on motivational factors which need have no relationship to intelligence. A variety of studies have suggested that there is a psychodynamic difference between the mobile and the nonmobile. Efforts have been made to develop personality tests that would locate achievement motivation as a specific personality attribute. Such studies have suggested that the upwardly mobile differ from the nonmobile and the downwardly mobile in having been trained for independence at an earlier time, in having heightened opportunities for interaction with adults while they were children, in having come from a family dominated by the mother rather than the father, in having learned to defer present gratifications in order to achieve later objectives, in having the capacity to deal with others in an instrumental rather than an emotional fashion, and in having higher rates of certain mental disturbances.

Research on the above set of personality variables seems to lead us away from sociological analysis. However, it can also raise the sociological approach to a more complex level of analysis than is found in studies (such as most of those reviewed in this book) which attempt to trace in behavioral terms the interlocking consequences of having a given position in society. The psychological studies suggest that although given social positions may tend to form certain personality types, the character structure of an individual cannot be determined directly from a knowledge of the social environment in which he developed. For example, in a family in which the father plays a weak role, or is not present, children may develop personalities which differ from those of children from families in which there is a strong father. Men raised in a family of the first type may be more mobile than those raised in the second. Given this hypothesis, the sociologist can study the conditions under which each type of family is found.

An indication of the way in which a knowledge of psychological variables may contribute to the analysis of a typically sociological topic can be seen in the study of mobile groups. There is evidence that certain ethnic groups—the Jews, the Scots, the Jains, the Parsees, the Armenians, the Japanese, and the Czechs—are more successful than other groups in enabling individuals to fill new roles in society. So far, the differences between these groups and others has been explained primarily in terms of attributes endemic in the situation of minorities. However, Jews in America tend to have higher intelligence-test scores than Gentiles, regardless of what social factors are controlled, and Scots have the same records in the British Isles.[67] In addition the Japanese-Americans have done much better in school than most other groups in the United States.[68] These groups also show a considerable capacity

[67] See Nathan Glazer, "Social Characteristics of American Jews, 1654–1954," *in* Morris Fine, ed., *American Jewish Year Book, 1955* (Philadelphia: Jewish Publication Society of America, 1955), pp. 3–42.

[68] William Caudill and George DeVos, "Achievement, Culture and Personality: The Case of the Japanese-Americans," *American Anthropologist*, 58 (1956): 1102–

to defer gratifications or not to indulge in them at all. The pattern
of inhibitions on extramarital sexual behavior of lower-class Japanese-Americans, Jews, and Scots resembles the middle-class pattern among other groups. Jewish family structure is of the type
which is regarded as favoring personalities with a capacity for
mobility—the strong-mother and weak-father family. All three,
Jews, Scots, and Japanese-Americans, stress early independence for
young children, a pattern which coincides with McClelland's assumptions concerning the background of men who are high in motivation for achievement. There are, of course, many more purely
sociological hypotheses which may account for the "success" of
these two groups. For example, both Jews and Scots are "peoples
of the book": the first completely literate peoples in Europe, since
both their religions enjoined them to be able to read regularly
from the Bible. The strong drive to learning which characterizes
both is probably strongly related to the positive value which they
give to religious education. The Japanese-Americans have also
placed strong emphasis on education as a means of advancement.

On a theoretical level, perhaps the most interesting effort to
bridge the gap between psychological and sociological research
may be found in the "reference-group theory," particularly as it
has been systematized by Robert K. Merton and Alice S. Rossi.[69] In
recent years sociologists and social psychologists have come to
recognize that a fuller understanding of many varieties of social
behavior requires a knowledge of the processes through which
men relate themselves to groups—groups to whose values they
refer their own behavior, and with whose members they compare
themselves in appraising various aspects of their situation. In explaining these processes, the term "reference group" has been used
in at least two different ways: we can utilize the convenient distinction of the *comparative* reference group and the *normative*
reference group.[70] To use a group of people as a comparative refer-

1126. This article describes the remarkable degree of upward occupational mobility achieved by Japanese-American families in Chicago.

[69] See esp. Robert K. Merton and Alice S. Rossi, "Contributions to the Theory of
Reference Group Behavior," *in* R. K. Merton, *Social Theory and Social Structure*,
rev. ed. (Glencoe: The Free Press, 1957), pp. 225–280, and R. K. Merton, "Conti-
nuities in the Theory of Reference Groups and Social Structure," *ibid.*, pp. 281–386.

[70] H. H. Kelly, "Two Functions of Reference Groups," in G. Swanson, *et al.*, *Readings in Social Psychology*, pp. 410–414.

ence group is to use it as a frame of reference within which to make some judgment.[71] To use a group as a normative reference group, on the other hand, is to take over its norms, to emulate its members. Applying the latter meaning specifically to social mobility, reference-group theory suggests that the potentially upward mobile usually reveal *anticipatory socialization*, that is, they absorb the norms and behavior traits of higher strata long before they have actually changed their social position. As Merton and Rossi have put it, such people "conform" to the norms of groups of which they are not yet members, thus becoming "nonconformists" within their group of origin.[72]

In presenting this theory, Merton and Rossi cite data from the "American Soldier" studies, which revealed that enlisted men whose attitudes on various military issues were closer to the attitudes of officers than to those of the average enlisted man, were much more likely to become officers than those who "conformed" to the enlisted man's scheme of values.[73] Other studies suggest that even where the Jews have been predominantly a low-income manual-worker group, they have behaved in many ways much more like the Gentile middle class than have the Gentile working class. In his study of an Italian slum in Boston, Whyte reported that the slum-dwellers who were upward mobile conformed to the norm established by the middle-class "Anglo-Saxon" social workers, and were rejected by their compatriots.[74] A recent study in Wales points out that the majority of the sons of low-level trade-union officers who are still working at their trade have middle-class occupations. The authors note that though most of the fathers are socialists and active in the Labor Party, their homes are furnished in middle-class style.[75] Kinsey's data, mentioned earlier, showed that the upward mobile followed the

---

[71] For use of the comparative-reference-group concept see S. M. Lipset, Martin Trow, and James Coleman, *Union Democracy* (Glencoe: The Free Press, 1956), pp. 111 ff.

[72] R. K. Merton and Alice S. Rossi, "Contributions to the Theory of Reference Group Behavior," p. 264.

[73] Samuel A. Stouffer, *et al.*, *Studies in Social Psychology in World War II. Vol. I, The American Soldier: Adjustment During Army Life* (Princeton: Princeton University Press, 1949), pp. 259–265.

[74] W. F. Whyte, *Street Corner Society*, p. 104.

[75] T. Brennan, E. W. Cooney, and H. Pollins, *Social Change in South West Wales* (London: C. A. Watts and Co., 1954), pp. 102 and 171.

restrictive sexual practices characteristic of higher strata while they were still part of the lower class. The studies of family size indicate that both upward-mobile workers and their parents usually accept the middle-class small-family norm. English children of small working-class families tend to accept the standards of middle-class children, both in worrying about their school work and in their propensity to join school clubs and societies; those coming from large families worry less, and are much likely to adopt middle-class patterns of behavior.[76]

Anticipatory socialization causes individuals to become "nonconformists" within their social group. The ability to function without strong primary-group ties can facilitate "nonconformity," and various psychological studies indicate that this ability is part of the personality syndrome of the upward mobile.

It should be noted, however, that although conformity to the standards of a group with higher status undoubtedly facilitates upward mobility, such conformity is not always a product of an orientation toward the higher-status group as a reference group, a possibility that is ignored in much of the writing on reference-group theory and mobility. Thus, lower-class individuals who exhibit good work habits, cleanliness, concern for personal appearance, and generally follow the established rules of "middle-class morality" are much more likely to move up in the social structure than those who reject these norms. The motivation to behave in this fashion may, however, have little or nothing to do with having a middle-class reference group, but may, for example, have developed out of the inner dynamics of a religious belief. Thus, ascetic sects which have arisen among the lower classes in various

---

[76] H. T. Himmelweit, "Social Status and Secondary Education since the 1944 Act," pp. 151–152. In addition, two American studies find that upward-aspiring boys of lower-class status tend to assume middle-class standards of participation in voluntary organizations and school activities. Beilin found that 84 per cent of the lower-class high school boys in his sample who were college oriented took part in extracurricular activities, compared to only 38 per cent of those who were not going to college. Harry Beilin, "The Pattern of Postponability . . . ," p. 42. Similarly, a study of adolescent boys in Michigan found that "boys with occupational aspirations above the level of their fathers' occupations are much more likely to belong to three or more youth groups than boys who aspired to the same level occupation as that held by their fathers." Survey Research Center, University of Michigan, *A Study of Adolescent Boys* (Ann Arbor: University of Michigan, 1954), cited in R. J. Havighurst and Bernice L. Neugarten, *Society and Education* (Boston: Allyn and Bacon, 1957), p. 53.

Protestant countries often insist that their members conform strictly to Christian principles, which, from another perspective, means conformity to middle-class standards. Similarly, the upward mobility of Japanese-Americans has been explained in terms of a "significant compatibility . . . between the value systems found in the culture of Japan and the value systems found in American middle class culture" rather than in terms of a conscious orientation of lower-status Japanese-Americans to the middle class as a reference group.[77] The study of anticipatory socialization should, therefore, always try to differentiate between that behavior which is manifestly anticipatory and that which is directed towards a different goal, even though both may serve the same function— that of preparing individuals to succeed in new roles.

Both reference-group theory and the data on role conformity, anticipatory socialization, and reference-group behavior suggest that by merging the sociological and psychological approaches to the study of social mobility we may be able to advance the study of the mechanisms by which individuals and groups reach their positions in the stratification structure.

[77] W. Caudill and G. DeVos, "Achievement, Culture, and Personality . . . ," p. 1107.

Chapter X | *Social Mobility and Social Structure*

The research—the national and local studies—reported on in this volume has been concerned with determining the sources of social mobility in an industrial society. One of the most significant problems that has been raised, but not answered, by this research, is that of the relation between social mobility and other features of the social structure. For example, in our discussion of American society we explored the relationship between mobility, the stability of democratic political institutions, and the persistence of ideological equalitarianism. This discussion, together with the comparative data on mobility rates, suggested that it is necessary to differentiate between actual rates of mobility and the prevailing beliefs about the equal or unequal distribution of opportunities. Apparently the same rates of mobility are compatible with quite different subjective appraisals of the available opportunities, and the reverse is perhaps also true, though more difficult to establish empirically. Clearly, further research is needed to discover what combinations of mobility rates and subjective evaluations have actually occurred, and to examine the consequences which different combinations have had. One may speculate, for example, that extensive publicity concerning famous cases of great mobility may sustain a strong belief in the availability of opportunities, even when there are few of them, and that such a belief may have a stabilizing influence on a society. On the other hand, a high rate of mobility may be a disruptive force in a society in which family background and inherited status are strongly emphasized.

Speculations of this kind are not just intellectual exercise; often they determine the direction that empirical research should take. At the present time, for example, there is great interest in the social and political effects of the industrialization of so-called underdeveloped areas, in what appears to be an important relationship between the consequent increase in rates of social mobility and the stability of social and political systems. Rapid industrialization has been said to have two clearly different consequences. On the one hand, the increase in the real income of the lower strata and in the rate of individual upward mobility that has accompanied industrialization in nations such as the United States and Great Britain has been held to be responsible for the emergence of stable democratic institutions: certainly, nations like Italy, Spain, and France, which did not industrialize as rapidly and successfully, have been troubled by deep-rooted social tensions and political instability. Hence, it is urged that the best way to stabilize democracy in countries like India and Indonesia is to facilitate their rapid industrialization. But, on the other hand, successful industrialization and high rates of social mobility have been said to produce structural instabilities and to disrupt orderly political process. The growth of radical political movements among newly created proletarian strata has been cited as evidence that the tensions created by industrialization may cause revolution and result in dictatorship. Russia, for example, was undergoing extremely rapid industrialization in the early years of the twentieth century, and the spread of strikes and the growth of revolutionary movements in that country were in many ways a result of industrialization.[1] In Norway, which was undergoing a comparable process of industrialization at the same time, the majority of the trade unionists and socialists joined the Communist movement.[2] There is a suggestion, moreover, that current efforts to stimulate industrialization in underdeveloped countries bring

[1] See Leon Trotsky, *History of the Russian Revolution* (New York: Simon and Schuster, 1937), pp. 33–51, for an excellent discussion of the relationship between industrialization and political protest.

[2] See Walter Galenson, "Scandinavia," in Galenson, *et al.*, *Comparative Labor Movements* (New York: Prentice-Hall, 1952), for a discussion of the effects of industrialization on the politics of the labor movement in Norway, Sweden, and Denmark.

about a repetition of this earlier pattern. The new industrial workers who are pulled or pushed into factories and cities from the rural villages of India or Indonesia supply the Communist party with a ready field for recruitment. It has also been pointed out that the rapid upward mobility that accompanies an expansion of the urban industrial economy does not necessarily contribute to political stability. The *arrivistes* often face social discrimination at the hands of the dominant classes, and adopt revolutionary doctrines and methods in the hope of doing away with traditional forms of domination, a pattern which many believe helps explain the French Revolution and later uprisings.[3] A somewhat analogous pattern may be observed in the newly industrializing countries, where increased educational opportunities seem to have created large groups of frustrated aspirants to high position, who find an outlet for their frustrations in revolutionary activity. So far there has been little effort to specify how the conditions under which industrialization and high rates of mobility tend to strengthen social and political stability differ from those under which they tend to undermine it.[4] Such specification is an important though formidable task of comparative social research.

Another question on which so little research has been done as to make speculation necessary, is this: How, and under what conditions, do attitudes toward social differences exacerbate or alleviate the tensions resulting from upward or downward mobility? Cultures which emphasize egalitarian values and the possibility of success for all, such as those of the United States

[3] Alexis de Tocqueville, *The Old Regime and the French Revolution* (Garden City: Doubleday Anchor Books, 1955); Elinor G. Barber, *The Bourgeoisie in 18th Century France* (Princeton: Princeton University Press, 1955).

[4] An early statement of these two possible effects of widespread mobility on the stability of social structures, from an individual point of view, is found in T. H. Marshall, "The Nature of Class Conflict," in T. H. Marshall, ed.; *Class Conflict and Social Stratification* (Ledbury: Institute of Sociology, Le Play House, 1938), pp. 110–111. "Some people hold that social mobility affords a safety-valve and helps to avert the threatened conflict. Although this is true up to a point, I think its importance can easily be exaggerated. Where individual mobility is automatic, or nearly so, class loyalty develops with difficulty. If every apprentice has a reasonable hope of becoming a master he will form his associations on the basis of his trade or profession rather than of his social level ... But where mobility is individual and not automatic but depends on the result of competitive striving, I am doubtful whether the same result follows. When the race is to the swift, the slow, who are always in a majority, grow tired of their perpetual defeat and become more disgruntled than if there were no race at all. They begin to regard the prizes as something to which they are entitled and of which they are unjustly deprived."

and the Soviet Union, presumably expose "failures" to greater problems of adjustment to their station in life than do societies which accept as right or as normal the assumption that most people will remain in the station in which they were born: clearly, cultures which emphasize success require that individuals be able to adjust to personal failure. A number of mechanisms may serve this need, of which two that seem particularly important in America may be briefly suggested here: (1) transvaluational religion, which teaches that the good rather than the rich will be rewarded in an afterlife; and (2) a high degree of child-centeredness that encourages parents to seek satisfaction in high aspirations for their children when their own personal goals have not been achieved. Both may be viewed as means of safeguarding society against instability. In America, for example, the depressed strata seem to have turned to evangelical religion rather than to radical politics;[5] in Russia, where political protest is forbidden, there is also some evidence of "a return to religion" among the poorer strata: and both societies—each in its own way—seem to place an extraordinarily high emphasis on a better life for children. It is in the societies of Europe and Asia where less emphasis is placed on equality of opportunity that left-wing political movements are strong among the lower strata—presumably because they teach that traditional inequities can be done away with by changing the social system. In general, it seems to be true that the depressed and the failures who have little hope of individual success have a strong faith either in radical politics or in an emotional religiosity, so that almost nowhere are the lower classes both moderate in their politics *and* indifferent to religion.

It is more difficult to speculate about the tensions brought about by upward mobility and the mechanisms by which people adjust to them. There is some evidence that stable societies with aristocratic traditions are quite able to deal with the problem of *arrivistes* with a minimum of strain.[6] Presumably the covert refine-

---

[5] Small sects grew in great numbers during the Depression.

[6] On the other hand, in the United States, which has no specific aristocratic tradition, would-be elite groups have striven to legitimize their precarious status by means of metropolitan social registers, the purpose of which is to exclude the "*nouveaux riches.*" For a discussion of the attempt to establish an elite aristocracy in America, see Oscar and Mary F. Handlin, "Cultural Aspects of Social Mobility," (Working Paper Five Submitted to the Fourth Working Conference on Social Stratification and Social Mobility, International Sociological Association, December

ment of invidious distinctions and the security felt by persons in
the upper strata make it easy for them to associate with persons
of lowly origin without fearing a loss of status for themselves.
Brotz' study, mentioned earlier, suggests this as one of the reasons
why Jews are more readily accepted by the British upper class
than by that of the United States,[7] though offhand one would
have expected the reverse: namely, greater rejection of the upward
mobile in a highly stratified than in an egalitarian society. More
generally, it may be suggested that the relationship between the
nouveaux riches and the old upper class and differences between
economic and social status in different societies are important
subjects for comparative research.[8]

Such research would have to examine the relations between
social mobility and the stability of not only an entire social structure but also the various groups it comprises. What is conducive
to stability, say, for American society as a whole may be disruptive
for particular groups or individuals, and vice versa. Thus, a high
rate of social mobility may make possible the personal growth of
one individual; strengthen the empty ambitiousness of another;
undermine the solidarity of trade-union organization; aggravate
the conflicts between new and old elites; create severe feelings
of insecurity and *anomie* among people who find that upward
mobility leads to social rejection; and so forth and so on.

1957). The most comprehensive work on the American upper class is E. Digby
Baltzell, *Philadelphia Gentlemen* (Glencoe: The Free Press, 1958).

[7] See Howard Brotz, *A Survey of the Position of the Jews in England* (New York:
American Jewish Committee, 1957; mimeographed), pp. 8–9. For comparable comments regarding the *lesser* exclusiveness of British as contrasted with American old-
family elites see James Bryce, *The American Commonwealth*, Vol. II (New York:
Macmillan, 1910), pp. 813–814, and Dennis W. Brogan, *U. S. A.: An Outline of the
Country, Its People and Institutions* (London: Oxford University Press, 1941), pp.
116–117.

[8] See also Tocqueville's telling contrast between the French and the English
aristocracy: "The reason why the English middle class, far from being actively
hostile to the aristocracy, inclined to fraternize with it was not so much that the
aristocracy kept open house as that its barriers were ill defined; not so much that
entrance to it was easy as that you never knew when you had got there. The result
was that everyone who hovered on its outskirts nursed the agreeable illusion that
he belonged to it and joined forces with it in the hope of acquiring prestige or some
practical advantage under its aegis. But the barriers between the French nobility
and the other classes, though quite easily traversed, were always fixed and plain to
see; so conspicuous, indeed, as to exasperate those against whom they were erected.
For once a man had crossed them he was cut off from all outside the pale by
privileges injurious both to their pockets and their pride." Alexis de Tocqueville,
The Old Regime . . . , pp. 88–89.

However intriguing such speculations are, the fact remains that very little is known about the relationship between rates of mobility and the stability of national social structures. In recent years we have come to see that stable social structures are compatible with much mobility, and unstable structures with little mobility, and that psychological tension can be found in stable as well as in unstable societies. Little as this advances our knowledge, at least it does away with some facile assumptions of the past. For example, in his studies of Newburyport, W. Lloyd Warner deliberately selected a community which he believed to exemplify the social stability of Yankee culture.[9] Yet, Oscar Handlin has pointed out, this city had an extremely high rate of in- and out-migration.[10] Warner's study would appear to demonstrate, therefore, that a community may have a large-scale turnover of population, with foreign-born immigrants replacing a large proportion of the natives, and yet retain indigeneous cultural characteristics. Present-day Germany presents still another example of a culture that has remained more or less unaffected by mass mobility. In less than a decade Western Germany has absorbed more than ten million people—absorbed them to such a degree that refugees are no longer an easily visible stratum in the society, and that the political party which was organized to represent their special interests lost all its parliamentary seats in the 1957 election. To sum up, mobility may have different effects on different social groups, on different societies, on different cultures, and on different individuals. The effect on each must be studied separately, not assumed.

SOCIAL MOBILITY OF INDIVIDUALS AND GROUPS

The problem of dealing with the effect of social mobility on the behavior of individuals and groups seems less difficult. Certain basic elements inherent in *all* stratified societies facilitate analysis. As Weber, among others, suggested, the stratification system must be thought of as containing a number of hierarchies which differ with each variation and combination of the basic stratification

[9] W. Lloyd Warner and Paul S. Lunt, *The Social Life of a Modern Community* (New Haven: Yale University Press, 1941), see especially pp. 38–39.

[10] See review by Oscar Handlin of "The Social Life of a Modern Community," *New England Quarterly*, Vol. 15 (1942): 556.

factors: status, class, and authority.[11] In every society social mobility may result in discrepancies among the different positions one person may hold in each of these hierarchies. As a man advances his economic fortunes, he may find himself excluded from certain social groups because of his "lowly" social origin or his ethnic background. Again, persons who have high social status may find that they are unable to earn a commensurate income. Every industrial society has many different hierarchies of income (or wealth) and of social prestige, in each of which an individual's position is determined by a different factor: family background, service rendered, consumption patterns, education, and so forth. Each of these hierarchies may be further differentiated by religious affiliation, ethnic origin, membership in associations, etc. Individuals or groups seldom occupy positions of the "same" prestige in all the hierarchies to which they belong.[12]

The phenomenon of status discrepancies is commonly recognized.[13] The terms *"nouveaux riches,"* "upstart," "social climber," "old family," "poor but genteel," all indicate awareness of the variation between positions in the economic and social hierarchies. Interpretations of the behavior of Jews, Catholics, or immigrants often reflect the fact that members of such groups may have low social status and, at the same time, high status in the economic hierarchy. The increased power of labor unions does

[11] Max Weber, *The Theory of Social and Economic Organization* (New York: Oxford University Press, 1947), p. 425, see also pp. 424–429, and Max Weber, *Essays in Sociology* (New York: Oxford University Press, 1946), pp. 180–195; see also Talcott Parsons, *Essays in Sociological Theory* (Glencoe: The Free Press, 1954), p. 388.

[12] For an early discussion of some of these and a number of other criteria of stratification which are relatively incongruent, see Robert Michels, "Beitrag zur Lehre von der Klassenbildung," *Archiv für Socialwissenschaft,* 49 (1922): 561–593. A theoretical analysis of the structural basis of the same phenomenon is provided by Georg Simmel's discussion of multiple-group affiliation and its consequences for individuals in modern society. Georg Simmel, "The Web of Group-Affiliations," in *Conflict and the Web of Group Affiliations* (Glencoe: The Free Press, 1955). See also S. M. Lipset and Hans Zetterberg, "A Theory of Social Mobility," in *Transactions of the Third World Congress of Sociology,* Vol. III (London: International Sociological Association, 1956) and S. M. Miller, "The Concept and Measurement of Mobility," *ibid.* A discussion of how these concepts might be used in comparative research may be found in S. M. Lipset and H. L. Zetterberg, "A Comparative Study of Social Mobility, Its Causes and Consequences," *PROD, Political Research: Organization and Design,* September, 1958, pp. 7–11.

[13] G. E. Lenski, "Status Crystallization: A Non-Vertical Dimension of Social Status," *American Sociological Review,* 19 (1954): 405–413; E. Benoit-Smullyan, "Status, Status Types and Status Interrelationships," *ibid.,* 9 (1944): 151–161.

not confer high status on the labor leader; the high prestige of such important occupations in the public sector of the economy as judges, professors, and research scientists, is not accompanied by high income; both are good illustrations of discrepancies in status.[14]

There seems to be clear evidence that in caste societies such as that of India not only does mobility take place within castes, but the castes themselves are mobile, thus creating a series of status discrepancies, since, as Srinivas points out, "not only do the various castes form a hierarchy, but the occupations practiced by them, the various items of their diet, and the customs they observe, all form separate hierarchies."[15] In the main, as in Western society, economic mobility is easier and tends to occur first. Castes which improved their economic position "wanted to stake a claim for higher status."[16] A change in power position may also result in upsetting the caste equilibrium. "The three main axes of power in the caste system are the ritual, the economic, and the political ones, and the possession of power in any one sphere usually leads to the acquisition of power in the other two. . . . Economic betterment, the acquisition of political power, education, leadership, and a desire to move up in the hierarchy, are all relevant factors in Sanskritization, [becoming like the Brahmans] and each case of Sanskritization may show all or some of these factors mixed up in different measures."[17]

The process through which a caste secures higher recognition in India is almost identical with the way in which a *nouveau riche* individual in the West puts forth his family's claim to upper-class status.

The group concerned must clearly put forward a claim to belong to a particular varna, Vaishya, Kshatriya, or Brahman. They must alter their customs, diet, and way of life suitably, and if there are any inconsistencies in their claim, they must try to 'explain' them by inventing an appropriate myth. In addition, the group must be content to wait an indefinite period, and during this period it must maintain a con-

[14] For a discussion of the discrepancy between the high status and the income of groups in the public sector see S. M. Lipset, "The Fuss about the Eggheads," *Encounter*, April, 1957, pp. 17–21.

[15] M. N. Srinivas, "A Note on Sanskritization and Westernization," *The Far Eastern Quarterly*, 15 (1956): 483.

[16] *Ibid.*, p. 492.

[17] *Ibid.*, pp. 483, 492.

tinuous pressure regarding its claims. A generation or two must pass usually before a claim begins to be accepted; this is due to the fact that the people who first hear the claim know that the caste in question is trying to pass for something other than it really is, and the claim has a better chance with their children and grandchildren. In certain cases, a caste or tribal group may make a claim for a long time without it being accepted . . . by other castes.[18]

The process of changing the position of individuals or castes in the system of stratification is bound to result in status discrepancies (lack of parallelism of status); the number of hierarchies in that system and the length of time necessary to stabilize shifts make them inevitable. Analyses of the strains resulting from such discrepancies can contribute much to an understanding of "deviant behavior" (deviant from the pattern of a given group) and of social change.

Political literature, in fact, contains many suggestions that class discrepancies—e.g., low social status and relatively high economic position—predispose individuals or groups to accept extremist political views. Thus, the French bourgeoisie in the eighteenth century developed its revolutionary zeal when it was denied recognition and social prestige by the old French aristocracy: wealth had not proved to be a gateway to high status and power, and the mounting resentment over this fed the fires of political radicalism. Almost the reverse of this process seems to have occured in Germany during the late nineteenth century: there the Prussian Junkers maintained their monopolistic hold on the army and the bureaucracy while the middle-class leaders of German industry bought land in order to acquire aristocratic titles and have access to positions at court and in the government. As Max Weber observed at the time, no one was as vociferous in his patriotism and as reactionary in his politics as the man of business who had acquired a title through letters-patent and who wanted to make people forget his bourgeois origin.[19] Political radicalization may also occur among social groups whose social and economic position is in jeopardy. Franz Neumann has suggested that in a number of European countries the middle class

[18] M. N. Srinivas, *Religion and Society Among the Coorgs of South India* (Oxford University Press, 1952), p. 30.

[19] See Max Weber, "Agrarstatistische und sozialpolitische Betrachtungen zur Fideikommissfrage in Preussen," *Gesammelte Aufsätze zur Soziologie und Sozialpolitik* (Tübingen: J. C. B. Mohr, 1924), pp. 389–392.

turned towards the extreme political right because they felt threatened by downward mobility, following leaders who attributed the actual or anticipated loss of social position to political conspiracies and placed the blame on a secret group of evil-doers.[20] Thus, political radicalization may occur because the status of social groups is imperiled, as well as because the aspirations of ascending social groups exceed their actual status in the society.[21] Such discrepancies among the several rank-orders of a group or individual clearly point to aspects of social mobility which tend to be neglected by studies that rely, implicitly or explicitly, upon a single-dimensional concept of social stratification.

Yet, it is evident from the studies reported in this book that the greater part of actual quantitative empirical research has been unidimensional rather than multidimensional. To contribute to the shift from unidimensional to multidimensional analysis we would like to discuss here, at the end of this study, several somewhat neglected dimensions of the relationship among occupational, economic, and power rank-orders and of the social differentiation which arises from them.

Occupational Mobility.—Any study of social mobility that is based on analyses of upward or downward occupational moves presupposes that there is popular consensus on the relative status of different occupations. This assumption is supported by a good deal of empirical evidence, albeit of a limited kind. Reference has been made to the survey of the National Opinion Research Center in which ninety occupations, ranging from Supreme Court Justice to shoe-shine boy, were ranked by a sample of persons from different sections of the country, from towns of different size, from different age-groups and sexes, and from different economic levels. There was considerable agreement among the persons who composed the sample despite differences in their social positions:[22]

---

[20] "Anxiety in Politics," *Dissent*, 2 (1955): 135–141.

[21] See the various essays in Daniel Bell, ed., *The New American Right* (New York: Criterion Books, 1955), for interpretations of McCarthyism which suggest comparable hypotheses.

[22] See NORC, "Jobs and Occupations," in Bendix and Lipset, eds., *Class, Status and Power* (Glencoe: The Free Press, 1953), pp. 415–416. A second NORC study asked individuals to locate occupations in the "upper class, middle class, working class and lower class" and this study produced considerable comparability with the first one among the rank-orders of occupations. See Richard Centers, "Social Class, Occupation and Imputed Belief," *American Journal of Sociology*, 58 (1953): 543–55.

a subsequent study has indicated that occupations not mentioned in the NORC survey can be fitted into the original rankings with high reliability.[23] Further, in 1946, a sample of college students ranked the status of twenty-five occupations in the same order as a sample of college students had in 1925, thus suggesting that such estimates are valid for a considerable period.[24] It has also been found that a similar consensus concerning the prestige of occupations exists among samples taken in ten societies: Great Britain, New Zealand, Germany, Japan, the Soviet Union, the United States, The Netherlands, Australia, Brazil and the Philippines.[25] The high degree of agreement in these evaluations suggests, as Inkeles and Rossi note, "that there is a relatively invariable hierarchy of prestige associated with the industrial system, even when it is placed in the context of larger social systems which are otherwise differentiated in important respects."[26]

This approach to occupational classification is theoretically neat and operationally easy. However, one must be aware that using it as a basis for study of mobility obscures such significant shifts as those involved in movements from a skilled manual occupation to a low-level white-collar position, or from either of these to modest self-employment.[27] Some of these occupations fall on

[23] G. E. Lenski, "*Status Crystallization.* . . . "

[24] See George S. Counts, "Social Status of Occupations," *The School Review*, 33 (1925): 16–27, and M. E. Deeg and D. G. Paterson, "Changes in Social Status of Occupations," *Occupations*, 25 (1947): 237–241. A number of other studies of occupational rankings by college students all obtain results which are comparable with those found in the first study by Counts.

[25] Alex Inkeles and Peter Rossi, "National Comparisons of Occupational Prestige," *American Journal of Sociology*, 61 (1956): 329–339; Ronald Taft, "The Social Grading of Occupations in Australia," *British Journal of Sociology*, 4 (1953): 181–187; Bertram Hutchinson, "The Social Grading of Occupations in Brazil," *British Journal of Sociology*, 8 (1957): 176–189; Edward A. Tiryakian, "The Prestige Evaluation of Occupations in an Underdeveloped Country: The Philippines," *American Journal of Sociology*, 63 (1958): 390–399; F. van Heek, *et al.*, *Sociale stijging en daling in Nederland*, Vol. I, (Leyden: H. E. Stenfert Kroese N. V., 1958, pp. 25–26.

[26] Inkeles and Rossi, "National Comparisons . . . ," p. 339.

[27] This point has been made by Colin Clark among others, in a discussion of the methodology of the British social-mobility studies: "Instead of the conventional grouping of occupations which many investigators have hitherto used they attempted to make a scientific grouping on the basis of the 'esteem' in which various occupations were held, as shown by the answers of a number of representative citizens interviewed. Unfortunately Professor Glass' conclusions led him to group together skilled manual workers, salesmen and clerical workers in one class in his list, which reduces its value for comparison with other countries." Colin Clark, *The Conditions of Economic Progress*, 3d ed. (London: Macmillan, 1957), p. 552.

the same prestige level and hence changes from one to another are not recorded as social mobility. In addition to studying the prestige of different occupations it is necessary also to study variations in *occupational settings,* that is, the kind of social structures in which occupations are found. Changes between occupational settings are important: white-collar workers behave differently from small businessmen or skilled workers and when a manual worker moves to a white-collar job he often feels and acts as if he has moved from one class to another although the prestige of his new occupation may be no greater than that of his old one.[28]

Some inferences about different occupational settings have proved to be useful in analyzing various other forms of behavior. Most sociologists in the United States consider that small-business ownership is a basically different occupational setting than white-collar employment, and that the latter, in turn, has predictable important effects on behavior that differ from the effects of manual employment. There is a lack of international agreement, however, on the categories to be used in delineating occupational settings. For example, European social scientists and census analysts usually agree in differentiating artisans—self-employed men who work with their hands, such as barbers, shoemakers, and tailors—from small businessmen who engage primarily in selling. The artisans are generally considered members of the working class; the shopkeepers are grouped with the middle classes. American social scientists, however, rarely distinguish between artisans and other self-employed persons. Similarly, in classifying occupations, most European surveys treat civil servants as a group distinct from white-collar workers employed in private industry, and also differentiate between free and salaried professionals, while Americans do not make these distinctions. It would be interesting to test the hypotheses that are implied by these different systems of classification. Are manual workers who become artisans in Europe less likely to change their political opinions than men in America who have made a similar shift? Specifically, do European workers who become artisans still vote for left-wing parties (Socialist or Communist) since they are still part of the "working class," and do comparable Americans, who

---

[28] See the discussion and evidence presented in chapter ii (pp. 14–17) on the saliency of the manual to nonmanual shift.

as artisans have entered the "middle class," change from the Democratic to the Republican party? Or, are European artisans less likely to adopt middle-class culture and ways of life than Americans? Are there greater differences between white-collar workers employed in government and private industry in Europe than in America?

The principal problem which has concerned social scientists who employ the occupational-prestige-ranking method is that of describing the amount of vertical mobility which takes place in a society. But questions such as these suggest a different approach, namely that of using an "objective" occupational classification that is based on the assumption that changes in the type and setting of work are also forms of social mobility. Horizontal mobility between two occupations on the same prestige level may require that an individual make a greater adjustment in his style of life, his interpersonal relations, and his attitudes, than a move up or down the prestige ladder. Clearly, if shifts which involve no change of prestige—from skilled work to small business; from rural work to urban work; or from manual to low white collar—have more effect on the behavior of individuals and the structure of a society than moves involving changes of prestige, there is something peculiar about a definition of social mobility that is couched purely in terms of prestige differences. We therefore suggest that a concern with the consequences of social mobility dictates the examination of at least two types of change in occupation: (1) shifts among occupational prestige groups; and (2) moves among objective occupational strata which do not necessarily involve changes in prestige position. Both types of analyses may prove fruitful in the same study.

Economic Rankings.—It is useful to separate *occupational* from *economic* status. A lawyer who lives in a suburban villa behaves in one way as a "lawyer" and in another as a "home owner." Economists have, for good reasons, differentiated between the status of individuals as "producers" (occupational hierarchy) and their status as "consumers." Although it is possible to establish a rank-order for both, it is not necessarily true that those who receive a high rating as "producers" will also receive a high rating as "consumers." By way of example, we shall comment briefly on the problem of consumer status.

Amount of *income* is not necessarily a good indicator of *consumption status*, or style of life, although it obviously sets the limit of a person's consumption. The way in which a man spends his income, rather than the size of that income, most often affects the social status he is accorded by others. The consumption standards of individuals will reflect their aspirations and reinforce or modify the prestige derived from their occupation alone. Thus, a study of the clothing habits of white-collar and manual workers reveals that, holding income constant, low-level white-collar workers have much more concern with styles of dress, cleanliness, and so forth, than do manual workers: they are much more likely to believe that how you dress affects your chances for social mobility.[29] As the clear correlation between income and occupational prestige declines, owing to rapid changes in relative income, men can often decide for themselves whether they will adopt the behavior patterns of one social class or those of another. For example, some skilled workers choose to live in working-class districts, others in middle-class suburbs.[30]

The recent changes in the income of different occupational groups in many Western countries point up the necessity of considering consumption as a distinct stratification category. In countries such as the United States, Sweden, Germany, the Netherlands, and Great Britain, the lower classes have improved their economic position, while the proportion of the national income going to the upper fifth of the population has declined.[31] A long-

---

[29] William H. Form and Gregory P. Stone, *The Social Significance of Clothing in Occupational Life*, Technical Bulletin 247 (East Lansing: Michigan State College, 1955), pp. 30–32.

[30] A study of San Francisco longshoremen has indicated that those who moved to homes outside the docks area after longshoremen's wages went up tended to be much more conservative politically than those who continued to live in the area. (Unpublished study by Joseph Aymes, former graduate student in Department of Psychology, University of California.)

[31] Robert Solow has recently surveyed the economic literature bearing on changes in income distribution in Europe and America. *A Survey of Income Inequality Since the War*, (Stanford: Center for Advanced Study in the Behavioral Sciences, 1958; mimeographed.) He reports that the percentage of the total income received before income taxes by the top 5 per cent *declined* between the late 1930's and the early 1950's in the United States (26.5 to 20.5), in the United Kingdom (29.5 to 20.2), in Germany (27.9 to 23.6), in the Netherlands (28.9 to 24.6) and in Sweden (28.1 to 17.0). See pp. 31, 41. Other data indicate that the percentage of the national income received in the form of wages and salaries has *increased* between 1938 and 1955 in the United States (68.1 to 76.7), in Belgium (45.7 to 53.9), in Finland (50.4 to 61.2), in France (52.0 to 59.1), in western Germany (55.4 to 63.6), in Italy (40–42 to 48–50), in the Netherlands (50.7 to 54.1), in Norway (50.2 to 55.4),

term full-employment economy combined with a reduced working-class birth rate has, in many countries, resulted in a large number of families headed by men in low-prestige occupations having higher incomes than many middle-class families, and in their children receiving a better education. The consequences of a change of relative income position may vary in different societies. For example, efforts to increase the proportion of workers' children attending college in Scandinavia has resulted in only moderate change since 1910, although real wages have increased greatly, the income gap between the working class and the middle class has narrowed, and education is free and subsidized.[32] In the United States, on the other hand, similar economic changes have been accompanied by a sizable increase in the proportion of workers' children attending colleges and universities.[33] It is plain that the size of income does not necessarily determine the consumption patterns of an individual or a group. Within each income bracket it is the

in Sweden (52.0 to 62.7), in Switzerland (49.2 to 58.5), and in the United Kingdom (62.7 to 71.1). The only country for which data exist in which the share of the employed did not increase in this period was Ireland. See pp. 13–15. It is important to note that the variations among countries in the proportion of self-employed, particularly in agriculture, make it impossible to compare the absolute magnitude of the shares received; see also Allan M. Cartter, "Income Shares of Upper Income Groups in Great Britain and the United States," *American Economic Review*, 44 (1954): 875–883.

[32] Sven Moberg, *Vem blev student och vad blev studenten?* (Lund: Gleerup, 1951). It should be noted, however, that the situation in Finland differs greatly from that in the other Scandinavian countries. "The Finnish secondary schools have promoted rapid social mobility, carrying increased numbers of students from humble social origins to their destinations in universities and professional careers . . . Three-fourths of the university students come from homes where the father has had no university training." The fact that more advantage is taken of educational opportunities in Finland than in the other Scandinavian countries is explained by the fact that "sending one's sons—and, more recently, daughters—to a 'learned' school has developed into a cultural pattern. It was originally a response of educated people, as well as enlightened farmers, to the challenge of the Russian period in Finnish history when no political avenues and too few business paths seemed open for young Finnish men, and when intellectual investments seemed more profitable." Heikki Waris, "Finland," *in* Arnold Rose, ed., *The Institutions of Advanced Societies*, (Minneapolis: University of Minnesota Press, 1958), pp. 224–225.

It is interesting to note that all of the European peoples who seem to excel in educational achievement, the Jews, the Scots, the Czechs (who have the highest rate of university education in Europe) and the Finns, seem to have developed their "love of learning" as oppressed national or religious minorities. For further bibliographical sources on mobility in Finland see Sven-Erik Astrom, "Literature on Social Mobility and Social Stratification in Finland, Some Bibliographical Notes," *Transactions of the Westermarck Society*, Vol. II, (Copenhagen: Ejnar Munksgaard, 1953), pp. 221–227.

[33] See chapter iii.

cultural background or the social aspirations of an individual family that influences the way income is spent, and that, rather than total income, determines a family's consumption class and often affects the social status it is accorded by others.

Social Class.—Much of the study of stratification in America has been concerned with social class. Social classes are usually defined as strata of society composed of individuals who accept each other as status equals, and are hence qualified for intimate association. Men may change their occupational status by changing their job, but they can improve their social-class position only by being admitted to relationships of intimacy with those who already possess a higher rank.

The stringency of the criteria which affect the individual's placement in a social class probably varies with the size of the community in which he lives, and the position of the class to which he aspires.[34] The smaller the community and the higher the social class, the more likely it is that an individual's rank is determined by his personal attributes. A more formal system is maintained by the upper strata in metropolitan American cities. The Social Register Association considers candidates for membership only after three or more members certify that the candidate is a person with whom they associate regularly and intimately. As one moves down the social-class ladder, and the size of the relevant classes becomes large, men employ more general attributes as criteria for placing an individual in the structure. In America, these include, in particular, occupation, income, education, consumption style, ethnic origin, and religion.[35] The social-class hierarchy is also the area where status symbols play their most important role. It is evident that movement up the social ladder is slower than movement up the occupational ladder, and that consequently, differentiation between the two can be a major means of locating status discrepancies. This fact is made evident in a recently published study of the Philadelphia elite, which analyzed in detail the accretions to membership in the *Social Register*. The author, E. Digby Baltzell, reports an increase of 68 per cent in the num-

[34] S. M. Lipset and R. Bendix, "Social Status and Social Structure," *British Journal of Sociology*, 2 (1951): 167–168.

[35] W. Lloyd Warner and Paul S. Lunt, *The Social Life . . .*, and W. L. Warner, *et al.*, *Social Class in America* (Chicago: Science Research Associates, 1949).

ber of families listed in the *Social Register* between 1900 and 1910. Admissions declined sharply with each succeeding decade, both absolutely and proportionately, so that between 1930 and 1940 the *Register* grew only 6 per cent. Baltzell comments that the admission trends suggest that "this upper class has developed into a more or less closed group over the years and that status within it is less and less achievable, or sought after."[36] Since the evidence dealing with mobility into the business elite (see chapter iv) indicates that this stratum is as open as it ever was, Baltzell's findings suggest that there may be a growing discrepancy between high economic class and high social status in America.

Although the existence of the *Social Register* makes possible comparative analysis within the United States of differentials in social class mobility at the elite level, it does not facilitate comparisons on a mass level or among countries. Studies of variations in the backgrounds of marriage partners is probably the best way to analyze not only mass mobility and variations in rates among nations, but also differences that develop over time.

Power Rankings.—Power rankings are based on those relationships between groups and between individuals that involve subordination of one to another. The power of an individual may be defined as a measure of the extent to which his position in society gives him the opportunity to impose his ideas upon others, and those having approximately the same power may be said to constitute a power class. In part, power classes cut across other strata. A labor leader may have a low occupational and social status and yet wield considerable political influence. A civil servant or parliamentarian may enjoy a high occupational status that gives him power over persons whose consumption standards or social positions are higher than his own.

The achievement of social mobility through the acquisition of power has been a subject that has been relatively neglected by research workers, probably because it is a fairly recent mass phenomenon. For example, when the various national labor movements began to rise to political power in the Western world their leaders were largely persons from the middle or upper classes, and workers were thus afforded little chance to attain positions

---

[36] E. Digby Baltzell, *Philadelphia Gentlemen*, p. 68.

of political power and prestige. But labor movements old enough to have a second or third generation have usually recruited leaders from their ranks, and given them an opportunity to advance socially and occupationally via the political ladder. Yet, this change in the leadership recruitment of the labor movement has very rarely been investigated. Since at least ten per cent of the members of trade-unions have held some union office—paid or unpaid—it is probable that this one form of power mobility plays an important role in the dynamics of social mobility: there are today over 65,000 local trade unions in the United States, each of which has a number of officers. Of course, politics, itself, may be even more important than the trade unions in providing opportunities for mobility through the acquisition of power. Various students of American politics have pointed out that different ethnic groups, in particular the Irish, have been able to improve their position through the medium of politics. In Europe, the Labor and Socialist parties undoubtedly give many lower-class persons an opportunity to secure power and status far greater than that which their economic position could give them.[37]

It is usually difficult to isolate those aspects of the social mobility of *individuals* which are due to changes of the power structure. However, changes in the relative power position of various groups are more easily ascertained: for example, the return to power of the industrialists in Germany after World War II, the decline of the gentry in England, and the manifest increase in the power of organized labor everywhere in the Western world. It is plain that individuals increase their power by belonging to these groups.

These considerations should make it apparent that the concept "social stratification" comprises a series of partly overlapping and partly conflicting rank-orders which, although they should be studied together, have so far been either treated singly or actually neglected.

---

[37] See W. Bloomberg, Jr., "The State of the American Proletariat, 1955," *Commentary*, 19 (1955): 213, for a discussion of the way in which union office leads to higher status. Some British and European studies have suggested that the children of socialist leaders of working-class origin often secure higher education and leave the working class, or that holding minor union office raises the level of aspiration of manual workers. T. Brennan, "Class Behavior in Local Politics and Social Affairs," in *Transactions of the Second World Congress of Sociology*, Vol. II (London: International Sociological Association, 1954), pp. 291–292; S. M. Lipset, Martin

Social Mobility as a Problem for Investigation

We have discussed briefly the relations between social mobility and social structure, about which little is known and much remains to be learned. We have also discussed the multiple rank-orders which constitute the social stratification of a society, but which have often been neglected in favor of a unidimensional approach to the rank-order of occupations. Though awareness of the limitation that such an approach imposes may aid in the development of a more refined method, we think it is also necessary to give attention to the intellectual rationale that is the basis for the assumption that studies of social mobility are worth pursuing at all. Since the findings of this study (especially those of the first part) raise certain pertinent as well as perplexing questions, it will be useful to give an evaluative summary of these findings at this point.[38]

The studies of the American business elite indicated that the opportunity to enter this elite from below has remained about the same *throughout* the process of industrialization, thus contradicting the frequently voiced opinion that it has become more restricted. We noted, however, that in the United States (and in other countries as well) access to the limited number of top-elite positions should be distinguished from movement into and out of the more numerous middle class. Regardless of how open the top elite is in any country, the number of persons who can achieve positions in it is not large enough to make it a goal toward which men may realistically work. Movement into upper-middle or intermediate positions, or from working class to middle class, or from the slums to the suburbs in one generation is attainable for millions. And these types of mobility may have a more significant effect on popular images of opportunity in a society—on whether people think it is "equally" or "unequally" distributed—than the actual rate of top-elite mobility. Such images, regardless of what the actual fact may be, affect the degree to which, in contemporary society, the lower strata accept as legitimate or just the present

Trow, and J. S. Coleman, *Union Democracy* (Glencoe: The Free Press, 1956); Robert Michels, *Political Parties* (Glencoe: The Free Press, 1949), pp. 280–281.

[38] For full conclusions of this study, see the conclusions at the end of each chapter.

distribution of rewards, and are thus of great significance to the stability of a given society. Since an emphasis on ability and achievement is inherent in industrial society, a lack of belief in the possibility of achievement may cause considerable resentment in the lower class.

Elite mobility, though not so important in affecting values as mass mobility, still has important consequences for the stability of ever-changing industrial societies. If "new men" are prevented from entering the ranks of the political elite, for example, the political leaders may become incapable of dealing successfully with the problems of the day, and the competence and leadership which develop outside may be used to build reform or revolutionary movements. Similarly, businessmen who have inherited their leading economic positions may often be less willing to accept innovations and take risks than those who have come into such positions through their own effort. It has been argued that Britain's decline as an economic power was in part due to the fact that, in the early twentieth century, British business leaders largely ran businesses they had inherited, and hence tended to follow traditional managerial practices, and also that revival of British industrial efficiency started after World War I, when "new men" began to assume positions of business leadership partly as a result of the many deaths among the scions of the old business elite during the war, and partly through the evolution of family-owned businesses into corporate enterprises. Similarly, the backwardness of French economy has been attributed to the predominance of family-owned business firms, and to the consequent absence of entrepreneurial innovation.[39]

---

[39] David Landes, "French Business and the Businessman: A Social and Cultural Analysis," *in* E. M. Earle, *Modern France* (Princeton University Press, 1951), pp. 334–353; John B. Christopher, "The Desiccation of the Bourgeois Spirit," *ibid.* pp. 44–57. While these discussions stress the influence of mobility on the innovating capacity of elite groups, Joseph Schumpeter strikes at the same problem from the other side: the relationship of successful innovation to mobility. "Family and social history show that, in addition to the elements of chance and success along wonted and ordained lines, the method of rising into a higher class which we are now discussing is of crucial importance—the method of striking out along unconventional paths. This has always been the case, but never so much as in the world of capitalism. True, many industrial families, especially in the middle brackets, have risen from small beginnings to considerable or even great wealth by dint of hard work and unremitting attention to detail over several generations; but most of them have come up indirectly from the peasantry—because one of their members

These broad questions are related to our tentative attempt to assess the implications of the nationwide studies of social mobility in the United States and in Europe (chapters ii and iii). Our findings support the thesis that social mobility is an integral and continuing aspect of the processes of urbanization, industrialization and bureaucratization.[40] For if there is no evidence indicating that social mobility declines as industrial societies mature, there is likewise no evidence that the highly industrialized societies of Europe have substantially less mass social mobility—as measured by shifts across the manual-nonmanual line—than the United States. Admittedly, though the findings help us attack widely held opinions, they are primarily negative: yet the finding that a high degree of social mobility is a concomitant of industrialization and bureaucratization has important implications for our understanding of modern society. In societies undergoing economic expansion, the demands of the privileged few for the lion's share of the economic benefits must be reconciled with the aspirations of individuals from the lower ranks who have the drive and talent to assume positions of leadership. Inherited privilege seeks to monopolize economic opportunities: economic expansion

has *done something novel*, typically the founding of a new enterprise, something that meant getting out of the conventional rut." Joseph Schumpeter, *Imperialism and Social Classes* (New York: Meridian Books, 1955), p. 133.

[40] That urbanization may be a determinant of occupational mobility independent of industrialization is indicated by a recent study in Poona, India. "In the present generation the tempo of change [of rates of social mobility] seems to have quickened, and this is reflected in the declining proportion of those engaged in unskilled manual work and increasing proportions among skilled and highly skilled and among clerks and shop assistants in the total occupational pattern: urbanization would thus seem to bring about the transformation of unskilled manual workers into other types of skilled, highly skilled, etc. workers even in centres like Poona, where the process of urbanization is not based on industrial development." N. V. Sovani and Kusum Pradhan, "Occupational Mobility in Poona City Between Three Generations," *Indian Economic Review*, 2 (1955): 36.

For detailed discussions of the effects of industrialization and urbanization in contributing to the growth of a middle class in various Latin American countries and the consequent increase in upward mobility see the following monographs, all under the editorship of T. R. Crevenna, *La Clase Media en Argentina y Uruguay* (Washington: Pan American Union, 1950); *La Clase Media en Mexico y Cuba* (Washington: Pan American Union, 1950); *La Clase Media en Bolivia, Brasil, Chile y Paraguay* (Washington: Pan American Union, 1950); *La Clase Media en Panama, El Salvador, Honduras y Nicaragua* (Washington: Pan American Union, 1950); and *La Clase Media en Colombia, Ecuador, y La Republica Dominica* (Washington: Pan American Union, 1951). Most of the essays in this series discuss at some length the motivation for upward mobility. Unfortunately none have explicit data.

endangers the position of the highly privileged by increasing the number of competitors for top positions. Societies as diverse as those of the United States, the countries of Western Europe, India, the Soviet Union, and South Africa encourage individuals to "aspire above the station" of their parents, because of the greater literacy and increased educational opportunities that are a concomitant of economic expansion. Education seems often to induce aspiration for even higher social rewards than are easily available.

The result is a typical dilemma, especially acute in societies like Soviet Russia and the Union of South Africa, where the phenomena of social mobility have become explosive political problems. Soviet writers have complained, for example, that too many Russian school children have their eyes set on important bureaucratic or military positions, and have castigated the school system for failing to make the children of workers and peasants proud of their fathers' *productive occupations.*[41] But this effort of the Soviet leaders to preserve the myth of the workers' state cannot be pressed too far, for as they encourage the aspirations of young people from low-status families they also encourage them to pride themselves on their achievement, to put as much social distance as possible between themselves and their humble background, and to impart to their children the benefits of their privilege. In the Union of South Africa the same problem arises, though it is at present being solved rather differently. The Nationalists, and most other white groups, wish to perpetuate the present inequality of races, but they also want to industrialize the country. And industrialization so increases the demand for labor, especially skilled labor, that the ruling groups of South Africa are forced to permit some of the Negro population to acquire some education and higher technical skills.

The proposition that the rates of economic expansion and industrialization are more significant in determining the extent of social mobility in a given society than variations in political, economic, or cultural value systems, has recently been forcefully reiterated by the eminent sociologist of the University of Warsaw, Stanislaw Ossowski.

[41] Alex Inkeles, "Social Stratification and Mobility in the Soviet Union: 1940–1950," *in* Bendix and Lipset, eds., *Class, Status and Power,* pp. 611–621.

A socialist system needs economic development even more than a capitalist one... such development is a necessary condition of its success and even of its existence. Therefore one of the immediate aims of the leaders of the socialist states was to reach the level of more advanced capitalist countries in industrialization, urbanization, development of communications, and mass education. *All these processes imply an increase in social mobility in socialist countries as well as elsewhere,* and since they were induced by social revolutions we can therefore postulate a plain causal relation between social revolution and—this increase of social mobility. *But it is the 'social-economic expansion' and not the revolutionary introduction of a socialist order which can be considered a necessary condition of this increase. Increased mobility of this type could have been accomplished also if the capitalist system had persisted: it could have been done, e.g., with the help of schemes like the Marshall plan.*[42]

Though industrialization requires a good deal of social mobility, the social context in which economic development takes place influences decisively the incidence of such mobility. There are requirements for fulfilling the new occupational roles which must be met, and the already existing distribution of skills, as well as the cumulation of advantages and disadvantages that is the heritage of different groups in society, determines which individuals will be able to meet these requirements. In order to understand the incidence of social mobility, it is necessary to specify both the requirements of different occupations and the structure of opportunities for (and barriers against) learning skills and filling the positions. A small businessman in the service and retail trades needs to meet few requirements; he needs little educational preparation, social grace, technical skill, and so on. On the other hand, a doctor must have a long education, must gain admission into medical school, must be accepted by his colleagues, etc. To be mobile in a bureaucratic hierarchy an individual must meet still other requirements. Consequently, the recruitment of men

[42] See S. Ossowski, "Social Mobility Brought About by Social Revolution," (Working paper presented at Fourth Working Conference on Social Stratification and Social Mobility, International Sociological Association, Geneva, December, 1957). (Our emphasis in the quotation.) It is true that Professor Ossowski does mention that there is a type of social mobility other than that resulting from socioeconomic expansion which is "due to the introduction of a new social system in the countries we are discussing, a system generally called 'socialism.' " We do not think we are doing violence to the content of this excellent article when we say that its implications are that this type of mobility is not, in fact, very important.

to each kind of position creates a different pattern of social mobility. Movement into high-status occupations is possible only for men of various general types, men who are more likely to be found in some social classes than in others.[43]

Perhaps the most important variable connecting the requirements of occupational roles with the distribution of people available for them is the differential distribution of opportunities for formal training, especially in the school system. Sons of skilled workers are more likely to know about apprenticeship programs and to be able to enter them than sons of men in other occupational groups. The sons of men in high-status occupations are not only more likely to be financially able to embark on long training programs, but are also more likely to get more moral support from their family.

Finally, on the subjective side of the process of social mobility, the way in which motivation for achievement and knowledge

---

[43] A summary and bibliography of the psychological literature on the personality characteristics of members of different occupations is found in Anne Roe, *The Psychology of Occupations* (New York: John Wiley & Sons, Inc., 1956), especially pp. 143–248.

Perhaps the best study by a sociologist relating occupational choice and aspirations to individual traits is the Cornell Value Study, which dealt with the determinants of the occupational choices of a national sample of college students. This study showed that job aspirations of students correlated with their values along three lines: self-expression, orientation to people, and extrinsic reward. There were great differences among those who chose different occupations. Thus, "the three occupations with the greatest proportion of those with high faith in people are social work, personnel work, and teaching; the occupations with the lowest proportion are sales-promotion, business-finance, and advertising-public relations. It may be noted that both sets of occupations involve working with people but that the *quality* of the interpersonal relationship differs basically. The relationship of the social worker, personnel worker, and teacher to the people with whom they primarily deal tends to be a *helpful* one (concern with the interests of the other); the relationship of the advertiser, businessman, and salesman tends to be a self-interested one (concern with the interests of the self.) It would appear that there is some tendency for those with differing degrees of faith in human nature to select occupational areas involving a *quality* of interpersonal relations consistent with this attitude." Morris Rosenberg, *Occupations and Values* (Glencoe: The Free Press, 1957), pp. 26–27. Those with little faith in people were also more likely to use unscrupulous methods on their jobs, believed more readily that it was who you knew rather than what you knew that counted, and had a stronger desire to get ahead. It is interesting to note that students oriented toward *medicine* as a career were high in having that complex of values associated with *little faith in people*. They were more like prospective businessmen and advertising executives than like those oriented to social work, scientific research, or teaching. This characterization of prospective physicians is paralleled by psychological studies which find them to be high on scales testing cynicism.

about the occupational structure is distributed partly determines the probability that a man can satisfy the requirements of a given occupation.

One of the main concerns of this book has been to suggest the way in which such factors as class, community of origin, and the circumstances surrounding entry into the labor market, affect social placement. As we see it, our findings call into question some basic value assumptions which appear to have been accepted by almost all research workers in this field during the past decade or more. It seems to have been assumed that rapid and increasing social mobility is a good thing because it increases the opportunities of the underprivileged and hence enlarges their freedom, while the corresponding reduction of privilege among the few does not seriously jeopardize their position." It now appears that this assumption may be questioned on several grounds.

The argument that increased social mobility will create a healthy society is part of the nineteenth-century intellectual tradition. Its rationale was strongest when the theory of increasing misery appeared most reasonable; that is, during the initial phases of the industrialization process, when it appeared to be true that "the rich got richer, and the poor got poorer." This theory appeared, and continues to be persuasive, in those societies in which the widening of opportunities produced by industrialization coincided with the amalgamation of aristocratic and newly rising bourgeois groups and hence with a stubborn retention of quasi-feudal privileges. Though evidence is lacking, it seems reasonable to suppose that such privileges actually retarded the growth of opportunity: even if they did not, it is quite undisputed that opportunities were

---

" We say "appear" and "seems to have" advisedly. Because the bulk of modern research on social mobility is published without any explicit statement of its intellectual rationale, our statement of this rationale is the result of inferences and impressions. It may be added in passing that in the absence of sufficient attention to ideas which justify research effort in given directions, these directions will be determined (even more completely than they would be otherwise) by such extraneous considerations as availability of funds, the ease of pursuing past efforts still further, etc. This is a good example of anti-intellectualism within the scholarly community, and we see no reason to assume that the fashions which influence research that has no intellectual rationale are in any way superior to the fashions which are no doubt operative when there is such rationale.

[45] For a survey of the extensive discussions of this theme going back to the eighteenth century, see Robert Michels, *Die Verelendungstheorie* (Leipzig: Alfred Kröner, 1928).

available only to those who accommodated themselves to a middle- and upper-class style of life, which, for many people at least, aggravated rather than alleviated their psychological problems. The bitterness of class feeling in many European societies certainly derives from the condescension and arrogance with which members of the old or new upper classes endowed all their contacts with "inferiors." The emancipation from such a condition of social subservience was identified with the widening of opportunities, and was given a humane and humanitarian significance which helped inspire generations of the socialist movement. Equalitarian principles tended to be formulated in negative terms and it was taken for granted that less inequality would increase the sum total of happiness and human welfare—which is, of course, a reasonable assumption when conspicuous inequalities cause unhappiness.[46]

But it appears hazardous to base future studies of social mobility on the intellectual legacies of a nineteenth-century political argument. If it is true, as we have tried to show, that all developed industrial societies are characterized by a high rate of social mobility, it becomes questionable whether further studies of this phenomenon should be based on the implicit simple assumption that more mobility is a good thing. Is it? To assume as much is to ignore the abundant evidence of the social and psychic cost of a high degree of social mobility: a cost that is probably high in terms of the combativeness, frustration, rootlessness, and other ills that are engendered, even if it be true that there has been no increase in the incidence of psychoses, as Goldhamer and Marshall have suggested.[47]

In saying this we do *not* imply that the price is *too* high, for we lack proper standards of comparison. Presumably, any reasonable estimate of the value of social mobility would depend not only on

---

[46] For a recent statement of this position, see C. A. R. Crosland, *The Future of Socialism* (London: Jonathan Cape, 1956), chaps. 9–11.

[47] See Herbert Goldhamer and Andrew Marshall, *Psychosis and Civilization: Studies in the Frequency of Mental Disease* (Glencoe: The Free Press, 1953). Melvin Tumin has recently questioned the assumption that more and more mobility is inherently a good thing. His article is one of the few detailed attempts to consider the negative consequences of social mobility. Melvin M. Tumin, "Some Unapplauded Consequences of Social Mobility in a Mass Society," *Social Forces*, 36 (1957): 32–37.

counting the real gains that result from a high rate, but also on a determination of the social and psychic burdens imposed where the rate is low More explicit empirical research on the gains and losses accruing from different rates of social mobility can certainly increase our understanding more than can a tacit assumption that the higher the mobility rate the better things are—though it will not resolve the moral issues which are at stake.

Such considerations should not cause us to overlook, moreover, the available evidence that points to causes of mobility and of "immobility" in industrial societies to which the liberal and socialist theorists of the nineteenth century paid scant attention. It was their contention that the prevailing inequality of opportunities led to a drastic underemployment of the talent available in the lower classes, and also fostered the growth of mediocrity and decadence in the middle and upper classes. The conservative counter-argument asserted that in the long run the talented would rise to the top, and that the prevailing inequality was both a necessary precondition for the development of the talent already at the top and a necessary bulwark against the dangers of rapid change. So far as empirical findings bear on this question, they tend to support the liberal position, though with two qualifications. First, the talent available in the underprivileged groups is perhaps not as great as the earlier optimism seemed to assume. And second, it seems appropriate to question the frequent assumption that the removal of talent from the lower classes (through the upward mobility of individuals) is *prima facie* a good thing; the gains arising from such mobility should be balanced, rather, against the detrimental effects of diminishing the stock of talent in the lower classes.

Our findings also suggest that at the bottom of the social structure the problem is not merely one of "natural endowment thwarted by inequality" as had been assumed previously. Although so much attention has been given to the task of disentangling native intelligence and environmental influences that the problem of differences in motivation for achievement has become a subject for research only in recent years, the preliminary survey given above suggests that the cumulation of disadvantages at the bottom of the social scale is in large part the result of a lack of interest in educational and occupational achievements. In a country which is second to none in its concern with mobility and personal attainment it is clearly insufficient to attribute this lack of interest solely to the environment. Could it be that here is a built-in safeguard that enables those who have it to shy away from the psychological burdens which mobility imposes? And is this reluctance to assume such burdens a counterweight that diminishes the effects on society of the social cost of high mobility?[48] Further studies might well explore such possibilities. But it is clear, at any rate, that we have traveled some distance from the viewpoints of the nineteenth century: for these considerations suggest that we should turn away from the quest for more mobility *per se* and concern ourselves with the conditions under which men acquire motivation for achievement; that instead of identifying greater equality of opportunity with human happiness, we begin to inquire into the dissatisfactions which are endemic in our social life, including those dissatisfactions which create a drive for achievement and are hence a source of both the assets and liabilities of social mobility.

---

[48] Hollingshead and Redlich have reported on some of the differences between men who are intergenerationally stable in class IV (largely skilled workers), and those who have moved up into the class from class V (the lowest). These differences present striking examples of some of the functions of immobility in society as well as of the dysfunctions of upward mobility both from the perspective of class solidarity and that of ego satisfaction. They report that the nonmobile workers are "satisfied with their 'way of life' and are not making sacrifices to get ahead. They have a sense of personal dignity and self-esteem which sustains them in their 'life position'; they also identify themselves with the working class in significantly larger numbers. On the other hand, 77 per cent of the 31 per cent who moved upward from Class V positions have 'sacrificed' to better themselves. They identify in significantly larger numbers with the middle-class rather than with the working or lower-middle classes. . . . These strivers are less satisfied with their accomplishments and roles in the community; also they expect more from the future than stable persons who tend to be content with things as they are." A. B. Hollingshead and F. Redlich, *Social Class and Mental Illness* (New York: John Wiley, 1958), pp. 104–105.

Appendix	*Intra-generational Mobility*
	in Great Britain, Japan,
	and the United States

The international comparisons reported on in chapter ii of this book deal with inter-generational mobility. Suggestive as these comparisons are, they are handicapped throughout by the fact that the studies that supplied the comparative data were undertaken for different purposes. Considerable reclassification of the original data was necessary in order to achieve any comparability, and although we proceeded with caution, our judgments were necessarily somewhat arbitrary and never entirely free from the danger of creating classificatory artifacts. We were, therefore, interested to find additional confirmation of our principal comparative conclusions after this volume had gone to press. This confirmation is contained in two studies of intra-generational mobility, one a survey of labor mobility in Great Britain, the other a study of social mobility in Japan.[1] Both studies collected data on the first and present job of respondents and thus permit a direct comparison of results, and also a very limited comparison with American data, since the Oakland study and a much earlier San Jose study (1934)[2] have information on these two career points.

[1] Both studies were received after the completion of this volume, but the unpublished British study was probably completed in the early 1950's. See Geoffrey Thomas, *The Social Survey: Labour Mobility in Great Britain, 1945–1949.* An inquiry carried out for the Ministry of Labour and National Service. (Mimeographed, no date); Kunio Odaka, ed., *Shokugyô to Kaisô* (Occupation and Stratification) (Tokyo: Mainichi Shimbunsha, 1958).

[2] P. E. Davidson and H. Dewey Anderson, *Occupational Mobility in an American Community* (Stanford: Stanford University Press, 1937).

288

The major conclusion drawn from our comparative survey of data on the occupations of fathers and sons was that advanced industrial societies possess similar rates of social mobility. This is supported by the fact that industrial societies as diverse as those of England, Japan and the United States show close similarity in the social distance which respondents in these countries have traversed in the course of their occupational careers.[3]

Further, both the English and the Japanese studies confirm our conclusions, that the first job was an excellent indicator of the "present" job, i.e., the occupational position at the time of the interview,[4] and that the line between manual and nonmanual work is the most important single career boundary set by the occupational structure in advanced industrial societies. The overwhelming majority of those who start in a nonmanual occupation remain there, and the same applies to those who begin their career as manual workers. For nonmanual workers the proportion is 77 per cent for England, 87 per cent for Japan, 81 per cent for Oakland, and 73 per cent for San Jose: for manual workers the corresponding percentages are, England, 79; Japan, 74; Oakland, 65; and San Jose, 75.

Despite this similarity of the data the four studies also reveal important differences. First, in Oakland and in Japan the rate of upward movement—from manual to nonmanual—was considerably higher than that of downward movement but in England and San Jose rates of upward and downward movement were virtually the same. Second, although the absolute percentages are quite

---

[3] In this case also an international comparison of data presents great difficulties. The English sample is representative of the national labor force. The Japanese study is based on a nation-wide sample, but it is not clear how representative this sample is. Comparable data of similar scope are not available for the United States and we are, therefore, forced to contrast the data for Oakland, which are fundamentally not really comparable since they are a sample of heads of families, and San Jose data secured in 1934, during the Depression, with the national samples for Great Britain and Japan. Some distortion is also introduced by the use of different classifications of occupations. For example, in the Oakland study foremen were counted under "skilled workers," and hence as manual; in England (and probably in Japan) they were classified as managerial, and hence as nonmanual.

[4] The intensive examination of the data on this contained in the Oakland study has not been included in the present volume, although there is a brief reference to it on p. 191. A detailed consideration of the "first job" as a predictor of the subsequent career is contained in Lipset and Malm, "First Jobs and Career Patterns," *American Journal of Economics and Sociology,* 14 (1955): 247–261.

similar, the data indicate that upward movement was highest in Oakland (35 per cent), intermediate in Japan and San Jose (26 and 25 per cent), and lowest in England (21 per cent). Note that the studies which used comparable methods of classifying rural and urban occupations secured very similar results. The studies of England and San Jose merged urban and rural occupations, and the mobility patterns reported are almost identical, both showing

TABLE A.1

RELATIONSHIP BETWEEN FIRST JOB AND PRESENT JOB AMONG
THOSE WHO BEGAN IN URBAN OCCUPATIONS
(Percentages)

Present job	Study and first job							
	England (1949)		Japan (1950)		Oakland (1949)		San Jose (1934)	
	Non-manual	Manual	Non-manual	Manual	Non-manual	Manual	Non-manual	Manual
Nonmanual........	77	21	87	26	81	35	73	25
Manual...........	23	79	13	74	19	65	27	75
Total............	100	100	100	100	100	100	100	100
Number..........	498	3,097	1,366	1,013	229	356	368	811

NOTE: Farm occupations eliminated from table in computing percentages in Oakland and Japan, but included in nonmanual or manual categories in England and San Jose.

more downward and less upward movement than either the Oakland or Japanese studies, which separated urban and rural occupations. Men who start as farm workers are less likely to secure nonmanual positions than are those who enter the labor market as manual workers; and farm owners, managers, and tenants are more likely to become manual workers if they move to the city than are men from the urban middle class.[5]

[5] It should be also remembered in this connection that the Oakland sample under-represented the lowest strata and that the actual rate of upward mobility is therefore probably lower than shown by the data. Thus, although the proportion of the sample who were employed in occupations which were classified as nonmanual was 30 per cent in England, and 49 per cent in San Jose, it was 60 per cent in Japan (eliminating the rural group, which we are not considering) and 57 per cent in Oakland. The Japanese study included a number of occupations under the category of "sales" which are classed as manual elsewhere. These differences in sample and classification, together with the variations in classifying farmers mentioned above,

Some refinement of these broad results is possible. The proportion of those whose first job and whose present job are in the same occupational group may be taken as a rough measure of career stability over time. To be sure, the occupational groups used for this purpose are very broad and a man may be quite mobile without ever leaving his group. On the other hand, he may have left his occupational group in the course of his career but have returned to it by the time of the interview. However, because there is no

TABLE A.2

PERCENTAGE OF RESPONDENTS WHOSE FIRST AND WHOSE PRESENT JOBS
WERE IN THE SAME OCCUPATIONAL GROUP, BY COUNTRY

Occupational group	England	Japan	Oakland	San Jose
Professional..................	80 (122)[a]	65 (332)	61 (39)	78 (81)
Clerical.....................	34 (376)	54 (584)	27 (190)	37 (242)
Skilled......................	53 (723)	57 (409)	53 (112)	47 (90)
Semiskilled..................	51 (1,154)	37 (553)	25 (125)	34 (273)
Unskilled....................	26 (1,220)	47 (152)	17 (119)	42 (448)

SOURCE—Data for this table are taken from Thomas, *The Social Survey*, p. 29 for England, from Lipset and Malm, "First Jobs," p. 251 for Oakland, from Odaka, *Shokugyō to Kaisō*, p. 94 for Japan, and from Davidson and Anderson, *Occupational Mobility*, p. 95 for San Jose. Only those occupational categories were selected from the four studies which for purposes of comparison required a minimum of reclassification.

[a] Figures in parentheses are the total number of respondents in each of the occupational groups. Thus, in England, 80 per cent of 122 professionals began their careers in a professional position, and so on.

reason to assume that in these respects industrialized countries differ from each other in some systematic way, the index may be considered a useful approximation.

In all four studies professionals show the greatest degree of career stability. The percentage of respondents who began their careers as professionals but are now manual workers is small (7 per cent for England, 4 for Japan, 6 for Oakland, and 10 for San Jose).[6] Career stability in clerical occupations is clearly greater in Japan than in England, Oakland, or San Jose (see table A.2). This is also reflected in the proportions of those who started in such occupations, but were doing manual work at the time of the interview (England, 28 per cent; Japan, 11; Oakland, 23; San Jose, 32). On the other hand, the barrier against the entry of clerical workers

make it impossible to conclude that the reported variations correspond to significant differences in actual rates of intra-generational mobility in the total population.

[6] The percentages discussed in this paragraph are taken from tables in the original publications which are not given here.

into the professions is high in all three countries. It may be added that the index of career stability of clerical workers would be considerably higher if adjacent categories like "sales" and "managerial" had been included, but problems of classification did not make this feasible.

The data for skilled workers present much the same picture in all four studies, but the data for semiskilled workers show important variations between England and the other countries, with more stability in England. In general, semiskilled and unskilled manual workers have a much better chance to rise within the manual division in Oakland. The chances for semiskilled and unskilled workers to enter clerical occupations are also greater in Oakland (11 per cent) and San Jose (13 per cent) than in England (2 per cent) or Japan (3 per cent).[⁷] The relatively few mobility chances for the English operative are shown by the fact that 51 per cent who start as semiskilled remain there and 16 per cent fall into unskilled work. In Oakland 25 per cent remain semiskilled and only 4 per cent become laborers, and in San Jose, even during the Depression, 34 per cent remained semiskilled and only 11 per cent fell into the unskilled category. Consequently 36 per cent of the Oakland and 30 per cent of the San Jose respondents who began in semiskilled jobs rose to the skilled level (reflecting in part our classification of foremen as skilled workers) compared to only 9 per cent for England. The data for Japan show rates of both upward and downward mobility of semiskilled workers that are closer to those in the two American cities than to those in England: 37 per cent remain in semiskilled work, 7 per cent fall to unskilled jobs, and 22 per cent rise to skilled trades.

The pattern for unskilled workers is similar to that for the semiskilled. Unskilled work is, however, less of a *cul de sac* in England, for only 26 per cent who begin there end there. But 68 per cent can rise no higher than semiskilled employment, while in Oakland those starting as laborers eventually spread themselves out quite evenly among the occupational categories: actually more end in the skilled and self-employed groups than in the unskilled and semiskilled. The fact that in Japan 47 per cent of those who begin in

---

[⁷] Here, and in the next paragraph, we cite figures not contained in our tables: they are, however, to be found in the original sources.

unskilled work remain there and only 13 per cent rise one step on the ladder to semiskilled work may not indicate a greater restriction of opportunities because in the Japanese study the occupational classification "unskilled" contains only the very lowest working-class jobs. San Jose figures are in part similar to those in Japan: 42 per cent stayed in the unskilled class and 17 per cent moved up only one notch to the semiskilled level. These figures, which are quite different from those of Oakland, probably reflect both the large number in San Jose for whom unskilled activity meant farm labor, and sharp differences in sample designs. It is significant to note that 26 per cent of the San Jose workers whose first job was unskilled manual labor did achieve nonmanual status.

Beyond these specific comparisons there is a more general point which is reinforced by the English study. Since the publication of our first article based on the Oakland study and throughout the research which went into this book, colleagues at home and abroad again and again expressed their astonishment at the high rate of job mobility we had found. As a rule, Europeans would say that although our finding might be true for the United States, it was not true of Europe, or if it was, that it was the result of wars and revolutions, not of the ordinary development of industrial society. In view of the evidence we had assembled, this reaction could only be interpreted as a sophisticated expression of the popular contrasts between America and Europe which have been a conversational standby for a long time. And now we have received direct validation of our interpretation. The English study mentioned above shows that in the postwar years 1945–1949, 3,685 men recorded 13,957 job changes, or 5.8 jobs per man.[8] Perhaps job mobility in England was especially high during the immediate postwar years, but this is certainly a secondary factor. Of the 19,000,000 employed persons in the Federal Republic of Germany in September, 1957, 11,500,000 (60.5 per cent) were working in the same enterprise as in January of that year, 6,400,000 (34 per cent) worked in a different enterprise than in January and, 1,100,000 (6 per cent) had been newly employed during this nine-month period.[9] And although we have not located comparable

[8] Thomas, *The Social Survey* . . . , p. 15.
[9] See *Offene Welt*, No. 54 (March/April 1958): 104.

data on labor mobility in France, one recent community study suggests an extremely high rate of geographical movement in that country. Over half the residents of the city of Vienne were born elsewhere, a fact which takes on even greater significance when it is realized that there has been no significant increase in Vienne's population since 1871.[10]

The comparison of such findings in different countries is difficult at present, but it is after all rather unimportant for social structure analysis whether the job mobility of one country exceeds that of another by a few percentage points. It is sufficient, but it is also necessary, to recognize that a high rate of social and labor mobility is a concomitant of industrialization regardless of political conditions.[11]

---

[10] Pierre Clément and Nelly Xydias, *Vienne sur le Rhône: La ville et les habitants, situations et attitudes* (Paris: Armand Colin, 1955), pp. 22, 32.

[11] Considerable material on the social origins, marriage patterns, and mobility opportunities of English clerical workers is contained in David Lockwood, *The Black-coated Worker* (London: George Allen and Unwin, 1958). Lockwood's findings, which appeared too late to be incorporated in the present volume, are in general quite consistent with the main generalizations reported in chapter ii. For example, he reports that 41 per cent of male clerks were sons of manual workers lower than foremen, that 40 per cent had fathers-in-law who were manual workers, and that the clerks were more likely to possess "the material concomitants of middle-class status—savings, house-ownership and suburban dwelling," and to identify with the middle class, than were skilled manual workers at the same or higher income level.

Indexes

Index of Names

(This index includes the names of authors cited in the text and in the notes.)

Subject Index

Aarhus, Denmark, 31, 45
Aberdeen, Scotland, 46, 235
Achievement motivation, 52, 238–240, 244–247
Age factors in mobility: of white-collar workers, 34; of businessmen, 173–174
Anomie, 252, 264
Anticipatory socialization, 257–259
Aristocracy, 2, 3, 48, 263–264
Armenians, 255
Asia, 263. See also India, Japan
Australia, 29 n., 67
Austria, 160 n., 199, 221
Authoritarianism as a consequence of social mobility, 71

Bavaria, 43–44
Belgium, 221, 238, 240, 273 n.
Bennington, Vermont, 71
Boston, 228, 230, 237, 242 n., 243 n.
Brahmans, 63, 267
Brazil, 30–31
Bureaucratization: as a major trend and cause of mobility in modern society, 11, 57–58, 280–281; of business careers, 128 n., 143, 177
Business aspirations, occupational differences in, 178–179
Business elite: American, career patterns of 103–104, methodological problems in the study of, 115–121, 124–125, 128–131, 133–135, 137 n., social origins of, 115–143, 208, education of, 126–127, colonial background of, 137,

career assistance and, 139–143; English, cotton industry, social origins of, 35, steel mill, social origins of, 36; international comparisons of the social origins of, 40–42
Business mobility: in American mythology, 82–83; in the United States, 101–104, 176–177; and career instability of businessmen, 170; age factors in, 173–174; as influenced by size of city of birth, 208; personality determinants and consequences of, 249–250, 251. See also Business elite, Self-employment, Small-business turnover

Career Patterns, 157–181: of the business elite, 103–104, 128 n.; of the self-employed, 176–177; father's occupation and, 184–189, 197–199; education and, 190–191, 197–199; first job and, 191, 289–293; community size and, 206–213; international comparisons of, 288–294. See also Intragenerational mobility
Caste system, mobility in the, 62–64, 267–268
Catholics, 49–56, 73, 104, 137–138, 266
Child-rearing practice and mobility motivation, 245, 248–249, 250–254, 256
China, 63–64 n., 74–75
Civil servants, social origins of, 39, 73
Class consciousness: as a function of contrast in life-style, 108–110; as related to occupation, 156